DIVINE DOMINION
AS IT PLEASES GOD

DR. Y. BUR

Divine Dominion: As It Pleases God®

Recovering the POWER Lost in the Garden of Eden

Copyright© 2025 by R.O.A.R. Publishing Group. All Rights Reserved.

Visit www.RoarPublishingGroup.com for more information. No part of this publication may be reproduced, stored in a retrieval system, or transmitted in any way by any means, electronic, mechanical, photocopy, recording, or otherwise, without the prior permission of the author except as provided by USA copyright law.

R.O.A.R. Publishing Group
581 N. Park Ave. Ste. #725
Apopka, FL 32704
www.RoarPublishingGroup.com

Published in the United States of America
ISBN: 979-8-9990619-1-1
$22.88

Send *As It Pleases God*®
***Book Series* and *Workbook* Testimonies, Donations, Questions, or Orders to:**

Dr. Y. Bur
R.O.A.R. Publishing Group
581 N. Park Ave. Ste. #725
Apopka, FL 32704
ROAR-58-2316
762-758-2316

✉ Dr.YBur@gmail.com

Visit Us At:

📷 **AsItPleasesGodMovement**
▶ AsItPleasesGod

🖥 DrYBur.com
🖥 AsItPleasesGod.com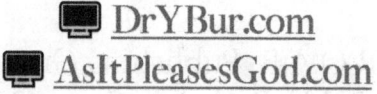

Please Donate

Please DONATE to this *Missionable Movement of God* as a GIVE-BACK to the Kingdom. Thanks for your support. Many Blessings.

AIPG Donation Link

Scan to Pay

As It Pleases God

ASITPLEASESGOD.COM

Available Titles

ASITPLEASESGOD.COM

Table of Contents

Introduction 11
Chapter One 19
  Divine Dominion ReDefined 19
    The Groundwork 21
    The Cancel Culture 25
    The Dominating Challenges 32
    Taking Authority 38
Chapter Two 47
  The Role of Free Will 47
    The Equation 54
    Overall Perceptiveness 58
    Self-Acceptance 62
    Running Our Own Race 65
    The Leading Edge 70
Chapter Three 77
  The Pitfalls of Manipulative Spirits 77
    The Signs of Manipulation 83
      Spiritual Manipulation Checklist 85
      A Manipulative Individual Checklist 87
    The Spirit of Jezebel 90
    The Spirit of Delilah 92
    The Spirit of Haman 98
Chapter Four 105

- Beyond the Church Walls 105
  - The Calculations of Men 113
  - Pulling Back The Curtains 114
  - Triggering Seeds 121
  - Spiritual Giftings 126
  - Divine Purpose 128
- Chapter Five 131
  - The Heart and Mind Posture 131
    - The Good Enough Test 133
    - The Quinternity Effect 135
    - The Difference 137
    - Speak and Document 139
- Chapter Six 143
  - Character and Worthiness 143
    - Inside Out 146
    - Unlimited Potential 148
- Chapter Seven 151
  - Navigating Life's Challenges 151
    - Spirit of Gratefulness 153
    - Representing the Kingdom 155
    - Divine Wisdom 157
- Chapter Eight 165
  - The Cost of Emotional Infections 165
    - Ace In The Hole 167
    - Carnality vs. Spirit Man 168
    - Victim No More 170

    When Triggered 180
    Privilege vs. Underprivileged 182
    For Show vs. For Sure 184
Chapter Nine 193
  Embracing the Fruits of the Spirit 193
    Tree of Life 198
    The Fruitful Prophet 205
Chapter Ten 215
  Spiritual Maintenance of the Psyche 215
    The Mind of Mankind 218
    The One-Up 221
    Warring Members 223
    The Tutor of Mankind 225
Chapter Eleven 237
  The Power of Oneness 237
    Spirit to Spirit 244
    The Fight 247
    In Him 249
Chapter Twelve 259
  The Clarion Call to Authority 259
    The Divine Mindset 265

AS IT PLEASES G⊙D MOVEMENT®

Introduction

The most relevant question on the table is, 'Do we as mankind have Divine Dominion?' In Earthen Vessels, the answer is a resounding 'Yes.' The Divine Sovereignty and Authority granted by God, our Heavenly Father and Creator, is a real factor hidden within our DNA. In addition, it is also often overlooked by us and miscalculated by Science, causing us to whitewash what is designed to liberate and facilitate.

For example, if we do not switch the light switch to the on position, we cannot benefit from the power that is already. So, suppose we do not switch our Spiritual Apparatuses on. In this case, we and Science will miss out on what is already hidden within our Genetic Design related to our Dominionatorial or Territorial Faculties. Then again, we may also find ourselves pointing the finger or passing the blame, similar to what Adam did to Eve in the Garden of Eden.

Why would we do such a thing as shift the blame when we own our truth? Every human being has Divine Instructions written from within, and the moment we disobey them, we will tend to project, blame, disassociate, or control as the void from within gets larger and more profound.

Introduction

How do we make Divine Dominion make sense, especially when we are not a part of the government? Unfortunately, this is how we are deceived. The government is an administration that administers rules, laws, and standards. Therefore, we as individuals possess our own governmental system from within that also contains selfish and selfless or ethical and unethical rules, laws, and standards that must remain BALANCED and RELATIONAL.

Simply put, we have Divine Dominion over ourselves, our lives, our homes, our families, our children, our reason for being, and our Predestined Blueprints. More importantly, we have the Divine Right to cover them with the Blood of Jesus to guide, protect, and govern with the Holy Spirit. However, we CANNOT violate the free will of mankind unless they are our children assigned to us by God, our Heavenly Father.

Taking authority over what DOES NOT belong to us or our Divine Mission can get us in a world of trouble, giving way to Jezebel's Controlling Spirit, Delilah's Manipulative Enticing Spirit, or Haman's Plotting Spirit. Are they real Spirits? Yes, they are real, operational, consuming, and contagious. The Biblical Stories about them are not mere stories; they are Divine Warnings designed to help us recognize when these types of Spirits are in operation within ourselves and others.

In this Book, *Divine Dominion: As It Pleases God®*, we are going to break down ordinary dominion, Divine Dominion, and excessive manipulative control from the pews to the pulpit and beyond, extending outside of the church's four walls. Is Divine Dominion reserved for Believers only? Divine Dominion (The Higher Calling) is available to all mankind, regardless of whether we are Believers or not. *"For He makes His sun rise on the evil and on the good, and sends rain on the just and on the unjust."* Matthew 5:45.

Most Believers want to bogart Divine Dominion while not using it properly for themselves or excommunicating those

Introduction

who know how to use it, *As It Pleases God*. As this unsettling and unnerving trend has emerged, here is the deal: First, God deals with Spiritual Principles, Laws, and Protocols according to His Divine Will. Secondly, He evaluates our Heart and Mind Postures to determine our worthiness or usability in His Divine Relational Dynamics. Thirdly, we benefit the most in Divine Dominion when we are selflessly operating in Purpose on purpose.

If we desire to become one of the Kingdom's Upper Echelons, we must consider our charactorial traits while working on them consistently for the Greater Good to uplift and empower others. Now, if for some reason we find ourselves degrading, disempowering, rejecting, or insulting others based on their condition, we can indeed bring that same energy into our lives. Therefore, it is only wise to explore the boundaries of dominion to ensure we are not crossing the line in another man's territory.

Why should we avoid unauthorized access into another man's territory? Unfortunately, it leads to corruption and bogus masquerades of power, rooted in fear, coercion, selfishness, and self-interest. Unbeknown to most, the Bogarting Spirit is always rooted in some form of underlying jealousy, envy, pride, greed, coveting, competitiveness, or lies. All of which causes us to intentionally attempt to capitalize on the obvious weaknesses of others to satiate the hidden longing from within.

How do I know so much about Divine Dominion? To get the Divine Information for this book, I saw a few jaded things that blew my mind with those in the pursuit of Spiritual Superiority, Titles, or Notoriety. To add insult to injury, they boldly alienated those who could offer invaluable perspectives or guidance, only to create a cycle of misinformation, confusion, disdainment, and misunderstanding. All of which were grafted with excessive manipulative control and marked

Introduction

with guilt, coercion, and division. I could not believe what my eyes were seeing, but I knew that the Divine Wisdom gleaned would override my experiences. So, with a mindset rooted in humility, I continued to glean the information to feed God's sheep to activate the Law of Reciprocity.

On this Spiritual Journey, going from ordinary authority to Divinely Sacred Authority, I will not be sugarcoating the truth about where we stand in the Eye of God. Why not? We are ultimately confused and blinded about who we are and why we are in the Eye of God while trying to control the narrative of what does not belong to us.

When life throws you a curveball, it is your responsibility NOT to leave empty-handed or empty-headed, nor should you leave dismayed, dismantled, discouraged, delusional, or disassociated. Even if you argue with loved ones or friends, have an unexpected job loss, have been lied to or lied on, have been ultimately betrayed, or experience sudden health issues, they all can make you feel like you have been blindsided. In these moments, it is crucial to understand how to navigate these challenges effectively, courageously, rationally, and steadfastly without becoming overwhelmed, brainwashed, or disillusioned.

Why should we not be affected, especially when we are thrown under the bus? In all actuality, life, in all its unpredictability, has a knack for throwing you under the bus from time to time to test or provoke you. In Earthen Vessels, it is natural to feel a whirlwind of emotions or become shocked, disappointed, and confused when faced with unexpected challenges. While being momentarily affected is humans, the goal is NOT to become infected, distracted, or sidetracked by negativity, debauchery, or shadiness.

How is it humanly possible not to become infected or impacted by the issues of life? First, you must acknowledge these feelings by taking Divine Dominion over them. Secondly, you must cast them down while replacing them

Introduction

with positive and fruitful characteristics or the Word of God. Thirdly, you must do all of such without allowing them to negatively dictate your actions, thoughts, beliefs, desires, words, or mindset. Lastly, you must do your absolute best to use the Fruits of the Spirit and behave Christlike.

Should it not be the Fruit of the Spirit instead of Fruits of the Spirit? I stand to be corrected in the earthly realm on the singular or plural use. But in the Spiritual Realm, the Fruit of the Spirit represents ONENESS. And if we are not ONE with the Holy Trinity in Spirit and Truth or operating in the Spirit of Righteousness at all times, it is best to indulge in a little Spiritual Maintenance.

For example, when maintaining a car, if a part needs replacing, we do not fix or replace the whole car; we deal with the PARTS to bring the car back into ONE STANDING. Just as a car requires regular maintenance to function optimally, our Spiritual Lives also demand ongoing attention and care by addressing the specific part that requires attention. Targeted Maintenance, as such, can also be applied to our Spiritual Journeys as well.

In the As It Pleases God® Movement, for the sake of our Divine Dominion, we break the Spiritual Fruits down into individualized fruits. Each Fruit of the Spirit (Love, Joy, Peace, Patience, Kindness, Goodness, Faithfulness, Gentleness, and Self-Control) represents a distinct aspect of our character that can be nurtured and developed according to Galatians 5:22. Why is this necessary? First, bad fruits or negative patterns are real. Secondly, utilizing the Fruits of the Spirit helps you to become a work-in-progress with the ability to transform obstacles and bad fruits into opportunities for growth to become ONE in Christ Jesus. Thirdly, there is no law against their use, empowering us to confront our weaknesses directly with outright authority.

Ultimately, to emerge stronger and wiser in the Eye of God, if we approach Oneness without breaking the Fruits of the

Introduction

Spirit down, *As It Pleases God*, we will have a hard time pinpointing our point of erring. To add insult to injury, we may lose our Divine Dominion over things we should dominate while dominating the people, places, and things we should take the L on, especially when they do not belong to us. Plus, negativity and debauchery have a knack for lurking in the shadows during tough times, waiting to sidetrack or trip us up as we inadvertently call good evil, and evil good.

According to the Heavenly of Heavens, based on the Divine Elements associated with your Divine Dominion, there is always a Spiritual Lesson, Blessing, Testing, or Wisdom hidden in all things, similar to a Diamond in the Rough. Why must we work so hard on ourselves to PLEASE God? Unfortunately, with all that He has created for our Heaven on Earth Experiences, we are the only vessel that veers away from how we were initially created, doing whatever we so desire.

As the Tree of Life is now within every human being, *As It Pleases God*, it is our reasonable service to extract the life-giving FRUITS designed to help us grow Mentally, Physically, Emotionally, and Spiritually in love, faith, truth, peace, and oneness. What does this mean in layman's terms? We must work on ourselves for ourselves, Spiritually Tilling our own grounds and becoming a selfless work-in-progress, *As It Pleases Him*, and NOT selfishly please ourselves or others with Him nowhere in the equation. Why must we PLEASE Him first? Without Him, there would be no us! Without Him, we cannot gain Divine Access to our Predestined Blueprint. Without Him, we cannot maximize our full potential.

What if we already have it going on, needing no help from God? Once again, this is how we are deceived! Without connecting to our Heavenly Father, we possess a longing from within the psyche that can only be filled by Him. On the other hand, if we are full of ourselves, then there are bigger underlying problems in need of Divine Reckoning. For this

Introduction

reason, 1 Thessalonians 5:6-8 advises: *"Therefore let us not sleep, as others do, but let us watch and be sober. For those who sleep, sleep at night, and those who get drunk are drunk at night. But let us who are of the day be sober, putting on the breastplate of faith and love, and as a helmet the hope of salvation."*

If we do not connect to God, *Spirit to Spirit*, the longing will remain hidden behind closed doors as we continue to lie to ourselves about what is really taking place from within, especially in the wee hours of the night. And, based on *Divine Dominion: As It Pleases God*® from the Garden of Eden Experience with Adam and Eve, no one is exempt from this. This longing from within is buried within the DNA of all mankind, provoking us to AWAKEN from our slumber. Here is what Romans 13:11-12 says: *"And do this, knowing the time, that now it is high time to awake out of sleep; for now our salvation is nearer than when we first believed. The night is far spent, the day is at hand. Therefore let us cast off the works of darkness, and let us put on the armor of light."*

With this Spiritual DIY Project, no one can do this for you besides you, in Earthen Vessel! *Divine Dominion: As It Pleases God*® invites each of you to reflect on the understanding of AUTHORITY and POWER. All of which pushes you to aspire to a mode of governance that is PLEASING to God. Above all, it is a Clarion Call to embrace your Quaternity Roles as sheep, shepherds, leaders, and followers like the Four Rivers of Eden, committed to walking in Divine Purpose and mutual respect for all mankind.

What makes the Quaternity Roles so important in the Eye of God? When it comes to *Divine Dominion: As It Pleases God*®, it appears that most of us have lost the charactorial element of HUMILITY. This one charactorial trait prevents us from tapping into our Highest and Greatest self, even if we appear to have it going on. When we are overshadowed or blinded

Introduction

by focusing on self-promotion, self-indulgence, and personal success without God in the equation or outright pimping Him, we set ourselves up for a rude awakening.

When becoming an idol in our own lives, we chip away at our own Cornerstone of Greatness, leading to a web of pridefulness and unrecognizable blind spots. We often deny this fact, but the truth is, it happens to us all. It is in our nature, and it must be contained to ensure we are not dominating the wrong people, places, and things. Plus, the fine line between healthy aspirations and unhealthy idolization can become easily blurred.

In addition, intricately woven into the fabric of our existence for a PURPOSE GREATER than ourselves, we may not always know who or what God is using to test, train, prepare, bless, challenge, or even demote us. It is within this uncertainty that it is only wise to exercise Divine Discernment to ensure we are not entertaining Angels in Disguise.

In the Eye of God, we must look beyond our immediate circumstances or conditions and Divinely Connect with the Spiritual Insights that guide our decisions and judgments, *As It Pleases Him*. As we navigate the complexities of life, those whom we may underestimate or misunderstand may be the Divine Answer to our prayers. So it behooves us not to overlook what is in plain sight while extracting the positive and converting the negative, unlocking the profound elements of Divine Wisdom woven into our daily experiences, thoughts, beliefs, words, and desires.

With this book, *Divine Dominion: As It Pleases God*®, with Dr. Y. Bur, The WHY Doctor, we are going to take a deep dive into unveiling and maintaining our POWER and AUTHORITY as our Divine Birthright. So, if you are ready, let us get our boots on the ground, doing what we were called to do.

Chapter One
Divine Dominion ReDefined

According to the Ancient of Days, the hidden desire to dominate is veiled within us all, even if we do not understand it or use it properly, *As It Pleases God*. This ever-present desire for dominance was often vital for survival back in those days, shaping us, societies, cultures, and relations, influencing everything, including our *Spirit to Spirit* Relationship with our Heavenly Father.

Now that we are out of the caveman days, removed from the primal instincts of our Ancestors or Forefathers, gaining unprecedented access to knowledge, insights, understanding, technology, and self-expression with a contemporary lifestyle, many of us seem to drift aimlessly. How so? We lack a well-defined sense of purpose and operate cluelessly and recklessly through life as if it owes us something.

With the desire to assert identity and ownership, we have gotten into the mindset of taking people, places, and things by force or manipulation without accounting for the cost or putting in the work, *As It Pleases God*. Here is what Luke 14:28-30 says about this serious matter: *"For which of you, intending to*

Divine Dominion ReDefined

build a tower, does not sit down first and count the cost, whether he has enough to finish it—lest, after he has laid the foundation, and is not able to finish, all who see it begin to mock him, saying, 'This man began to build and was not able to finish.'"

The unregulated desire for dominance or control without the understanding of its dual nature, can put us into a serious pickle with God, our Heavenly Father. Why is this a problem for Believers in the Eye of God? We as humans are just existing, not knowing or caring about our reason for being or our Predestined Blueprinted Purpose. Yet, we want to 'Name it and claim it,' forcing the Hand of God without fully knowing the reasons why we are doing so or even preparing ourselves, *As It Pleases Him*. Here is what Proverbs 24:27 taught me about the importance of preparing: *"Prepare your outside work, make it fit for yourself in the field; and afterward build your house."*

In preparing this chapter, *As It Pleases God*, we are going to have a *Spirit to Spirit* discussion about:

- ☐ The Groundwork
- ☐ The Cancel Culture
- ☐ The Dominating Challenges
- ☐ Taking Authority

Without laying *The Groundwork* or a stable foundation, *As It Pleases God*, we can easily slip and fall Mentally, Physically, Emotionally, and Spiritually, creating all types of avoidable or unnecessary issues, and complicating our lives further with *The Cancel Culture* Phenomenon.

In the journey of Spiritual Growth and Understanding, we all have our own missions, be it personal or Divine, and it demands our attention. With the initial steps to get the ball rolling, we are going to prepare with the information on the

Divine Dominion ReDefined

Principled Mindset of God to ensure that the *Spirit to Spirit Engagement* can occur properly. In our discussion regarding the ReDefining Process and *The Dominating Challenges* we may face, our Spirit Man already knows this information, so there is no need to DEFINE what is already; we simply need a reminder.

For our Spiritual Maturing Process, *As It Pleases God*, we are just AWAKENING what is written on the Tablet of our Hearts, and we only need to *Take Authority* in Earthen Vessels.

The Groundwork

While laying the Spiritual Platform and Groundwork for my life, it was not easy at all. Still, being that I was in Purpose on purpose, I had Divine Dominion to create a strong and stable edifice with my Mind, Body, Soul, and Spirit, which is my symbolic House or Temple. So, it was and still is my responsibility to ensure that it becomes MEANINGFUL and SUSTAINABLE according to Kingdom Standards that are PLEASING to God, my Heavenly Father.

Even though I get laughed at, mocked, talked about, and underestimated for using Proverbs 24:27, the Spiritual Principle for PREPARATION and PRIORITIZATION, I still do not relent to human reasoning. I target the Spiritual Aspects, allowing the Holy Trinity to dumb whatever it is or is not down for me with a Heaven on Earth Mindset and Heart Posture. With God at the forefront, I continue to analyze, research, brainstorm, and even seek advice while putting my hands to the plow and not turning back with my lips zipped.

What is the big deal about not turning back, especially when operating in a deficit? According to Luke 9:62, *"No one, having put his hand to the plow, and looking back, is fit for the kingdom of God."* The commitment to move forward in the Spirit of Excellence without bickering, fussing, fighting, or complaining means a lot in the Kingdom. And if we want the Divine Secrets, Wisdom, Treasures, and Understanding of all things Spiritual, we do not need to be perfect; we must develop the MINDSET OF EXCELLENCE amid our issues, hiccups, or mess-ups.

In my ReDefining Process, although unnerving and treacherous at times, I could not afford to turn my back on the innocent sheep who are in desperate need of this Divine Information for a time such as this. Therefore, in my condition, with all of my issues, and regardless of how my life appeared to the naked eye, I pursued and moved forward in the Spirit of Excellence despite the naysayers, manipulators, and dream killers. I must say, beyond a shadow of a doubt, the timeless SUSTAINING POWER from the Heavenly of Heavens did not miss a beat. With this being said, I am pretty sure by now that you would definitely agree!

At the core of investing, planning, and preparing for harvest amid a famine, I continue to plow, *As It Pleases God*. Now, the fields of Divine Information and Wisdom that I harvested over the years have become ROOTED and GROUNDED, setting the stage for success on my behalf and that of others. In addition, I have included all types of Spiritual Seeds activating the Law of Reciprocity to BUILD and PREPARE the lives of others until the end of time.

Is it not being a little arrogant when proclaiming to build and prepare the NEXT in line? Absolutely not! It is called UNWAVERING DEDICATION. I am committed to feeding God's sheep, *As It Pleases Him*, and I am also all in on being selflessly about His Business. Now the question is, 'Are you all in?' Then again, 'Is He all into you?' Wait, wait, wait, do not answer this question yet, let us talk a little more.

Every remarkable transformation ordained by the Heavenly Father comes at a price or sacrifice. I stand as a Testament to this, having paid a high price to evolve into the woman that I

Divine Dominion ReDefined

am today. The trials I faced were gruelingly painful and exhausting, but the invaluable lessons granted me a portion of Divine Wisdom, Understanding, and Authority that is undeniable and unrelenting.

In laying *The Groundwork*, if the Nuggets of Divine Wisdom from my story can save even one person from enduring the struggles I have faced, then every iota of my suffering was well worth it. Our experiences in life will often hold the keys to healing ourselves for the sake of others. Then again, what hurts us will also contain the catalyst for healing us as well. Due to God's Divine Grace and Mercy, this is where Divine Dominion comes into play, allowing us to glean and overcome through the POWER of our Testimony.

Back in the day, when laying *The Groundwork*, I did not have this type of information at my fingertips. As a Believer, it was my responsibility to present the information in the way that I needed it back then in my good ole days, without a whole lot of fluff and stuff. I needed solid, profound, relevant, proven, and guaranteed information, and this is what I give. And now that it is available to all mankind, the Floodgates of Wisdom have opened up for our sake with forward-looking faith.

What if we do not know what to say when speaking? Then hold your tongue. James 1:26 says, *"If anyone among you thinks he is religious, and does not bridle his tongue but deceives his own heart, this one's religion is useless."* When engaging in Divine Wisdom, the Holy Spirit will often test us in this manner to see if we will engage in lying rambling. Really? Yes, really! The lies we tell under pressure have astounded me. Instead of saying, 'I do not know,' 'Give me a minute,' 'I am not sure,' or 'Let me get back with you,' we begin making up stuff to make ourselves appear better than we are.

I cannot tell you how many times I have been written off as being unwise, dumb, or flighty for not knowing or remembering certain things or information. Above all, I am

Divine Dominion ReDefined

okay with people labeling me however they feel. Why do I not defend myself or attempt to prove them wrong? Because they are entitled to their own opinions. Plus, I know about the power hidden in having free will, and if I deprive them of it, my Divine Wisdom, Understanding, and Gleaning Faculties can become keeled. In addition, God has given every human being something to work with, and if they cannot see what I am working with, I do not force it; I LEARN!

Nevertheless, when the Holy Spirit speaks through me, all of those negative attributes go out the window. Luke 12:12 even states: *"For the Holy Spirit will teach you in that very hour what you ought to say."* If the Holy Spirit is not revealing, then it is our responsibility to hold our tongues. For example, when writing, if I am not getting Divine Downloads from the Heavenly of Heavens, I do not write anything. Instead, I may use my creativity in other ways to keep my mind busy and my creative juices flowing until the Voice of God begins to speak to me, *Spirit to Spirit.*

What if Believers do not respond to this information? Divine Wisdom is not by force; it is a free-will offering to those who are willing to receive. Here is the deal: I authentically present my hard-earned wisdom to the masses, and whatever is done with the information, I still gain my Spiritual Brownie Points with zero shame attached. What does this mean in layman's terms? Ultimately, how others respond to the information I share is beyond my control. What truly matters is the intention, as well as the heart and mind posture behind it. In addition, I also approach all things with 1 Thessalonians 5:11 on the table, sharing what I am given freely. It says, *"Therefore comfort each other and edify one another, just as you also are doing."*

To ensure that *The Groundwork* is laid effectively, we must prepare and document, *As It Pleases God.* If we do, here is the enforceable Spiritual Seal according to Matthew 7:24-25.

Divine Dominion ReDefined

"Therefore whoever hears these sayings of Mine, and does them, I will liken him to a wise man who built his house on the rock; and the rain descended, the floods came, and the winds blew and beat on that house; and it did not fall, for it was founded on the rock."

Whereas on the other hand, the ones who laughed, mocked, and underestimated the Hand of God based on my condition left zero fields, and zero gleaning faculties, and were forgotten by those whom they tried to impress with material gain. Clearly, with this analogy, I wish the best for everyone and do not invoke any ill will; however, if we do not prepare *The Groundwork* and refuse to document, *As It Pleases God*, here is what can happen according to Matthew 7:26-27. *"But everyone who hears these sayings of Mine, and does not do them, will be like a foolish man who built his house on the sand: and the rain descended, the floods came, and the winds blew and beat on that house; and it fell. And great was its fall."*

When there is a fall from within with personal failures, insecurities, and vulnerabilities from our fears, weaknesses, and shortcomings, we may find ourselves attempting to cancel others with or without just cause. The need to reinforce our own values and beliefs does not mean we should engage in *The Cancel Culture*. Why not? We could be treading on dangerous ground if we engage. According to the Heavenly of Heavens, we do not know what God is using to Spiritually Teach, Train, Guide, Chastise, or Develop us or them unless He advises us on the matter. So, let us dig a little deeper into this issue to ensure we are properly informed from a Spiritual Perspective.

The Cancel Culture

In a society increasingly divided, pressured, and manipulated, we have somehow bought into *The Cancel Culture* Phenomenon, judging the mistakes of others without accounting for our own. If my memory serves me correctly, Romans 3:23 says, *"For all have sinned and fall short of the glory of God."*

What if we have no sinful ways, thoughts, or desires as Believers? One of the biggest downfalls of mankind surrounds the deceptive lies we tell ourselves to justify our behavioral manifestations and charactorial quirks. With all of our known and unknown mishaps, 1 John 1:8 also calls us out on this matter: *"If we say that we have no sin, we deceive ourselves, and the truth is not in us."*

In the same way that we cancel others, what if God withdrew His Divine Hand from us? Unfortunately, we, as human beings, would cease to exist. Yet, His UNFAILING LOVE grants us the Breath of Life, and we are deadset on taking it from another person Mentally, Physically, Emotionally, or Spiritually. How do we make this make sense? In all simplicity, the works of the flesh contribute to hurting others, especially when our conscience is keeled.

What are the works of the flesh? According to Galatians 5:19-21, here is what we must know: *"Now the works of the flesh are evident, which are: adultery, fornication, uncleanness, lewdness, idolatry, sorcery, hatred, contentions, jealousies, outbursts of wrath, selfish ambitions, dissensions, heresies, envy, murders, drunkenness, revelries, and the like; of which I tell you beforehand, just as I also told you in time past, that those who practice such things will not inherit the kingdom of God."* If we are engaging in any of these things, we have no reason to participate in *The Cancel Culture* movement. Really? Yes, really!

Divine Dominion cannot remain in a place where we cancel others for the same things we are secretly or openly guilty of. Although we can have normal dominion based on the Laws of the Land; however, the Heavenly Elements of Divine Dominion based on the Spiritual Laws, Principles, and Protocols cannot remain until we awaken from our slumber. Why is this such a big deal? Galatians 6:7 says it best

Divine Dominion ReDefined

regarding one of the highest Spiritual Principles regarding Spiritual Duality given to mankind: *"Do not be deceived: God is not mocked; for whatever a man sows, that he will also reap."* The moment we think we are exempt, we will 'get got' by the enemy's wiles.

Why would we 'get got' by exempting ourselves? We have the 'Instead Factor' working against us unless we willfully reverse it from negative to positive. Here are a few examples, but not limited to such:

- ☐ Instead of canceling, we should be healing.
- ☐ Instead of judging, we should be more understanding.
- ☐ Instead of hating, we should be more loving.
- ☐ Instead of being sad, we should be more joyful.
- ☐ Instead of being chaotic, we should be more peaceful.
- ☐ Instead of being impatient, we should be more patient.
- ☐ Instead of being detestable, we should be more kind.
- ☐ Instead of being bad, we should be good.
- ☐ Instead of being unfaithful, we should be more faithful.
- ☐ Instead of being abrasive, we should be more gentle.
- ☐ Instead of being reckless, exercise self-control.
- ☐ Instead of being helpless, we should be more helpful.

Here is my question with the 'Instead Factor' on the table: 'How is it possible to Heal the Land when we are canceling the people, places, and things sustaining its viability?'

In today's swiftly changing social landscape, we are becoming so sensitive or offended by everything. With these ungoverned emotions, we participate in *Cancel Culture* to destroy and disrupt while avoiding the Spiritual Principles associated with building, growing, and establishing, *As It Pleases God*.

Divine Dominion ReDefined

Without an intense debate about who is right or wrong, how do Bloodwashed Believers approach the issues of canceling people? We must approach carefully and strategically with the Fruits of the Spirit and behave Christlike. For me, I approach with fact-finding and relevant questions, in the Spirit of Lovingkindness. Instead of arguing, I believe in fostering constructive dialogue with an understanding of growth or cultivation. I refuse to engage in nasty, negative, hasty, and hot-headed responses that lead to fear, division, condemnation, and all types of things that God hates. When things get heated, I will do a few things:

- ☐ I will walk away, shaking the dust off my feet. According to Matthew 10:14, it says, *"And whoever will not receive you nor hear your words, when you depart from that house or city, shake off the dust from your feet."*

- ☐ I will remain silent. Here is what I repeat over and over according to Psalm 141:3, *"Set a guard, O Lord, over my mouth; keep watch over the door of my lips."* Here is the reason WHY I repeat this over and over until the Holy Spirit consumes me with the Spirit of Peace: *"He who guards his mouth preserves his life, but he who opens wide his lips shall have destruction."* Proverbs 13:3.

- ☐ I will respond kindly and respectfully to deflate the situation. Here is WHY: Proverbs 16:24 says, *"Pleasant words are like a honeycomb, sweetness to the soul and health to the bones."* *"A soft answer turns away wrath, but a harsh word stirs up anger."* Proverbs 15:1.

Is this not being weak? No, it is a matter of exhibiting strength, especially with my tongue. Here is what Proverbs

Divine Dominion ReDefined

18:21 shares with us about our hidden power: *"Death and life are in the power of the tongue, and those who love it will eat its fruit."*

Trust me when I say this: It takes a lot of self-discipline to walk away with a target on your back, to hold your tongue when you are intentionally provoked, or to be nice to an outright jerk with a smile on your face. Above all, here is what Matthew 7:6 taught me: *"Do not give what is holy to the dogs; nor cast your pearls before swine, lest they trample them under their feet, and turn and tear you in pieces."* For this reason, I do not force my Spiritual Gifts on anyone; they must want it for themselves to receive the Divine Impartation from the Heavenly of Heavens. But know this: When I walk away, I take my BLESSINGS, WISDOM, and DIVINE COVERING with me, period!

Listen, when dealing with *Divine Dominion: As It Pleases God*®, we do not need to contend or stand against anyone or anything when we do a few things, but not limited to such:

- ☐ When we OPERATE *As It Pleases God.*
- ☐ When we USE the Fruits of the Spirit faithfully.
- ☐ When we BEHAVE Christlike.
- ☐ When we STAND on the Word of God.
- ☐ When we COVER ourselves with the Blood of Jesus.
- ☐ When we ALLOW the Holy Spirit to guide, provide, and protect.
- ☐ When we REVERSE bad to good, negative to positive, wrongs to right, losses to wins, and so on.
- ☐ When we REPENT and FORGIVE consistently.

In addition to this list, we must also know what perturbs our Heavenly Father. Why must we know what He does not like? Spiritually Speaking, it is designed to ensure that we do not begin to fight against or cancel ourselves without knowing it, while overlooking our own flaws. Nor do we want to perpetuate a cycle of negativity, hatefulness, debauchery, and bitterness, vilifying others.

What is the big deal, especially when having free will to vilify whomever we please? To write about vilification effectively means that I have to endure this type of canceling culture based on the things I write about today. Now, to answer the question: Having free will does not mean we should bite the hand feeding us. Plus, our differences must be respected, even if we do not agree, especially when we are sitting around doing NOTHING for the Kingdom of God while twiddling our thumbs, knowing nothing about our reason for being or our Divinely Blueprinted Purpose. Yes, I said it...Once again, we should not be canceling anybody when we are confused about why we are here in the first place, when we are not in Purpose on purpose, when we refuse to confront our own shortcomings, or when we fail to understand what God hates.

One of the most explicit lists of what God hates can be found in Proverbs 6:16-19. The passage states: There are six things the Lord hates; yes, seven are an abomination to Him:

- ☐ A proud look.
- ☐ A lying tongue.
- ☐ Hands that shed innocent blood.
- ☐ A heart that devises wicked plans.
- ☐ Feet that are swift in running to evil.
- ☐ A false witness who speaks lies.
- ☐ And one who sows discord among brethren.

When dealing with pride, deceit, violence, discord, or disregard for God's Divine Creation, we are quick to get a side eye from Him, especially when Romans 12:18 says, *"If it is possible, as much as depends on you, live peaceably with all men."*

Divine Dominion ReDefined

Why are we getting a side eye from God, primarily when we are doing our best as Believers? First, in doing our best, here is what 1 Corinthians 15:33 advises: *"Do not be deceived: 'Evil company corrupts good habits.'"* Secondly, He did not establish us in Earthen Vessels to bring His Kingdom down to please ourselves. Thirdly, He did not design us for our Heaven on Earth Experiences to leave Him out of the equation as we become our own demigods, doing whatever, whenever, however, wherever, whyever, and with whomever.

According to the Heavenly Expectations of humanity, God placed us here to build His Kingdom, *As It Pleases Him*, in the Spirit of Righteousness, Integrity, Love, and Unity with a *Spirit to Spirit* Relationship with Him. Without justice, repentance, forgiveness, humility, mercy, or a *Spirit to Spirit* Relationship with Him, conflicting desires for power, money, sex, understanding, and connection will grab hold of us. When we risk becoming ensnared by conflicting desires, it can symbolically become the vise grip known for leading us further away from the Kingdom and His Divine Presence.

As we face the daily struggles of conflicting desires, needs, and wants, we inadvertently stub our own toes when the newness wears off. For sure, these known or unknown yearnings, while deeply human, can lead us astray into the lust of the eyes, the lust of the flesh, and the pride of life, headfirst. Many chase after them, believing that success in these areas will bring happiness and fulfillment. Whereas, in the Eye of God, they are only fleeting, cultivating a sense of emptiness once the emotional high wears off.

Unfortunately, this profound sense of disillusionment produces a form of secret isolation and dissatisfaction within the psyche of mankind. If not rectified accordingly or if the state of mental disarray is not addressed properly, we will find ourselves bonding with people, places, and things, zapping our personal power. In many cases, these toxic attachments serve as coping mechanisms, which often lead to unmet expectations, ungratefulness, dissatisfaction, and warped perspectives plagued with negative thoughts, words, and feelings. If they are not reversed from negative to positive or if we do not break the toxic cycle, *The Dominating Challenges* will escalate until we reclaim our *Divine Dominion: As It Pleases God®*.

The Dominating Challenges

In *ReDefining Divine Dominion* in a way that is palatable and effective, we must willfully RECLAIM our lives and AWAKEN from our slumber with a commitment to activate the Law of Reciprocity to build and enrich another. By upgrading ourselves from a lower conscious state of being, we can dominate our challenges with Divine Preciseness, getting to the core or seed of whatever issues we face.

What if we choose not to upgrade or elevate our level of consciousness, *As It Pleases God*? We have free will to increase, decrease, or remain the same. However, He is not going to come down to our level to appease us, nor will He force us to use what He has already provided in Earthen Vessel.

How do we know when *The Dominating Challenges* are getting the best of us? The psyche knows...and we do not need confirmation from anyone because it is conveyed in our thoughts, actions, reactions, words, beliefs, biases, perceptions, weaknesses, and traumas. If one does not believe this, please allow me to query the psyche for a moment:

- ☐ Are you resentful toward anyone or anything?
- ☐ Do you overly worry about negative things?
- ☐ Are you suspicious of everyone you meet?
- ☐ Do you get angry quickly?
- ☐ Are you overly jealous?
- ☐ Do you envy those who possess more than you?

Divine Dominion ReDefined

- ☐ Are you secretly insecure or shy?
- ☐ Do you fear what you do not understand?
- ☐ Are you extremely competitive?
- ☐ Do you allow your ego to get the best of you?
- ☐ Are you humble?
- ☐ Do you feel better when you lie?
- ☐ Are you battling with a negative addiction or habit?
- ☐ Do you often engage in acts of rebellion?
- ☐ Are you very indecisive?

Answering these questions proves that the psyche knows more than we think. Why is this the case? By Divine Design, the psyche holds the unconscious SEEDS of our motivations, fears, proclivities, unresolved issues, aspirations, conflicts, triggers, and memories, even if we do not remember them.

Beneath the layers of consciousness, the human psyche is complex, unique, capitalistic, and poignant, doing what it takes to get our undivided attention by creating patterns. Even though it is a part of our nature, if we do not control it, it will control us with the reservoir of our positive and negative experiences. In addition, it also possesses an interplay that can work for or against us to feed our fleshly wants, needs, desires, and habits to reel us in or hang us out to dry.

If we want to recognize and address our unresolved feelings, uncontrollable mental chatter, underlying habits, cycles of disobedience, or unresolved traumas, we must begin to deal with the psyche and its fleshly ways. What if we know nothing about the psyche of mankind? It is time to get in the know to avoid the unconscious bouts of self-sabotage, blocked inner compass, warring from within, and distorted senses. All of this prevents us from becoming truly Spirit Led, *As It Pleases God*! Blasphemy, right? Wrong! Galatians 5:17

Divine Dominion ReDefined

says, *"For the flesh lusts against the Spirit, and the Spirit against the flesh; and these are contrary to one another, so that you do not do the things that you wish."* Then again, here is what James 4:1 says, *"Where do wars and fights come from among you? Do they not come from your desires for pleasure that war in your members?"*

Whether or not we confront or deny our truths, we can feel the tugging from within. Even when we sugarcoat, lie, or deny the internal warring process, the complex interplay of psychological and biological responses continues, releasing a cascade of chemicals within the body, with or without our permission.

When we lie to ourselves, the brain does not merely conjure up untruths, masks, or fairytales, only. It engages in a series of cognitive processes that trigger emotional and physiological responses. Moreover, it facilitates the conflict between the truth and the deception, creating our very own built-in lie detector test, which stimulates the release of stress hormones, primarily cortisol and adrenaline, leading to feelings of anxiety and discomfort.

Besides, in our quest to understand ourselves from the inside out, our psyche holds many of the answers we are desperately searching for. We simply need to MASTER how to ask the right questions without justifying or lying to ourselves while getting out of our own way.

How do we begin the process of getting out of our own way as Believers? First, if we begin by ReDefining our self-talk from negative to positive, wrong to right, unjust to just, bad to good, and so on, we can change our lives for the Greater Good. Secondly, if we activate the Law of Reciprocity, giving in the area of our needs, it can assist in this process as well.

How do we make giving make sense, especially when we can barely help ourselves? In the Eye of God, whatever we need, we must be willing to give it with no strings attached. For example, when faced with *Dominating Challenges*, here is a

Divine Dominion ReDefined

list to help break negative stigmas or attachments, but not limited to such:

- ☐ If we need love, give it.
- ☐ If we need hope, give it.
- ☐ If we need peace, give it.
- ☐ If we need joy, give it.
- ☐ If we need patience, give it.
- ☐ If we need kindness, give it.
- ☐ If we need goodness, give it.
- ☐ If we need faithfulness, give it.
- ☐ If we need gentleness, give it.
- ☐ If we need self-control, give it.
- ☐ If we need support, give it.
- ☐ If we need a shoulder to lean on, give it.
- ☐ If we need a hug, give it.
- ☐ If we need mercy, give it.
- ☐ If we need forgiveness, give it.
- ☐ If we need gratefulness, give it.

These intangible free will offerings break more yokes than we could care to imagine. Although this is not a long list, still, if we master this list alone, it will indeed change the trajectory of our lives, guaranteed.

What makes this list work so well for Believers? Once we release a free-will offering into the atmosphere with goodwill, *As It Pleases God*, it must find its way back to us based on the Law of Reciprocity. Plus, it reverses the negative controlling factors associated. For instance, with the desire to be understood with a sense of belonging, if we do not exercise self-control, our mental chatter and headspace can become consumed with desires or mental playbacks before the action, habit, or yoke of domination occurs. Whereas, if we exercise

Divine Dominion ReDefined

the use of self-control with ourselves and others, we can regulate our mental playback, reversing it from negative to positive at the drop of a dime.

The challenge lies in finding a balance between what to dominate and what NOT to dominate. What is the difference? One provides a BRIDGE, getting and preparing us for our NEXT, making us relevant, usable, obedient, and pleasant. The other one provides a PIT to stifle and blind us with all types of yokes, traumas, and issues, making us toxic, dull, stiffnecked, and lukewarm. In *Divine Dominion ReDefined*, we as Spiritual Beings having a human experience must determine which one will dominate based on our free will.

Negating the Spiritual Principles of mutual respect and cooperation, while thinking we are above God or becoming demigods for followers, clicks, and status, can lead to unethical thoughts, practices, and desires. And then we dare to engage in justifying our blatant idolatrous efforts and put God on the back burner as if He is secondary or ranking Him very low on our personalized hierarchy. All of this leads to destructive behaviors, thoughts, beliefs, words, desires, and demeanor, making us secretly or openly oppressive, exploitative, and violent while appearing right in our own eyes. For this reason, God is calling for Divine Dominion to become ReDefined for those who have a willing ear to hear, thus saith the Lord of Hosts.

When dealing with *Divine Dominion: As It Pleases God*®, we all have something to '*Give Back*' to the Kingdom of Heaven as a token of appreciation. Now, we may not all know what it is, and for this reason, in this chapter, the goal is to help narrow this down, ensuring we develop a clear image of our Divine Blueprint to ReDefine what is already.

Why does *ReDefining Divine Dominion* require a shift in mindset? The concept of Divine Dominion has been thwarted by the underlying elements of control, tainting our Spiritual

Divine Dominion ReDefined

Relationship with our Heavenly Father. Therefore, it is only wise to ReDefine ourselves to a form of stewardship or servanthood instead of engaging in blatant idolatry or becoming demigods to control the narrative. Is this Biblical? I would have it no other way. Mark 10:44-45 says, *"And whoever of you desires to be first shall be slave of all. For even the Son of Man did not come to be served, but to serve, and to give His life a ransom for many."*

In addition, John 12:26 also says, *"If anyone serves Me, let him follow Me; and where I am, there My servant will be also. If anyone serves Me, him My Father will honor."* *"But he who is greatest among you shall be your servant."* Matthew 23:11. So, when someone approaches me with the mindset of being the best thing since sliced bread, and cannot serve another, I do not believe them! Why not? To become the Crème de la Crème of the Kingdom, servanthood is not an option; it is a prerequisite.

Am I pulling for straws with Kingdom Prerequisites? Absolutely not! In the Eye of God, our Heavenly Father, mere rhetoric is not going to cut it, nor will it prevent the enemy from targeting us! In addition, good works and public displays of faith to show off do not guarantee Kingdom Acceptance or Usability. We need Spiritual Fruits to sustain our *Spirit to Spirit* Connection, and we must behave Christlike to truly represent the Kingdom, *As It Pleases God*.

If we continue to play church or keep pretending while selfishly consuming our own fruits, leaving rotten fruits all over the place, playing with God, or pimping Him out, here is what Matthew 7:21-23 has to say about this RELATIONAL DISCONNECT. *"Not everyone who says to Me, 'Lord, Lord,' shall enter the kingdom of heaven, but he who does the will of My Father in heaven. Many will say to Me in that day, 'Lord, Lord, have we not prophesied in Your name, cast out demons in Your name, and done many wonders in Your name?' And then I will declare to them, 'I never knew you; depart from Me, you who practice lawlessness!'"*

Divine Dominion ReDefined

The concept of servanthood might seem counterintuitive for some, especially when possessing a posh image of delusion. However, within the Spiritual Realm of Divine Leadership, Authority, and Greatness, we SERVE to LEAD in the Spirit of Excellence, *As It Pleases God*.

Taking Authority

As we all know, life is often a winding road, filled with twists, turns, roadblocks, and dead ends. If or when we get off course, we do not want to run to God to have a pity party with a sense of entitlement, especially if we are dead set on doing what we want to please ourselves. For this reason, it is imperative to seek clarity, wisdom, and understanding with a level of accountability and humility that turns our weaknesses into strengths and failures into purpose.

According to the Heavenly of Heavens, to have authority over our lives, choices, and destinies, we must become guided by Spiritual Principles, Laws, and Protocols with a Spiritual Awakening Process. If not, instead of having dominion, we become minions (followers) falling for the okey doke when we should be becoming Doers of the Word of God.

Understandably, we all have issues in need of reckoning, but we should not wait until the last minute to work on them. Why should we not put off working on ourselves? We can block or delay our Divine Blessings, Spiritual Preparation, or Training. Plus, we do not want to be ill-prepared when evilness attacks us from the inside out, and then we try to play cleanup when the Wrath of God is upon us. In my opinion, this is similar to King Saul's experience in 1 Samuel 16, where the Spirit of God departs from him, and something evil tortures his psyche to no avail. The moment we think we are any different from Saul or we get a free pass on willful disobedience, we will 'get got' by the enemy's wiles. How so? We will eventually turn on ourselves without realizing it!

Divine Dominion ReDefined

Having *Divine Dominion: As It Pleases God*® does not grant free rein over the Earth to control and terrorize others. Instead, it places an obligation on humanity to act ethically, respectfully, and rationally with a Spiritual Framework and Balance of the Kingdom. In the same way that when building a house, we need a solid foundation and frame with all types of checks and balance systems in place for stability, we are no different. When embracing Divine Dominion, we must do likewise in the Realm of the Spirit.

As stewards in Earthen Vessels, when *Taking Authority*, we must begin Spiritually Tilling our own grounds to ensure we are up to par to lead by example amid distractions and challenges. Just as farmers prepare their fields to ensure a fruitful harvest, we too must do likewise.

Taking Authority is not merely about having control or influence, as most would think. According to the Heavenly of Heavens, it is about embodying the Kingdom Principles, exhibiting integrity, compassion, and resilience in getting the job done from start to finish.

What if we have a problem completing projects? Outside of having a medical condition limiting us, the act of leaving projects unfinished is most often associated with a few items, but not limited to such:

- ☐ The lack of motivation or poor time management.
- ☐ The lack of control or planning.
- ☐ The lack of focus or clarity.
- ☐ Unregulated stress and anxiety.
- ☐ Perceived limitations or setbacks.
- ☐ Mental blockages or brain fog.
- ☐ Unclear goals or objectives.
- ☐ Overwhelming confusion or frustration.
- ☐ Loss of interest or support.
- ☐ Insufficient resources.

Divine Dominion ReDefined

- ☐ Fear of judgment, rejection, or being ridiculed.
- ☐ Internal or external distractions.
- ☐ Fear of success, winning, or completion.
- ☐ Excessive burnout, exhaustion, or loss of energy.
- ☐ Ungoverned indecisiveness or skepticism.
- ☐ Ulterior or manipulative motives.
- ☐ Unfulfilled expectations.
- ☐ An underlying reason to return.

When we have a history of starting what we cannot finish, we often run into a brick wall, suffering multiple failures and setbacks, openly or privately. Why would this happen? It is due to some form of underlying disobedience relating to the hidden elements of selfishness intertwined in our senses, habits, or lusts.

In the Eye of God, when it comes to our domain or dominion, what we DO determines the MAIN thing, especially in the areas where we hold INFLUENCE or AUTHORITY. Our actions or reactions set the stage for what's to come, regardless of whether we are dealing with our personal, business, relational, or work-related affairs. This Spiritual Principle also applies to societal issues and governances, or markets, products, and customer relations, even if we deny or downplay its existence. When *Taking Authority* on any level, what we DO or fail to DO within these boundaries determines who we are, positively or negatively.

For example, if we are comfortable with serving others or behaving shotty as if we are doing them a favor, then that is who we are. Conversely, if we are more comfortable with serving others or behaving integrally, doing everything in the Spirit of Excellence with goodwill, then that is who we are. The bottom line is that our method of operation says a lot

Divine Dominion ReDefined

about our character without us having to say one word. Really? Yes, really!

If one does not believe what we DO determines the MAIN thing, let us take a look at Luke 6:43-45 on how our actions and behaviors shape our character. *"For a good tree does not bear bad fruit, nor does a bad tree bear good fruit. For every tree is known by its own fruit. For men do not gather figs from thorns, nor do they gather grapes from a bramble bush. A good man out of the good treasure of his heart brings forth good; and an evil man out of the evil treasure of his heart brings forth evil. For out of the abundance of the heart his mouth speaks."*

For me, I pay attention to what a person does or refuses to do before I believe what comes out of their mouth. I learned this Spiritual Principle from Proverbs 14:15. It says, *"The simple believes every word, but the prudent considers well his steps."* Does this make us suspicious of everyone? No, it makes us pay attention and examine our fruits and theirs as well.

Our fruits do not lie, but the tongue will lie at the drop of a dime! Is this not why Psalm 34:13 says, *"Keep your tongue from evil, and your lips from speaking deceit."* For this reason, in the ReDefining Process, Ephesians 2:10 gives us a little pep talk, letting us know this: *"For we are His workmanship, created in Christ Jesus for good works, which God prepared beforehand that we should walk in them."*

All in all, the good is already within each one of us; we simply need to *Take Authority* and bring it forth, *As It Pleases God*. If we do not make a willful effort to bring it forth, the bad can dominate the Mind, Body, and Soul by reason of omission, ratting us out in due season. Please allow me to Spiritually Align the ratting process according to Kingdom Standards: *"He who walks with integrity walks securely, but he who perverts his ways will become known."* Proverbs 10:9.

Divine Dominion ReDefined

In the ReDefining Process, what would cause the hidden elements of selfishness to occur, ratting us out? It will vary from person to person, situation to situation, mindset to mindset, lesson to lesson, and so on. From the Garden of Eden to the present, when it comes to selfishness and disobedience, we do not get a free pass. So, the cause of the ratting out process could be due to a few things, but not limited to such:

- ☐ We have the wrong motives or heart posture, causing us to manipulate, scheme, bully, or use others.

- ☐ We are following the vision of another while hiding or shying away from our Divine Blueprint just to feel accepted, fit in, or prove our loyalty.

- ☐ We lack passion or the get-up-and-go, contributing to greediness, ungratefulness, or laziness.

- ☐ We are trying to recreate the wheel based on some form of superficial worldly expectations or idolatry.

- ☐ We are negative or doubtful while NOT creating a win-win out of everything, or we refuse to develop a Positive Mental Mindset.

- ☐ We have not taken the time to mind-map or journal the instructions or pointers given, only to find ourselves wandering in circles without a Plan of Action.

- ☐ We are not learning, growing, and sowing back into the Kingdom while believing we were self-created. And, from my perspective, had it not been for God's GRACE and MERCY, we would not be where we are today.

Divine Dominion ReDefined

- [ ] We are consumed Mentally, Physically, Emotionally, and Spiritually with jealousy, envy, pride, and coveting, blocking access to our Spiritual Gifts.

- [ ] We are exhibiting competitiveness, causing all forms of disobedience and uncooperativeness.

- [ ] We are oblivious to exhibiting the Fruits of the Spirit or behaving Christlike while negating to perfect our people skills.

- [ ] We are operating in an unrepentant or unrelenting Spirit.

- [ ] We have not involved the Holy Trinity in our Spiritual Giftings as if we were self-made.

In *Divine Dominion ReDefined*, self-improvement and self-discovery are needed with Divine Insightfulness. Although self-belief, self-trust, and self-understanding provide *The Opportunity* for us to become better, stronger, and wiser, *As It Pleases God*. Still, we must also add Him to our equational efforts.

Yes, we are taught to trust God, have faith in Him, and understand His Divine Ways. However, we are not often taught to truly believe in ourselves, trust our instincts, master our senses, and understand the Spiritual Compass that lies within. In the Eye of God, all of these attributes underscore the immense power in participating and shaping our outcomes while confronting our doubts, challenges, weaknesses, fears, and idiosyncrasies.

Do we really possess power as Believers? Absolutely. We have regular power, and then we have Divine Access to

Divine Dominion ReDefined

Supernatural Power as well. We simply need to know it beyond a shadow of a doubt and own it, *As It Pleases God*. 2 Timothy 1:7 says: *"For God has not given us a spirit of fear, but of power and of love and of a sound mind."*

The POWER and OPPORTUNITIES are hidden within each one of us based on our commitments, character, and fruits. And then, our LEVEL of power is determined by our Divine Blueprint and whether we are in Purpose on purpose. What does this mean? Our Divine Purpose has a level of PROTECTION and POWER that we can only tap into by ENGAGING with it, *As It Pleases God*. Blasphemy, right? Wrong!

If you think you are big and bad enough to intentionally hurt someone who is in their Divine Purpose or who is Divinely Appointed by the Heavenly of Heavens, then carry on and see what happens. I promise what I am saying will make a believer out of you! For the record, the Wrath of God is not something you want to contend with, especially when your ego is pumping you up to become an untouchable demigod. Psalm 105:15 even warns us about this matter: *"Do not touch My anointed ones, and do My prophets no harm."*

As a Word to the Wise, the way God operates, you will not know who possesses the Real Power unless the Holy Spirit reveals it to you. According to the Heavenly of Heavens, they will NEVER look the way we envision Divine Power and Authority. For their protection, they will move in SILENT HUMILITY. So much so that you will think they are weak, timid, and oblivious to what's really happening. Nevertheless, amid the wolves in sheep's clothing, they are wise as a serpent and gentle as a dove, as stated in Matthew 10:16.

When dealing with *Divine Dominion: As It Pleases God*®, it is always WISE to do good to all and be kind to everyone. God will NEVER put Divine Power into the hands of a reckless fool. Why not? First, it is dangerous, like a double-edged but

Divine Dominion ReDefined

teachable sword. Secondly, they will think they are above Him while doing and saying things to benefit themselves at the expense of the innocent. Thirdly, they can NEVER outdo or outsmart God Almighty, even on their best day. However, if man gives their earthly power over to a reckless fool who is full of folly, then that is their free will choice, and God will allow it to teach us a valuable lesson regarding how FAITH and DOMINION really work.

Conversely, if someone is self-appointed, man-appointed, cheated their way to the top, and has all types of rotten fruits all over the place while behaving badly, engaging in all types of debauchery and idolatrous efforts, the enemy will have a field day with them. Why would this happen to a Believer? They lack Kingdom Authority! We cannot cast down our enemies by behaving like them. Even though we have free will, we must behave UNLIKE them, and *As It Pleases God* to Spiritually Counteract and harness real Spiritual Power on HIGH.

Can we really counteract the wiles of the enemy as Believers? Absolutely! We have the right to agree or disagree; however, most of us do not understand what to counteract because the enemy can appear amid fear, anxiety, or insecurity. Surely, all of these can become problematic for us, but we still must engage in *Taking Authority* over all forms of negativity. When rejecting negativity, we do not need to become combative, loud, rude, or pretentious. Just reverse it kindly and smoothly, like honey dripping from a honeycomb.

For example, if someone says, 'You are unattractive to me.' I would say, 'I am beautiful in the Eye of God. Thus, He makes everything beautiful in its Divine Timing, and He does not make mistakes.' In closing, I would wrap up my response with an open-ended, redirecting question of concern, provoking the element of thought, such as: 'What do you think about how God sees beauty?' 'How do you feel about

Divine Dominion ReDefined

God's beauty residing from the inside out?' Or, then again, I may flip the script by asking, 'Would you agree?'

What is the purpose of gaining agreement in the reversal, canceling, or counteracting? Once the negative forecaster comes into agreement with our positive reversal, it creates a double-seal. How so? They came into agreement with the positivity that we interjected to intercept their debaucherous attempts. With this approach, more than likely, they will move on to an easier victim. What if they do not? Unfortunately, due to *The Role of Free Will*, they will begin to turn on themselves from the inside out with all types of insecurities and negative mental chatter.

Dr. Y. Bur

www.DrYBur.com

Chapter Two
The Role of Free Will

One of the most profound Spiritual Principles that we are seldom taught is *The Role of Free Will*. The illusion of freedom shrouded in chains of limitations makes us complacent without wanting to interject Spiritual Intervention until we become yoked to the core. Regardless of whether we are deprived of our free will or deprive others of their free-willed choices, accountability remains the same because we were not created as robots.

According to Scripture, we were created with dominion according to Genesis 1:26-27. *"Then God said, 'Let Us make man in Our image, according to Our likeness; let them have dominion over the fish of the sea, over the birds of the air, and over the cattle, and over all the earth and over every creeping thing that creeps on the earth.' So God created man in His own image; in the image of God He created him; male and female He created them."* Nowhere does it say, God created robots! However, He has given us the power to create robots, but we were not designed as such; we were designed with the free will to obey or disobey, to agree or disagree, to love or not

The Role of Free Will

to love, to want or reject, to participate or not to participate, and so on.

As we navigate the complexities of our existence or what we think about our Creator, He has given us normal assignments and Divine Assignments. Even if we ignore them, opt out, or check out, they still exist, awaiting our free will participation.

For instance, normal assignments are associated with our day-to-day operations, such as raising our children, taking care of our homes, assisting our spouses, carrying out certain tasks, and so on. Our Divine Assignments are associated with our reason for being and contain a Predestined Blueprint that comes through Him, by Him, for Him, and In Him with a Quaternity-Based Spiritual Seal. Is this Biblical? Absolutely! Jeremiah 1:5 says, *"Before I formed you in the womb I knew you; before you were born I sanctified you; I ordained you a prophet to the nations."* Where is the Divine Quaternity in this Scripture?

- ☐ He FORMED.
- ☐ He KNEW.
- ☐ He SANCTIFIED.
- ☐ He ORDAINED.

In *Divine Dominion: As It Pleases God*®, this is the Spiritual Process that will occur when we become wholeheartedly WILLING and ABLE to walk in Purpose on purpose. Unfortunately, it is the SANCTIFYING part that causes most of us to run for the hills.

In my opinion, if we desire to run to the hills while exercising free will, we need to make sure we run to the right hilltop when seeking protection and refuge. From experience, I must say that God does His greatest works when we are in the wilderness, wandering in the desert, in a famine, or when

The Role of Free Will

activating Psalm 121:1-2 when possessing the PROMISE, *"I will lift up mine eyes unto the hills, from whence cometh my help. My help cometh from the Lord, which made heaven and earth."*

In the hidden Spiritual Quaternity of the hills, if we willfully and faithfully develop The-Lord-Will-Provide Mindset, He will move Heaven and Earth for us with a ram in the bush. I extracted this Spiritual Reference from Genesis 22:14, where it says, *"And Abraham called the name of the place, The-Lord-Will-Provide; as it is said to this day, 'In the Mount of the Lord it shall be provided.'"* When combining the righteousness of our free will with The-Lord-Will-Provide Mindset, *As It Pleases Him*, it rattles the Heavenly of Heavens with a Clarion Call to come to see about us.

When we bring our willing faith and willful obedience together, Divine Provisions must come forth. How do I know? Psalm 37:5 says, *"Commit your way to the Lord, Trust also in Him, And He shall bring it to pass." "I have been young, and now am old; Yet I have not seen the righteous forsaken, Nor his descendants begging bread."* Psalm 37:25. Conversely, if we lack faith and are disobedient to the Will and Ways of God, Divine Provisions can indeed be withheld until we awaken from our slumber. Hebrews 11:6 says, *"But without faith it is impossible to please Him, for he who comes to God must believe that He is, and that He is a rewarder of those who diligently seek Him."* So, in *The Role of Free Will*, if those Divine Rewards are not flowing, we must check to see if our faith is PLEASING to Him.

What is the big deal, especially when Abraham has nothing to do with us? Fortunately, we are living in the Promises of Abraham. Nevertheless, in the same way that God tested him when stepping into uncertainty, we will be tested as well to gauge our unwavering trust in Him, the amount of trust we have in ourselves, and the level of trust we have in others.

The Role of Free Will

What is the purpose of God testing us? First, it is used to prepare us. Secondly, to see if we would faithfully trust Him more than we trust ourselves or others with sacrificial obedience. If He is not first above all else or if we refuse to obey Him, it is back into the Spiritual Classroom for preparatory updates on charactorial reformation and to strengthen our faith. Here is what Proverbs 3:5-6 taught me in my Divine Reformation Process: *"Trust in the Lord with all your heart, And lean not on your own understanding; In all your ways acknowledge Him, And He shall direct your paths."*

Our Forefathers did not have the luxuries that we have today, but they were all so FAITHFUL and POWERFUL in the Eye of God. Yet, in today's day and age, we have Divine Access to more in and out of the Kingdom, but for some odd reason, we do less with what we have been GRACED to possess in Earthen Vessels. How so? Based on our free will, here are a few things to consider, but not limited to such:

☐ We have the Blood of Jesus as Spiritual Atonement, allowing us to go to God for ourselves, *Spirit to Spirit*. Revelation 1:5-6 clues us in on how important the role of our Mediator is to Him. *"And from Jesus Christ, the faithful witness, the firstborn from the dead, and the ruler over the kings of the earth. To Him who loved us and washed us from our sins in His own blood, and has made us kings and priests to His God and Father, to Him be glory and dominion forever and ever. Amen."* According to the Heavenly of Heavens, we fail to use our Go-between as He intended. While, at the same time, willfully not REPENTING or FORGIVING ourselves and others for the same things we are secretly or openly guilty of.

☐ We have the Holy Spirit to guide, teach, and provide for us. With His on-demand or on-call Divine

The Role of Free Will

Presence, when we encounter trials and tribulations, we panic or spaz out as if He does not exist. Then again, if we do usher in His Divine Presence, we do not listen, learn, or obey Him as we should while trying to fix ourselves and others on our own without Him. On the other hand, we may begin self-medicating with people, places, and things to replace Him. According to the Heavenly of Heavens, when in this state of being, we willfully lie on the Holy Spirit while opting to remain stiffnecked, dull, or lukewarm, and sometimes avoiding the Spiritual Classroom altogether.

☐ We have the Fruits of the Spirit to help us build our charactorial skills to become Christlike and to gain Divine Favor. Yet, we are clueless about them or how to use them while willfully opting to remain jealous, envious, confused, greedy, pompous, and covetous.

☐ We have the Word of God to guide us with Spiritual Principles, Testaments, and Instructions. Yet, what do we do? We extract what we want while discarding what we really need while debating and dividing ourselves over who is right or wrong. 2 Timothy 3:16-17 even says, *"All Scripture is given by inspiration of God, and is profitable for doctrine, for reproof, for correction, for instruction in righteousness, that the man of God may be complete, thoroughly equipped for every good work."*

In my opinion, if we have not taken the time to document our Testament or Testimony, we should not engage in judging or degrading the Word of God. Why not? Or better yet, do we not have free will to do so? Yes, we do have free will; however, if they (the Writers of the Bible) took the time to document what they have

The Role of Free Will

learned and we have not, then whose words are more powerful?

Our words do not add up to a hill of beans, especially if they are lost in the wind of life or go undocumented! With all due respect, if our stories die with us or we refuse to share our story, then we must ask ourselves, 'Am I living in vain?'

Remember, the Word of God lives on with or without us...use it to bring life by saying this consistently: *"Your word is a lamp to my feet and a light to my path."* Psalm 119:105. It contains invaluable WISDOM that will change the trajectory of our lives, guaranteed.

Oddly enough, the underlying truth is that we DO NOT want to experience the liberating power of free will Mentally, Physically, Emotionally, or Spiritually. Why do we subconsciously do this to ourselves? First, we are not taught about this stuff. Secondly, it may require self-restraint or self-sacrifice, so we settle for the yokes of bondage without really knowing what we are doing or the reasons why.

I must say, the funny thing about all of this is that we desire FINANCIAL FREEDOM over all else. I am sometimes baffled by how this often pans out, but it is a topic in need of addressing. So, in this chapter, we are going to get down to the nitty-gritty, taking our understanding of free will to the next level.

The Role of Free Will refers to the birthright of mankind to make genuine choices that should not be constrained by internal or external influences, intangible or intangible forces, and predetermined or coincidental outcomes, regardless of our foreknowledge, back knowledge, or assumed knowledge. All this means is that as a part of being human and based on the Spiritual Law of Duality, we have the Divine Right to

The Role of Free Will

choose between right and wrong, good and evil, just and unjust, positive and negative, and so on. Even if we are clueless about what we are agreeing to, it is also our responsibility to get an understanding. Here is the Spiritual Seal from Proverbs 4:7: *"Wisdom is the principal thing; therefore get wisdom: and with all thy getting get understanding."*

With all the information presented before us, good, bad, or indifferent, we must be free to choose, and we must also be ready to bear the positive or negative consequences of our choices, actions, and decisions. Conversely, suppose we do not have all the information. In this case, it is also our responsibility to ask fact-finding questions to make the appropriate assessment or decision, and then do this:

- ☐ Add God into *The Equation*.
- ☐ Evaluate *Overall Perceptiveness*.
- ☐ Practice *Self-Acceptance*.
- ☐ We must *Run Our Own Race*.
- ☐ Remain on *The Leading Edge*.

At a glance, we may feel that we exercise free will in our thoughts, actions, decisions, and words. However, many of these choices are influenced by conditioning, traumas, societal expectations, environments, and, most of all, our ego.

Our free will is indeed the Cornerstone of Greatness hidden within all mankind, giving us the ability to navigate or propagate according to our likes, dislikes, desires, and aspirations. Although trauma, hiccups, and conditioning can sometimes hinder this vital aspect of the personal growth and fulfillment process. Still, it cannot stop us if we refuse to allow it to do so. Listed below are a few things to do, but not limited to such:

The Role of Free Will

- ☐ Add God into *The Equation* of all things.
- ☐ Operate *As It Pleases Him*.
- ☐ Relate to Him *Spirit to Spirit* when praying.
- ☐ Plead the Blood of Jesus as Spiritual Atonement.
- ☐ Invite the Holy Spirit into all things.
- ☐ Repent of known and unknown sins.
- ☐ Forgive everyone, even if they do not deserve it.
- ☐ Become a work-in-progress.
- ☐ Use the Fruits of the Spirit faithfully.
- ☐ Behave Christlike.
- ☐ Read and use the Word of God.

Will this list really work for us? Absolutely! If it works for me, it will work for anyone who is selflessly willing to PLEASE God. Here is the request from Colossians 1:10: *"That you may walk worthy of the Lord, fully pleasing Him, being fruitful in every good work and increasing in the knowledge of God."*

The Equation

If we have not noticed by now, God will not violate our free will. Now, if we make the wrong choices, remove Him from *The Equation*, or turn a deaf ear to Him, becoming disobedient, rebellious, or stiffnecked, the Divine Mantle can pass to the next in line. From my perspective, this type of Spiritual Transfer of a Divine Mantle is similar to the anointing of David after the downfall of King Saul. Let us align this pivotal transition accordingly. *"So, he sent and brought him in. Now he was ruddy, with bright eyes, and good-looking. And the LORD said, 'Arise, anoint him; for this is the one!' Then Samuel took the horn of oil and anointed him in the midst of his brothers; and the Spirit of the LORD came upon David from that day forward. So, Samuel arose and went to Ramah."* 1 Samuel 16:12-13.

The Role of Free Will

According to the Heavenly of Heavens, in *The Equation* of Life, the same recipe of Divine Favor designed for elevation can also contain the same ingredients that can become disastrous for us. Really? Yes, really! When we become disobedient to the expectations of stewardship while willfully misaligning with the Divine Will of God, as Saul did, our instigated shortcomings of irresponsibility can create a homecoming for our replacement. Proverbs 17:15 also says, *"He who justifies the wicked, and he who condemns the just, both of them alike are an abomination to the Lord."*

In the Eye of God, a call to leadership in any capacity, regardless of who we are, why we are, or where we are, it is indeed a call to humbly serve others, to uplift them lovingly, and to be a BEACON of Light, Courage, and Hope. If not, rest assured that when intentionally terrorizing innocent people without just cause due to our underlying fears, pride, and idiosyncrasies to build our personalized Tower of Babel, God will eventually change the language on us. Also, He will create all types of chaos in our system of conveyance while reversing our destructive, underhanded, and distractive efforts, making an example out of us, similar to what occurred with King Saul.

How do we redeem ourselves when thinking and operating disobediently? First, we must repent and seek God, our Heavenly Father. Secondly, we must become willing to purify ourselves from the inside out from the negative characteristics causing us to become the enemy turned inward. Thirdly, we must aim to PLEASE God and operate with wisdom, compassion, integrity, and justice for all mankind. In reflecting on our own lives, 2 Corinthians 5:9 tells us exactly what to aim for when redeeming ourselves: *"Therefore we make it our aim, whether present or absent, to be well pleasing to Him."*

When dealing with *The Equation*, outside of the lack of love or the overzealous effects of having too much of it, there are a few negative characteristics we must deal with. What if we

The Role of Free Will

choose not to deal with our negative attributes? With *Divine Dominion: As It Pleases God*®, we still have free will to deal with them or not. Nonetheless, with greater accountability as Believers, listed below are a few things that can happen when allowing negativity to fester and brew without positive counteractions, but not limited to such:

- ☐ We can become overly possessive or aggressive.
- ☐ We can become consumed with jealousy or envy.
- ☐ We can become unnecessarily codependent.
- ☐ We can have control and dependency issues.
- ☐ We can become insecure, unsure, and uncomfortable.
- ☐ We can fear loss or rejection.
- ☐ We can suffer from secret or open imbalances.
- ☐ We will need constant validation.
- ☐ We can suffer from unrealistic expectations.
- ☐ We can suffer from emotional delusions.
- ☐ We will begin to ignore negative character traits.
- ☐ We can experience inner longings or loneliness.
- ☐ We can experience stunted growth or backwardness.
- ☐ We can experience a barrage of rotten fruits.
- ☐ We can become yoked to the core.
- ☐ We can become easily soul-tied.

The dynamics of hidden anger, greed, and resentment are the second most profound contributors to the issues we are facing today, breaking the broken bond of relationships ranging from the worldly to the Spiritual Realm. What is the first contributor to our issues? The lack of love or too much of it.

Most would think we should cut off relationships with the worldly, especially when we develop a Spiritual Relationship, and this is so far from the truth. Why is this not true? God owns it ALL, giving some form of LIGHT to every man! As

The Role of Free Will

Believers, we are to set boundaries, *As It Pleases God*, based on whether they are dimming or brightening our LIGHT and vice versa. Plus, most of His sheep are clueless or are on Spiritual Milk, and they need SHEPHERDS like us to teach, guide, and nurture them to digest the Spiritual Meat of the Word of God. But let us align this accordingly, *"All things were made through Him, and without Him nothing was made that was made. In Him was life, and the life was the light of men. And the light shines in the darkness, and the darkness did not comprehend it. There was a man sent from God, whose name was John. This man came for a witness, to bear witness of the Light, that all through him might believe. He was not that Light, but was sent to bear witness of that Light. That was the true Light which gives light to every man coming into the world."* John 1:3-9.

In the Kingdom, we must learn how to deal with anyone on any level, be kind, strong, and consistently diligent, use the Fruits of the Spirit, and behave Christlike, especially when our experiences can range from totally uplifting to downright unpleasant. Why must we remain the bigger person when dealing with mean, nasty, and rude people? Once again, we are the Earthen Vessel used to draw people into the Light, *As It Pleases God*. I know it can become challenging at times, but as we navigate our own paths, we must become willing to work on ourselves daily to endure the wiles of the enemy on a moment-by-moment basis.

What is the purpose of consistently working on ourselves to become better, stronger, and wiser, *As It Pleases God*? Our known and unknown enemies will change their strategy at any given moment. In stark contrast to what is conveyed by them, we must be ready, willing, and prepared with positive reinforcement to rise above the undercut or uppercut designed to break our stride, test our level of patience, or shatter our humility.

According to the Heavenly of Heavens, we will be faced with negativity and we will encounter the elements of

The Role of Free Will

unfairness and injustice. Still, when adding God into *The Equation*, we do not have to engage in such behaviors, regardless of how others behave. Unbeknown to most, the moment we take a stand for unselfish and wholehearted righteousness, our psyche stands at attention, waiting for instructions.

Now, suppose we fail to feed the psyche with the proper instructions, *As It Pleases God*. In this case, with the lack of positive counteractive input, the psyche is designed to revert to its default mechanism, biases, conditioning, or the path of least resistance, thwarting our understanding, truth, or *Overall Perceptiveness*. In addition, it will also inadvertently make us appear difficult or mean-spirited based on the perception of the individual on the receiving end. For this reason, it is always WISE to use the Fruits of the Spirit to establish Divine Balance within the perceptive factors across the board.

Overall Perceptiveness

What does our *Overall Perceptiveness* have to do with *Divine Dominion: As It Pleases God*®? To possess Divine Dominion over something or someone, we must PERCEIVE it or them correctly. As Spiritual Beings having a human experience, in the pursuit of understanding ourselves and our senses, we must become perceptive to function properly in the Realm of the Spirit. If we do not perceive correctly, our Spiritual Discernment Faculties or Compass can become keeled or rusty.

As a result of our *Overall Perceptiveness* being warped in the Eye of God, we will find ourselves calling evil good and good evil with a Spiritual Woe attached. Is this Biblical? I would have it no other way. *"Woe to those who call evil good, and good evil; who put darkness for light, and light for darkness; who put bitter for sweet, and sweet for bitter!"* Isaiah 5:20.

The Role of Free Will

According to the Heavenly of Heavens, we are required to UNDERSTAND and INTERPRET the people, places, and things around us through observation, intuition, and insight for the unveiling of our Heaven on Earth Experiences. Now, the problem is that when we are Spiritually Blind, Deaf, or Mute, we do not often see clearly, hear correctly, or speak wisely simultaneously.

How does seeing, hearing, and speaking apply to a Believer's perceptiveness? The best way for me to explain this is to use the 'See Saw' Analogy. For instance, we may see something correctly, while at the same time, we hear it wrong because our trauma has overshadowed what we saw clearly. As a result, we begin talking crazy, saying things that inflict more trauma on ourselves and the ones on the receiving end. Therefore, in the Eye of God, being that we got one thing right and two things wrong, we are then ushered back into the Spiritual Classroom for charactorial updates.

Why would we need updates, especially when having free will or when we are entitled to our own feelings? It is due to our negative 'up and down' thoughts, words, actions, biases, conditioning, traumas, and communicative efforts that DO NOT align with the Spiritual Fruits of someone having Divine Dominion over something or someone, *As It Pleases God*. In keeping things simple with this matter, Matthew 12:34 has a questionable statement for us: *"How can you, being evil, speak good things? For out of the abundance of the heart the mouth speaks."*

Perception in itself has a lot to do with how we are perceived and plays a critical role in shaping our understanding of the people, places, and things around us. Actually, it influences our beliefs, experiences, and environments and how we interpret our actions, thoughts, beliefs, desires, words, and intentions. In addition, our perceptions are also subjected to worldly or deceptive

The Role of Free Will

measures, especially if the Word of God or the Fruit of the Spirit is not interjected into *The Equation*.

When we do not understand others due to their differences, we will naturally perceive them as problematic based on our motives. At its core, two individuals can witness the same event and walk away with two totally different experiences based on their mindset, thoughts, beliefs, experiences, traumas, conditioning, and so on. For this reason, we must exercise extreme caution to determine whether we are using a positive perception or a negative one.

What is the purpose of Believers governing their perceptions? Our perceptions are not always accurate or foolproof. Frankly, our perceptions can lead to a lot of folly, misjudgments, misconceptions, lies, biases, negativity, and missed BLESSINGS.

The bottom line is that we are designed to make a difference in our ability to understand, convey, redirect, and articulate on behalf of the Kingdom. Now, in the process of this Spiritual Manifestation, we need the Holy Spirit and the Blood of Jesus to keep us on a straight and narrow path. If we decline in this formality, our perceptions can indeed get in the way of our genuine efforts, sometimes turning negatively awkward.

We have all found ourselves at some point thinking we are doing the right thing, but according to the Kingdom, *As It Pleases God*, our motives were all wrong. Or, we found ourselves feeling as if we were wrong in our charactorial approach or sight; yet, in the Kingdom, it was the right thing to do. How do we make this make sense in real life? For example, we have someone being mistreated, rejected, and hung out to dry. Yet, this person feels like a fool for extending mercy, forgiveness, and compassion when the person attempting to assassinate them falls into their own trap.

The Role of Free Will

As this individual exhibits the Fruits of the Spirit, *As It Pleases God*, they still feel a little perturbed, wanting to stay mad, or want the person on the giving end to feel their pain. Still, their conscience will not allow them to treat others the way they were treated. So, they decide to take the high road in their approach, behaving Christlike to reap the Spiritual Fruits and Blessings of their Divine Obedience.

In *Divine Dominion: As It Pleases God*®, we do not want to give the enemy any justifiable leverage to pounce upon or yoke us for behaving in an ungodly, negative manner, clouding our sense of reasoning and good judgment. What does this mean for Believers? Frankly, this is when we are acting and behaving foolishly, supposedly in the Name of God, which only opens the door for other hypocritical behaviors, causing the Kingdom to frown upon our reckless folly.

We, as parents or guardians, attempt to save our children from the world, but we fail to train them on how to deal with, maneuver through, contend among, abound from, or create a win-win amid dire defeat. Nor do we educate them regarding their *Overall Perceptions*, whether good, bad, or indifferent. As a result, they create their own perceptive system that may or may not have anything to do with the Kingdom of Heaven, yet it appears right in their own eyes, but all so unappealing in the Eye of God.

According to scripture, we must train ourselves and our offspring to become sanctified by Divine Truths instead of worldly deception. Is this Biblical? I would have it no other way, *"But now I come to You, and these things I speak in the world, that they may have My joy fulfilled in themselves. I have given them Your word; and the world has hated them because they are not of the world, just as I am not of the world. I do not pray that You should take them out of the world, but that You should keep them from the evil one. They are not of the world, just as I am not of the world. Sanctify them by Your truth. Your word is truth. As You sent Me into the world, I also have sent them into*

The Role of Free Will

the world. And for their sakes I sanctify Myself, that they also may be sanctified by the truth." John 17:13-19.

Self-Acceptance

In a society that often measures success by external accomplishments, wealth, status, fame, fortune, and titles, one of the worst feelings to experience is to win in the eyes of men and feel like a loser from within. What is even worse is when we experience the symptoms of a bona fide loser behind closed doors with our family members. Why would this happen? The reasons will vary, but most often, it is due to a few factors:

- ☐ We do not match the image portrayed.
- ☐ We are pressured to fit into a certain mold.
- ☐ We have too many masked lies.
- ☐ We behave hypocritically.
- ☐ We are being absolutely fake or wishy-washy.
- ☐ We are too gullible.
- ☐ We have unrealistic expectations.

At its core, according to the Ancient of Days, *Self-Acceptance* involves recognizing our strengths and weaknesses without judgment. While simultaneously developing a work-in-progress mindset for Spiritual Growth, *As It Pleases Him*, to avoid the Spirit of Insecurity from possessing us.

Can the feeling of insecurity really engulf us as Believers? It happens to us all, especially when God is not in the equation of what we are doing, saying, becoming, establishing, or conveying. More importantly, if we are engaging in the things He hates, then negative feelings will come with the territory, even if we pretend to have it going on. Unfortunately, this is how we find ourselves in a realm of pretense, putting on all

The Role of Free Will

types of masks and grappling with self-doubt, over-the-edge anxiety, bad habits, and a sense of unfulfillment.

In the Eye of God, we should never allow the appearance of anyone to deceive us, including ourselves. It is the character traits and heart posture that determine the 'yea or nay' in or out of the Kingdom of God. Thus, *Self-Acceptance* is crucial, especially when life is lifing, and the Vicissitudes and Seasons of Life are doing their job. If we do not accept ourselves, be it good, bad, or indifferent, we will become prone to people-pleasing or seeking validation.

In the relentless pursuit of perfection, if we do not take the opportunity to become a work-in-progress, *As It Pleases God*, we may find ourselves between a rock and a hard place. Why would this occur, especially when putting in the work? It is not humanly possible to achieve perfection without God Almighty, being out of Divine Purpose, or not knowing our reason for being. As a result, the longing within the psyche will remain, nudging us away from worldliness to Godliness.

We can debate *Self-Acceptance* issues all we like; it does not change the fact that we are Spiritual Beings having a human experience. Nor does it exempt the fact that we are all fearfully and wonderfully made according to Psalm 139 with a unique Spiritual Blueprint. Thus, failures and setbacks will occur from the least to the greatest as training and preparation for our NEXT.

According to the Heavenly of Heavens, there are components of freedom and wisdom hidden in all of our imperfections. Here is what 2 Corinthians 12:9-10 shares with us: "But He said to me, *'My grace is sufficient for you, for My strength is made perfect in weakness.' Therefore most gladly I will rather boast in my infirmities, that the power of Christ may rest upon me. Therefore I take pleasure in infirmities, in reproaches, in needs, in persecutions, in distresses, for Christ's sake. For when I am weak, then I am strong.*"

The Role of Free Will

If we are strong or weak 100% of the time, there is something wrong. There must be a balance between the two. Why must balance occur in mankind? Based on the Spiritual Law of Duality, we all have a little bit of this and a little bit of that in us, and it is our responsibility to know and understand the difference and counteract it. Plus, it carries vital information on what to do next as it relates to our Divine Dominion or Spiritual Authority over whatever it is or is not. For instance, if we do not know the difference between right and wrong, wrongness will prevail until we counteract it with righteousness. If we do not know the difference between being hateful or loving, hatefulness will prevail until we counteract it with love.

So you see, any negative attribute carries its own solution, similar to the venom of a snake carrying its own antidote. According to Spiritual Principles, if we do not know this information, we cannot heal ourselves as we should. Why not? Because we are so consumed with denying who we are, as if God made a mistake when He created us. For me, to become Dr. Y. Bur, the WHY Doctor, I had to accept my flaws and all, extract the WISDOM hidden in everything, and activate the Law of Reciprocity.

And now, the Floodgates of Heaven have opened a Portal of Divine Wisdom for a time such as this to Heal the Land. Had I refused to do so, hiding under a rock, feeling ashamed, wounded, or defeated, you would not be reading this book right now. Being that I did not give up for your sake, do not dare think about giving up on yourself, not now and not ever! Take authority over whatever it is or is not, and reverse it positively, *As It Pleases God*. If you do not know the opposite of something, here is what you need to do, but not limited to such:

☐ Google it.

The Role of Free Will

- ☐ DOCUMENT your findings.
- ☐ FIND the Scripture about it.
- ☐ PRAY, REPENT, and FORGIVE.
- ☐ COVER yourself and it with the Blood of Jesus.
- ☐ GIVE it to the Holy Spirit for guidance.
- ☐ USE the Fruit of the Spirit.
- ☐ BEHAVE Christlike.
- ☐ ACTIVATE the Law of Reciprocity (Share).

When you put in the work to research, document, and reverse positively, God will honor your good works. All in all, this means you do not need to be perfect; you just need a paper trail of your work-in-progress intents to PLEASE Him, and He will do the rest. I am living proof!

Before moving on, I want to share what Henry Ford once said: *"If you think you can or think you can't, you will always be right."* He also said, *"Failure is only the opportunity to begin again more intelligently."* If you do not examine the reason behind your WHY, you may miss out on valuable information, preventing you from *Running Your Own Race*. When running in or out of the Kingdom of God, know this: You are the best and only you that you have; make the most of it, leaving a HOT TRAIL of Divine Wisdom behind to help the next person.

Running Our Own Race

When thinking about *Running Our Own Race*, it can come off as a little selfish at times. However, if we do not run it for ourselves, then who will do it for us? My point exactly: NOT A SINGLE PERSON! The ideal way is to run with the correct heart and mind posture, *As It Pleases God*, while operating in the Spirit of Righteousness.

The Role of Free Will

When wholeheartedly embracing our Spiritual Journey or when embarking upon *Divine Dominion: As It Pleases God*®, in His Divine Eye, pursuing our goals, passions, and ambitions is not always an act of selfishness. It could very well be a selfless act designed to feed His sheep or to train us on how to deliver them. Then again, without being excessively influenced by others' expectations or societal pressures, it could also be a necessary step toward personal growth, development, fulfillment, well-being, and Divine Purpose. All of which depends on our commitments. And for the sake of Divine Dominion, our commitments are not always created equal. For example, we can be committed to helping others, and here is what happens when we need help:

- ☐ No one is available to assist.
- ☐ We have to seemingly beg for help.
- ☐ People are too busy.
- ☐ People look at us as if we are an inconvenience.
- ☐ We are mocked for needing help.
- ☐ People try to manipulate or gaslight us.
- ☐ They will make us the last priority.

All of this will happen when there are half-hearted commitments on the table. Still, if we desire to *Run Our Own Race*, we cannot become sensitive or offended when this happens, even when we are justified to do so. Here is the deal: When we are in Purpose on purpose, God will send us help in His timing. Therefore, we must exercise patience amid the waiting process while continuing to prepare ourselves, doing what we can. If we cannot do something, then do not worry about it. Simply pray, place it in the Hands of God, and do something else in the meantime.

The Role of Free Will

When *Running Our Own Race*, why are commitments important? In a microwave world where we want everything right now without building relations, we are forced to compare and compete instead of committing, learning, and growing. In accordance with our DNA structure, we were created as relational beings. The moment we remove this element, people, places, and things will appear burdensome to us if there is no immediate benefit associated. In this state, even if it is the right thing to do, we will engage in wrongness or debaucherous acts to get rid of whatever or whomever.

Unfortunately, this has happened to me a lot...I have been used for my kindness, or my kindness has been mistaken for a weakness. Above all, in *Running My Race*, I operate in the Spirit of Excellence, *As It Pleases God*, using the Fruits of the Spirit. All this means is that I am not going to hand someone something in shambles, sucker-punch them, or engage in bait-and-switch tactics; I am going to give them my best. If I cannot, then I will advise them in advance.

Conversely, when I needed help, I was handed below-the-standard stuff as if I were not worthy of EXCELLENCE or common courtesy. Although grateful amid all, I remained Divinely Observant to protect myself and my Spiritual Gifts. In some cases, I was abandoned or rejected altogether. Yet, I remain their go-to for genuine help. Instead of them finding another go-to, they are hellbent on draining me with their recklessness. I must say, in all caps, THE DEVIL IS A LIAR! Is this not being a little mean-spirited? Absolutely not!

Picturesquely, if someone is pouring pure, clean water into someone to keep them Spiritually Hydrated, and they, in return, intentionally pour out dirty, contaminated water with a muddy substance, is it wise to continue to pour into them? The answer is 'NO.' In the same way that I have mastered *Running My Own Race*, they must learn how to do likewise without dragging me through the mud and spitting in my face.

The Role of Free Will

I have enough documented and proven information to ensure that no WILLING person is left behind, including them.

Amid all the mud and sludge, do you think it stops me from operating in the Spirit of Excellence? Absolutely not! I am here for the stories to feed God's sheep and perfect my Spiritual Fruits, *As It Pleases Him*. Plus, it lets me know what and who I am dealing with. Beyond a shadow of a doubt, Matthew 7:20 does not lie: *"Therefore by their fruits, you will know them."* It is not wise to go by what people are committed to saying; we must PAY ATTENTION to what they are doing! When dealing with a commitment on any level, it is always better to say less and do more than to say more and do less.

How is commitment defined for Believers? A commitment is a profound dedication to a person, place, thing, cause, activity, goal, or mission. Listed below is a Commitment Checklist on how it is extended to include other things, but not limited to such:

- ☐ A commitment to God.
- ☐ A commitment to ourselves.
- ☐ A commitment to others.
- ☐ A commitment to a relationship.
- ☐ A commitment to our families.
- ☐ A commitment to our homes.
- ☐ A commitment to a mission.
- ☐ A commitment to a job.
- ☐ A commitment to like-mindedness.
- ☐ A commitment to excellence.

The commitment or promise goes far beyond mere intentions; in the Eye of God, it represents an ACTIVE CHOICE. Yes, indeed, it is a free-willed choice to take consistent actions toward something or someone that can work both positively

The Role of Free Will

and negatively. Here is a choice blueprint from Deuteronomy 30:19: "*I call heaven and earth as witnesses today against you, that I have set before you life and death, blessing and cursing; therefore choose life, that both you and your descendants may live.*"

In living real life, when *Running Our Own Race*, most would think love is an emotion, but it is an actual CHOICE that may or may not involve emotions. Why not? It is tied to our conscience, which inadvertently feeds our senses. If it is not governed properly and positively, *As It Pleases God*, negativity and unrighteousness will allow our senses to usher in the lust of the eyes, the lust of the flesh, and the pride of life. Sadly, this is where we become controlled by power, money, sex, status, clicks, and likes. Unfortunately, this is where we go on mere feelings, real or imagined, or infatuation, and not FACTS or TRUTH.

For instance, we do not need to involve our emotions to exhibit lovingkindness; it is already embedded into the conscience. For this reason, Galatians 5:13 says, "*For you, brethren, have been called to liberty; only do not use liberty as an opportunity for the flesh, but through love serve one another.*"

Now, on the other hand, if the conscience stops working, then we have a real problem. What does this mean? It means that the psyche is out of control, and we need to reel ourselves in before we self-destruct. Clearly, I do not wish ill will upon anyone, so let us take it to Scripture: "*Let no one say when he is tempted, 'I am tempted by God'; for God cannot be tempted by evil, nor does He Himself tempt anyone. But each one is tempted when he is drawn away by his own desires and enticed. Then, when desire has conceived, it gives birth to sin; and sin, when it is full-grown, brings forth death.*" James 1:13-15.

By embracing our individuality, a commitment to whatever, whomever, wherever, however, or whyever comes

The Role of Free Will

with the territory! As we *Run Our Own Race*, it is imperative to know what we are committed to and what we are not.

What do our commitments have to do with anything? We all have commitments to something or someone. In contrast, we need the right commitments to *Run Our Own Race*, capitalizing on the challenges and opportunities for Spiritual Growth, *As It Pleases God*. Here is what 1 Corinthians 9:24-27 advises: *"Do you not know that those who run in a race all run, but one receives the prize? Run in such a way that you may obtain it."* Moreover, with structure and focus, this mindset helps to make the weak strong, the strong humble, and the humble effective, placing them on *The Leading Edge*.

Regardless of who we are or why we are here in Earthen Vessels, when we hold ourselves authentically accountable and push through challenges, we can overcome anything, including procrastination. In addition, when we Spiritually Till our own grounds, putting in the work, we can develop new skills, glean valuable information, enhance our problem-solving abilities, and learn important lessons to activate the Law of Reciprocity. Once this occurs, *As It Pleases God*, nothing or no one can hold us back or stop us from achieving the desires of our hearts.

The Leading Edge

When positioning ourselves to be on *The Leading Edge*, we must fine-tune our VISION. Our Spiritual Vision, to be exact! When we are in such a position, we do not want to fall off the cliff with our worldly rationales. Instead, we want to VIEW people, places, and things from a Spiritual Perspective before our human perspective does its calculations.

What is the big deal about the calculations associated with our Spiritual Eye? First and foremost, according to scripture, we must understand, *"For where your treasure is, there your heart*

The Role of Free Will

will be also." Matthew 6:21. Secondly, *"The lamp of the body is the eye. If therefore your eye is good, your whole body will be full of light. But if your eye is bad, your whole body will be full of darkness. If therefore the light that is in you is darkness, how great is that darkness!"* Matthew 6:22-23. For this reason, Spiritual Blindness is nothing we would want to play around with. Why? It contaminates the human psyche with the lust of the eyes, the lust of the flesh, and the pride of life through our senses, causing us to become caught up or soul-tied without us realizing we are.

What can we do to position ourselves to develop our Spiritual Eyes, Ears, Language, and Stance from a Heavenly Perspective? Listed below are a few ways to do so, but not limited to such:

- ☐ We must cease from bragging about what we do for others while expecting our Spiritual Rewards from the Kingdom. It helps us to do away with false expectations and disappointments associated with feeling used. Meanwhile, when we do whatever with no strings attached, we allow the Heavenly of Heavens to usher in the people, places, and things money cannot buy while establishing true Spiritual Value. *"Take heed that you do not do your charitable deeds before men, to be seen by them. Otherwise, you have no reward from your Father in Heaven."* Matthew 6:1.

- ☐ We must redirect our charitable deeds as being the right thing to do, without seeking accolades from others or becoming a hypocrite behind someone's back. *"Therefore, when you do a charitable deed, do not sound a trumpet before you as the hypocrites do in the synagogues and in the streets, that they may have glory from men. Assuredly, I say to you, they have their reward."* Matthew 6:2.

The Role of Free Will

- [ ] When we decide to help someone genuinely, we do not have to seek approval from others to do the right thing proactively. We are Blessed to be a Blessing; therefore, if we allow others to judge our Blessed Provisions, we can miss the Spiritual Mark or Cue. *'But when you do a charitable deed, do not let your left hand know what your right hand is doing."* Matthew 6:3.

- [ ] We must understand that sharing without seeking attention gives us a platform to become openly Blessed without any shame attached. *"That your charitable deed may be in secret; and your Father who sees in secret will Himself reward you openly.* Matthew 6:4.

- [ ] We must not seek to impress others with our ability to pray. It usually causes us to pray amiss because we are often using our personal prayers for the wrong reasons, and God weighs the heart's intent. So, we must be careful with community prayers to ensure we do not become hypocritical in our approach. *"And when you pray, you shall not be like the hypocrites. For they love to pray standing in the synagogues and on the corners of the streets, that they may be seen by men. Assuredly, I say to you, they have their reward."* Matthew 6:5.

- [ ] We must seek to have our private time alone with God. It builds our *Spirit to Spirit* Relations and our inside voice. It helps us to recognize the Voice of God when He is speaking and how to tune out, avoid, or redirect negative chatter. *"But you, when you pray, go into your room, and when you have shut your door, pray to your Father who is in the secret place; and your Father who sees in secret will reward you openly."* Matthew 6:6.

The Role of Free Will

- ☐ We must communicate with God without saying the same thing over and over. The issues of the heart will vary, and if we are repenting about the same things, it means growth is not taking place, or we are lying to ourselves. *"And when you pray, do not use vain repetitions as the heathen do. For they think that they will be heard for their many words."* Matthew 6:7.

- ☐ We must come clean with the issues of the heart. God knows what we are dealing with; He is waiting for us to admit, understand, and regraft it, doing our part in the process without whitewashing. *"Therefore, do not be like them. For your Father knows the things you have need of before you ask Him."* Matthew 6:8.

- ☐ We must direct our prayers toward Heaven. If not, we subject our prayers to becoming misdirected, not knowing who we are praying to. *"In this manner, therefore, pray: Our Father in heaven, Hallowed be Your name."* Matthew 6:9.

- ☐ We must avail ourselves to having our Heaven on Earth Experience while availing ourselves to the Will of God. We have free will to choose whether we desire a worldly or Heavenly Experience, and being in the Will of God. If we do not choose, we subject ourselves to the worldly system due to our lack of clarity. *"Your kingdom come. Your will be done on earth as it is in Heaven."* Matthew 6:10.

- ☐ We must ask for our daily bread or our portions while repenting and forgiving ourselves and others. It clears the Spiritual Channels, allowing us to receive or

The Role of Free Will

download from the Heavenly of Heavens. *"Give us this day our daily bread. And forgive us our debts, as we forgive our debtors."* Matthew 6:11-12.

☐ We must ask for the Leading and Deliverance of the Holy Spirit to ensure we do not subject ourselves to worldly temptation designed to sift us Mentally, Physically, or Emotionally. While simultaneously redirecting all things back to the Kingdom of Heaven, securing or Spiritually Sealing our position in Christ Jesus. *"And do not lead us into temptation, but deliver us from the evil one. For Yours is the kingdom and the power and the glory forever. Amen."* Matthew 6:13.

We have all recited the Lord's Prayer without understanding the reasons behind the *'Why.'* Well, today, we now know the importance of doing certain things in the Realm of the Spirit from a *Heavenly Perspective*. We can tiptoe around whatever we like, but when it comes down to the Heavenly of Heavens, we must follow Spiritual Protocol. It prevents us from being yoked, soul-tied, oppressed, or deceived because *"No one can serve two masters; for either he will hate the one and love the other, or else he will be loyal to the one and despise the other. You cannot serve God and mammon."* Matthew 6:24.

We must also keep in mind that when going about our daily duties or activities, we cannot change others. We can only change ourselves from within while impacting others outwardly. What if we have children? Here again, we must change ourselves and impact them outwardly.

We must lead by example, because children see who we are, not for who we pretend to be. And they will emulate accordingly. For example, if they see us faking, they will learn this behavior, even if they pretend to be authentic. Now, if we

The Role of Free Will

pride ourselves on being transparently authentic, becoming a work-in-progress, and solving problems in real-time, they will follow suit. Yes, we must be strong for our children, but if we do not teach them how to solve issues from the inside out, they will suffer inner weaknesses, trying to appear strong.

What is the big deal, especially when we have free will to raise our children the way we like? Of course, we do have the right to do whatever we like; however, from a *Heavenly Perspective*, here is the deal: *"Every plant which My heavenly Father has not planted will be uprooted. Let them alone. They are blind leaders of the blind. And if the blind leads the blind, both will fall into a ditch."* Matthew 15:13-14. Therefore, it is always best to reel ourselves in with the Fruits of the Spirit and Christlike Character to ensure we are using and sharing them with all we come in contact with.

What if we fall short? All we need to do is identify our point of erring, repent, forgive, learn, and self-correct. Plus, we can also repeat this scripture over and over to Spiritually Reset ourselves: *"Glory to God in the highest, and on earth peace, goodwill toward men!"* Luke 2:14. Does it work? Absolutely. The Heavenly Host used this in praising God, and if it worked for them, it would work for us, helping us to avoid *The Pitfalls of Manipulative Spirits*.

When on *The Leading Edge*, here are a few underlying questions to ask when falling short, but not limited to such?

- ☐ What was the inspiration that originated from God?
- ☐ How does God inspire us through this?
- ☐ What did we learn from God?
- ☐ How did we learn from Him?
- ☐ What correction occurred?
- ☐ Why did the correction occur?
- ☐ How did we become a better person because of this?
- ☐ What is our give-back as a result of this situation?

The Role of Free Will

- ☐ How did we apply the Fruits of the Spirit?
- ☐ How does this make us more Christlike?
- ☐ What is the win-win?
- ☐ How can we use this for the Greater Good?

Can these questions really get the ball rolling when on *The Leading Edge*? Absolutely! These are trigger questions derived from the Word of God, and if we engage in *Spirit to Spirit* Relations *As It Pleases Him*, the Voice from Within will speak loudly. But, of course, only loud enough for us to hear.

What if we omit documenting? We have free will to do whatever we like to do; however, to avoid documenting is like having to ask a person repeatedly for the same information. It not only wastes your time but also the time of the person you are asking for information that you failed to document. Moreover, it can lead to misunderstandings, avoidance, and confusion, causing people to withhold information, especially in a professional setting.

In addition, it creates an unprofessional image, disrespectfulness, and folly on our behalf, leading to frustration, loss of trust, and credibility. Then again, it can also introduce *The Pitfalls of Manipulative Spirits* into our lives by reason of omission.

Chapter Three
The Pitfalls of Manipulative Spirits

From the Garden of Eden until this very moment in time, at the core of Manipulative Spirits lie the seeds of deception, deceiving the deceivable and tricking the trickable. These negative seedlings present themselves in a manner that is seemingly beneficial, logical, good, or attractive, drawing individuals into their pitting web, similar to what happened to Adam and Eve in the Book of Genesis. In this chapter, we are going to discuss *The Pitfalls of Manipulative Spirits* to ensure we avoid the tantalizing snares designed for us to forfeit our Divine Dominion.

With the inborn desire to dominate, we will do one of two things: we either seek to dominate or risk becoming dominated, positively or negatively. Now, nestled between these twofold desires lies a complex phenomenon known as MANipulation. To be clear, this is not SPIRITipulation, and we must know the difference, or we will 'get got' by the enemy's wiles.

The Realm of the Spirit can plant seeds, but it is the human vessel that carries out the mission, action, or intent. So, when

The Pitfalls of Manipulative Spirits

we say the Devil made me do it, unfortunately, this is a lie. He may have planted the seed, but we have free will to do or not to do, say or not to say, feed or decline to eat, cast down or come into agreement, and so on. Up until this very moment, I have not seen the Devil put his hands on anyone, not even one! It is 'We The People' in Earthen Vessels that carry out his agenda and then cry Holy, Holy! God, God! Help, Help! Jesus, Jesus! Why, Why!

Is this not being mockingly, insensitively mean, rude, and disrespectful? Once again, I am not here to sugarcoat the truth, and my experiences have made me an excellent TEACHER with Spiritual Milk and Meat for the masses, so I pull no punches whatsoever. Nor am I down for the deceitful okey doke! To avoid *The Pitfalls of Manipulative Spirits*, I pay attention to character traits, mindsets, actions, and heart postures, and not what is being said by a person only. Actually, I hone in on what is not being said first and then what is said secondly. James 1:22 clearly says, *"But be doers of the word, and not hearers only, deceiving yourselves."* All this means is that we must align the Word of God with our character traits, *As It Pleases Him*.

What if we do not know the Word of God? We must make our best attempts, doing our due diligence. Still, know this: *"For it would have been better for them not to have known the way of righteousness, than having known it, to turn from the holy commandment delivered to them."* 2 Peter 2:21. According to the Heavenly of Heavens, we must at least TRY. What if we cannot read or we do not have time? Then listen to the Bible on audio, or we can use our phone app. The key is to find a way to get the WORD. If not, we will become seemingly unstable or double-minded in the Eye of God, limiting how much we can profit from our trials. Really? Yes, really! James 1:8 even says, *"He is a double-minded man, unstable in all his ways."*

The Pitfalls of Manipulative Spirits

What if we are not unstable, operating very wisely? I am not here to judge or determine the stability of anyone because, according to the Cycles and Seasons of Life, we will ALL have our moments of triggering instability. Now, this is where I come in...I want to know what is done in these moments behind closed doors when no one is looking or in the veil of the night. I want to know the thoughts that are chatting away from within. I want to know the silent words that are being whispered.

In our moments of crushing or pruning, Galatians 5:15 says, "*If you bite and devour one another, beware lest you be consumed by one another!*" Unfortunately, this is how *The Pitfalls of Manipulative Spirits* get in the back doors of the Mind, Body, Soul, and Spirit. Through our willful participation, it places a justified yoke of possession to facilitate debauched agendas while appearing right in our own eyes. As a result, we turn on ourselves and cannot tell a soul about the Spiritual Warring taking place from within, as it seeps into our Bloodline. Is this real? It is as real as the Breath of Life!

In the same way that Jacob wrestled with an Angel to release himself from his old nature in Genesis 32:22-32, do we think we get a free pass? With our Heaven on Earth Experiences, when dealing with identity, struggles, yokes, transformation, or our quest for Divine Purpose on any level, we will encounter some form of resistance with the threat of breaking. All of which will result in some form of Battle Scars or a Limp, signifying and reminding us of the experience. Although we may not look like what we have been through, when dealing with God Almighty, He likes to establish Cornerstone Reminders, ensuring we do not attempt to recreate what He deemed as FINISHED or take the credit.

Why is resistance testing necessary, especially when dealing with *The Pitfalls of Manipulative Spirits*? It is designed to test our limits, resilience, and bounce back. Truthfully, with

The Pitfalls of Manipulative Spirits

the survival nature of mankind and the way we were prewired from the Beginning, we do not really know what we will or will not do when under pressure or when dealing with uncertainty, famine, and fear. Spiritually Speaking, in a world bombarded with status, competition, and comparison, or when dealing with King Nebuchadnezzar's Spirit of Idolatry, until we are thoroughly tried, tested, and put through the fire like Shadrach, Meshach, and Abednego in Daniel 3:16-28, we will not know if we will be consumed or if the Fourth Man will be in the fiery furnace with us.

In my opinion, the overall concept of Divine Dominion is like a battle between God's Divine Logic and man's selfish, idolatrous logic. When facing our Heavenly Father, *Spirit to Spirit*, it is only wise to know and understand what the Word of God is saying to the CHURCH while COVERING ourselves with the Blood of Jesus to avoid *The Pitfalls of Manipulative Spirits*.

Should Believers already be covered by the Blood of Jesus? Yes, we are covered if we use it properly and *As It Pleases God*. Suppose we use it to manipulate, defame, hurt, abuse, or enslavely use His precious sheep for our selfish benefits. In this case, the BLOOD will work against us, even if we think we have it going on.

How is it humanly possible for the Blood of Jesus to work against mankind when He died for us? The Blood redeems us from physical death and destruction, allowing us to go to God, our Heavenly Father, for ourselves, *Spirit to Spirit*. But it does not exempt us from Spiritual Laws, Principles, and Protocols unless we are actively using the Fruits of the Spirit according to Galatians 5:22.

For the record, regardless of what we think or believe, Living by the Spirit, *As It Pleases God*, and living for ourselves to please ourselves are two different things in the Eye of God. What is the difference? One is FOR Him, with the mindset

The Pitfalls of Manipulative Spirits

that everything we do, say, or become affects us and those around us. And the other is IN SPITE of Him, where nothing we do, say, or become can affect us or those around us. Even though we are entitled to both simultaneously, we often do not realize how the DUALITY plays out in the Realm of the Spirit. So, let us go deeper!

Now, suppose we reject or abuse the Free Will Offering of the Blood of Jesus, choose not to use the Fruits of the Spirit, or opt out of behaving Christlike. In this case, we will inadvertently deceive ourselves only to deceive another. How so? The impact will occur from within the human psyche, pitting us against the man and the beast from within (the good and evil side of us), similar to the Plague of the Firstborns in Exodus 12:12. *"For I will pass through the land of Egypt on that night, and will strike all the firstborn in the land of Egypt, both man and beast; and against all the gods of Egypt I will execute judgment: I am the Lord."*

How does the firstborn apply to us? We are Spiritual Beings having a human experience. Simply put, we are Spirit first and human second. For our sake, this is why we must be born again in Spirit, and this is why John 3:3 says, *"Jesus answered and said to him, 'Most assuredly, I say to you, unless one is born again, he cannot see the kingdom of God.'"* And then, after being questioned by Nicodemus, He reaffirms His statement by saying, *"Most assuredly, I say to you, unless one is born of water and the Spirit, he cannot enter the kingdom of God."* John 3:5.

The Spiritual Duality of mankind should not be taken for granted, nor should it be left unmanned or uncorrected. Plus, if we think for a moment that the other side of us does not exist, we are sadly mistaken. John 3:6 gives us a big clue regarding our Spiritual Duality, yet we overlook it time and time again: *"That which is born of the flesh is flesh, and that which is born of the Spirit is spirit."* For this reason, it is wise for us to use the Blood of Jesus as Spiritual Atonement to tame the unruliness that lies within. For our Divine Dominion and Protection, it (The Blood of Jesus) helps us to Spiritually Seal the Passover Exemption on the Tenth Plague from Exodus 12:13. It says, "*Now the blood shall be a sign for you on the houses where you are. And when I see the blood, I will pass over you; and the plague shall not be on you to destroy you when I strike the land of Egypt.*"

What if Passover does not apply to us because we are not in Egypt, and this is the Old Testament, so we are not under the Law? We have free will to believe what we like, but the BLOOD still works regardless of whether we believe it does or not. Based on Spiritual Principles and Obedience, from bondage to freedom, "*Just as Moses lifted up the snake in the wilderness, so the Son of Man must be lifted up, that everyone who believes may have eternal life in him.*" John 3:14-15.

Our Divine Deliverance, Crossing, or Rescue is within our reach or capacity, even if we do not realize it as of yet. According to the Heavenly of Heavens, we are required to use what is in our hands with Divine Authority to part the Red Sea on our obstacles or hindrances, dividing past from present, *As It Pleases God*. If not, the bullified enemy, real or imagined, will chase us down like a dog, Mentally, Physically, Emotionally, Spiritually, or Financially. At the same time, we may retreat with our tails in between our legs as if God is not who He says He is, especially if we lack understanding in this area.

Conversely, if we allow the Spirit of Deception to override the BLOOD covering the doorpost of our Mind, Body, Soul, and Spirit, then have at it. Know this: it has a direct target for our sanity and peace within our environments, including homes and relationships. From the lips of the ONE that FULFILLED THE LAW, here is what Matthew 12:25 says to us: "*But Jesus knew their thoughts, and said to them: 'Every kingdom divided against itself is brought to desolation, and every city or house divided against itself will not stand.'*"

The Pitfalls of Manipulative Spirits

The Divine Memorial has been established for us to allow people, places, and things to PASS OVER or CONSUME US. If we willfully choose not to enforce it, *As It Pleases God*, then we have no right to complain, fuss, or fight. Before moving on, please allow me to Spiritually Align the Divine Memorial: *"So this day shall be to you a memorial; and you shall keep it as a feast to the Lord throughout your generations. You shall keep it as a feast by an everlasting ordinance."* Exodus 12:14.

The Signs of Manipulation

When dealing with *Divine Dominion: As It Pleases God®*, we must become very cautious about being manipulated or becoming a manipulator. In a world increasingly interconnected by diverse beliefs, varying perspectives, and assorted practices, the Spiritual Framework for growth and understanding requires an acute awareness of manipulation at its core. We have been brushing over this matter for far too long, and now it is attempting to lay claim to our love, freedom, and respect for all.

Here is the deal: Manipulation is a subtle and often sneaky tactic used by individuals or groups to influence our words, thoughts, feelings, beliefs, biases, cultures, and behaviors with or without our consent. The process of shifting from empowerment to control is not what God had in mind for us, especially when tying guilt or shame to non-compliance and violating free will.

Unbeknown to most, on the flip side, manipulation in itself, with or without our consent or agreement, is considered an entrenched belief system of witchcraft. Yes, I said it! It is what it is, and it carries Spiritual Consequences and Repercussions for negatively or deceitfully controlling or influencing without an agreement to do so. How so? In the Eye of God, manipulation and coercion are a form of rebellion or disobedience according to the Word. 1 Samuel 15:23 gives us a heads-up: *"For rebellion is as the sin of witchcraft, and stubbornness is as iniquity and idolatry. Because you have rejected the word of the LORD, He also has rejected you from being king."*

Even though King Saul was the example set for us in 1 Samuel, the Spiritual Principle is still in motion until this very day, doing what it is designed to do. What are Spiritual Principles designed to do for all mankind, especially Believers? Spiritual Principles, Laws, and Protocols were created to weed out or prune those who are engaging in such malice behaviors without corrective measures, such as REPENTING and OBEYING. Here is what Proverbs 3:11-12 says, *"My son, do not despise the chastening of the Lord, nor detest His correction; for whom the Lord loves He corrects, just as a father the son in whom he delights."*

On the other hand, with agreed participation in willful manipulation, conniving, and scheming, the culprit planting the negative seeds may get a slap on the wrist. At the same time, even if we are not the culprit, we can also become Spiritually Chastised for not self-correcting, dying a slow death from the inside out. Clearly, I do not wish death upon anyone, so let us take it to Scripture: Revelation 21:8 says, *"But the cowardly, unbelieving, abominable, murderers, sexually immoral, sorcerers (witchcraft), idolaters, and all liars shall have their part in the lake which burns with fire and brimstone, which is the second death."*

What if we are not in the Revelation Time Frame? Unfortunately, this is where we are once again deceived. Revelation is indeed upon us...The UNVEILING is NOW. If we do not self-correct, *As It Pleases God*, the psyche will make us feel like we are walking dead, while yet still alive. We can pretend it is not happening, but it is happening in real-time, right before our very eyes, with mass MANipulation like never before.

How do we know when we are being manipulated? We know when someone is pulling our strings, we often ignore it

The Pitfalls of Manipulative Spirits

for love, comfort, status, fame, money, image, fear, or out of idolatry. Plus, being that everyone is different and dealing with different issues, it will vary, but it will target a weakness, insecurity, or vulnerability. Nevertheless, to invoke self-awareness or recognize the patterns, here are a few indications of being Spiritually Manipulated, or when we are being manipulative individuals. However, this does not always apply to those with medical conditions or when taking certain medications, but not limited to such:

Spiritual Manipulation Checklist

- ☐ When being *Spiritually Manipulated*, we will become Mentally, Physically, Emotionally, or Spiritually drained or exhausted. To combat this, it is essential to establish strong personal boundaries and protect our energy from negativity, chaos, debauchery, hatefulness, or confusion.

- ☐ When being *Spiritually Manipulated*, we may feel the need to become isolated, cutting ourselves off from people, places, and things we enjoy. All of which are rooted in disloyalty, distrust, delusion, or paranoia, making us feel alone, unsupported, or forgotten. To combat this, we must maintain open lines of communication with loved ones and actively foster good, positive relationships.

- ☐ When being *Spiritually Manipulated*, we may find ourselves on a constant cycle of making bad, hasty, or rushed decisions, stubbing our toes royally. Approaching people, places, and things without clarity creates problems for us, Mentally, Physically, Emotionally, Spiritually, and Financially. To combat

The Pitfalls of Manipulative Spirits

this, we must take a pause, reflect, gather information, weigh the benefits or drawbacks, build a system, set goals, and add the Holy Trinity into the equation. By adopting a mindful decision-making strategy as such, we can think on our feet when the enemy begins to whisper sweet nothings.

- ☐ When being *Spiritually Manipulated*, we may get caught in a cycle of fear and anxiety, zapping our confidence in ourselves and others. All of this leads us to withdraw from social interactions, hesitate before making necessary decisions, and question our abilities with doubtfulness, creating all types of known and unknown shackles. To combat this, we must proactively address our fears and anxieties, *As It Pleases God*, reverse them to a positive, create a win-win, and remain calm using the Fruits of the Spirit.

- ☐ When being *Spiritually Manipulated*, we may get trapped in a period of stagnation or stunted growth while being bombarded with distractions. To combat this, we must become good stewards over our time and set realistic boundaries to ensure we are growing, sowing, and becoming, *As It Pleases God*.

- ☐ When being *Spiritually Manipulated*, we may find ourselves grappling with being excluded, rejected, abandoned, or unaccepted due to feelings, thoughts, and beliefs of unworthiness. To combat this, we must overcome the impostor syndrome while removing all the masks and fake facades. We cannot lose being our authentic selves while using the Fruits of the Spirit and behaving Christlike.

The Pitfalls of Manipulative Spirits

- ☐ When being *Spiritually Manipulated*, we are consumed with perfectionism or showing off with an underlying bed of insecurity. To combat this, we need to get rid of the performance mindset to develop a work-in-progress, purposeful, and result-oriented mindset while approaching everything and everyone in the Spirit of Excellence, while giving and doing our best.

A Manipulative Individual Checklist

- ☐ When we are the giver or the receiver of guilt tripping or gaslighting (invoking doubt), and twisting facts without asking fact-finding questions.

- ☐ When we are the giver or the receiver of withheld information to control someone, as if they are not worthy of getting the information or facts.

- ☐ When we are the giver or the receiver of emotional blackmail or being unnecessarily pressured, giving ultimatums with phrases such as, 'You better do this; if not, this will happen!'

- ☐ When we are the giver or the receiver of inconsistency, saying one thing and doing another. For instance, they treat us a certain way when they are with us, but treat us differently when others are present.

- ☐ When we are the giver or the receiver of the silent treatment, we withhold our communicative efforts to punish or control the narrative. We were created as relational beings, so communication should become an ultimate priority in any relationship.

The Pitfalls of Manipulative Spirits

- ☐ When we are the giver or the receiver of playing the victim or making others appear crazy or delusional to cover up our issues, quirks, or debaucherous efforts.

- ☐ When we are the giver or the receiver of love bombing, while showing affection and attention, and dropping them like a bad habit once we get what we want.

- ☐ When we are the giver or the receiver of negative affirmations, character assassinations, and critical feedback, to degrade instead of uplifting.

- ☐ When we are the giver or the receiver of changing the subject without advising the other party of the redirect, like cutting them off as if what they are saying is not important.

- ☐ When we are the giver or the receiver of making people feel obligated to us while playing all types of mind games.

- ☐ When we are the giver or the receiver of projecting or playing the blaming game.

- ☐ When we are the giver or the receiver of over-sensitivity or hypersensitivity.

- ☐ When we are the giver or the receiver of jealousy, envy, and pride, disguised as being helpful with ulterior motives and incorrect heart postures.

- ☐ When we are the giver or the receiver of instigated drama, chaos, or confusion.

The Pitfalls of Manipulative Spirits

- ☐ When we are the giver or the receiver of demanding loyalty from others, especially when it is a free will commodity.

- ☐ When we are the giver or the receiver, we use the past to control, downplay, or dominantly powerplay.

- ☐ When we are the giver or the receiver, playing the victim becomes our way of eliciting sympathy and avoiding accountability.

- ☐ When we are the giver or the receiver of selective memory, to avoid or enforce agreements or to get out of participating in certain events.

- ☐ When we are the giver or the receiver, by outright playing dumb to gain sympathy or control, especially when we have messed up.

- ☐ When we are the giver or the receiver of using third-party control, such as 'Mom or Dad said...', 'The boss said...', 'The Pastor said...'

Whether we are the giver or receiver, we must begin to set boundaries of free will and respect to AWAKEN our inner strength. In addition, even if people attempt to use our condition as a weakness, we must remain PEACEFUL and PLEASANT without becoming angry, abusive, defensive, or passing the blame. Then again, after stating the facts, sometimes the healthiest thing for the sanity of the Mind, Body, Soul, and Spirit is to extend distance without allowing unlimited access to our positive energy source.

The Pitfalls of Manipulative Spirits

The Spirit of Jezebel

The best way to protect ourselves from becoming the manipulator or manipulatee is to identify the signs and dangers of Jezebel's controlling Spirit. For those who think *The Spirit of Jezebel* is about being a loose woman, well, please allow me to give a brief update on this disembodied entity that is causing us to scramble for our sanity and dominion.

Spiritually Speaking, *The Spirit of Jezebel* is nothing new; however, it intends to dominate or undermine others using deceit, intimidation, anger, rage, bullying, or seduction while recruiting others to do its bidding. With the same debauched character traits, it leaves rotten and mangled fruits all over the place and then plays the victim. In addition, it has the audacity to point the finger through judging, projecting, blaming, or playing possum, as if it has done no wrong while assuming zero accountability. If this is you, keep reading...if this is within someone close to you, then pay close attention.

In the landscape of our relationships and personal interactions, *The Spirit of Jezebel* can reside in both males and females alike. How is this possible? This Spirit is a genderless PRINCIPALITY; therefore, it must operate in a vessel containing the Breath of Life to manifest itself. With some form of agreement of entry on our behalf, it can do what it does through us because of us. Blasphemy, right? Wrong. Amos 3:3 clearly says, *"Can two walk together, unless they are agreed?"*

The Spirit of Jezebel cannot possess us without us agreeing in some way, shape, or form. Sometimes, this is through our words, thoughts, beliefs, desires, actions, reactions, or trauma. Basically, at any point of entry, *The Spirit of Jezebel* will shoot its shot unless we erect a blockade, reversing or rejecting it. Then, it will move on to an easier target, trying us again when we are weak, vulnerable, pressured, needy, or desperate. For our sakes, this is why Ephesians 6:12 says, *"For we do not wrestle*

The Pitfalls of Manipulative Spirits

against flesh and blood, but against principalities, against powers, against the rulers of the darkness of this age, against spiritual hosts of wickedness in the heavenly places."

Keep in mind that this Spirit knows more about Spiritual Principles and Laws than we do. Really? Yes, really! Listen, although we call it *The Spirit of Jezebel*, it has been roaming the Earth for a long time. Frankly, it made its stapled hierarchal appearance with Jezebel in 1 Kings and 2 Kings of the Bible.

As Jezebel sought dominion as the wife of King Ahab of Israel, she promoted the worship of Baal and influenced her husband to defy God Almighty. In the same way she swayed her husband, she sought to do likewise to the Prophets of the Lord. If she could not, she persecuted, outed, and threatened them, provoking fear and mass manipulation, causing disbelief and idolatry in Israel.

Jezebel was so manipulative, conniving, and ruthless that she had the Men of God afraid of her. Above all, they were afraid to correct her while running into hiding until the threat was gone. Sadly, this is still happening today, and if we do not take *Divine Dominion: As It Pleases God*®, we will allow *The Spirit of Jezebel* to dominate as we sit back and watch, saying, 'Where is God?'

Without laying paws on anyone, according to the Heavenly of Heavens, God needs all Boots on the Ground with a National Day of Praying, Fasting, Repenting, and Forgiving from the North, South, East, and West. In Divine Quaternity, these FOUR ELEMENTS are needed in FAITH to Heal the Land, *As It Pleases Him*. If one thinks this is a joke, here is the Spiritual Seal from 2 Chronicles 7:14, *"If My people who are called by My name will humble themselves, and pray and seek My face, and turn from their wicked ways, then I will hear from heaven, and will forgive their sin and heal their land."*

For the UNITY of mankind, Divine Hope, Restoration, and Renewal are our Spiritual Portion. Still, in the Eye of God, we

The Pitfalls of Manipulative Spirits

must TRANSFORM the Mind, Body, Soul, and Spirit, *As It Pleases Him* to usher in His Divine Promises, Provisions, and Nourishment according to Revelation 22:2. *"In the middle of its street, and on either side of the river, was the tree of life, which bore twelve fruits and each tree yielding its fruit every month. The leaves of the tree were for the healing of the nations."* How do we bring this to real life? Here are a few tips to nurture our Tree of Life to avoid *The Pitfalls of Manipulative Spirits*, but not limited to such:

- ☐ Become a good listener.
- ☐ Speak clearly and concisely (Do not talk too much).
- ☐ Remain relevant and on point.
- ☐ Do not overtalk people, cutting them off.
- ☐ Respect the feelings of others.
- ☐ Think before speaking.
- ☐ Do not assume...ask fact-finding questions.
- ☐ Do not insult others based on opinions.
- ☐ Avoid jumping to conclusions.
- ☐ Maintain eye contact while communicating.
- ☐ Invite interactive feedback.
- ☐ Add a little humor to interactions.

As we strive to embody our fruits, *As It Pleases God*, we must also pay attention to *The Spirit of Delilah*. Why? She has an agenda as well, and we do not want to get caught up, especially with our senses, desires, habits, or feelings!

The Spirit of Delilah

Delilah's manipulative, seductive nature is not limited to females alone; it can possess males as well. Whether we are fully clothed or barely clothed, this swaying Spirit does not discriminate. It will use and influence any willing vessel from

The Pitfalls of Manipulative Spirits

the pews to the pulpit and beyond based on their TYPE. You know what I am talking about...we all have our types, even if we pretend we do not. Whether it is short, tall, thick, thin, dark, light, pretty, handsome, unattractive, or quirky, our preferences shape our attraction to others in irrefutable ways, sometimes without even realizing it.

According to our DNA, human attraction is a complex interplay of psychological, biological, scientific, and emotional factors that intertwine our experiences, whether good, bad, indifferent, or denied. When we are attracted to people who fit a certain mold, pattern, or standard outside of God, our Heavenly Father, we can sometimes get duped, limited, or yoked by *The Spirit of Delilah*. How so? They will appear Heaven Sent but demonically induced or manifested by our unrestrained or selfish wants, needs, weaknesses, and desires to feed our egos while initiating a downfall from the inside out. Unfortunately, this primarily happens when we do not selflessly add God into the equation, *As It Pleases Him*.

To be clear, just because we have our dresses long and britches pulled up does not mean that we are not under the influence of *The Spirit of Delilah*. She has a long, gentle hand, grabbing hold of us in ways that make us quiver. How do we make this make sense? For instance, while we are pointing the finger at the obvious, *The Spirit of Delilah* is doing its job inconspicuously to accomplish its agenda through seductive charm on the psyche, extracting our secrets as leveraged control.

Unbeknown to most, the allure of a Delilah Spirit often lies in its ability to appeal, entice, and manipulate the taste buds of an individual, feeding the lust of the eyes, the lust of the flesh, and the pride of life. This manipulative, seductive 'only fans' quality can mask toxic traits, blinding our sense of good judgment. And, sometimes, blocking our common sense, making it difficult to see the true nature of the individual.

The Pitfalls of Manipulative Spirits

Although I am tempted to talk about Samson and his issues, we will not. Being this chapter is about *The Pitfalls of Manipulative Spirits*, let us stick to *The Spirit of Delilah* to ensure we understand what God wants Believers to know for a time such as this.

What is the big deal regarding *The Spirit of Delilah*? When we are choosing external factors such as skin colors, eye colors, hair textures, teeth alignment, or designer labels over internal factors such as heart and mind postures, character, and fruits, the Delilah Spirit is indeed making its mark, getting us caught up like Samson, resting our heads in the wrong laps.

It is not just men resting their heads on the wrong laps; women are more apt to do so due to the shortage of the male species and desperation. Unfortunately, it is through fear, desperation, hurt, and a desire to be loved that feeds *The Spirit of Delilah*. Although there are more traits, in the Eye of God, these are the major players that give this Spirit permission to possess us.

What if *The Spirit of Delilah* does not possess us? I am not here to determine who is possessed or not; I am just the Messenger. Still, if we cannot keep our dresses down and our britches up, or we enjoy sleeping with ladi, dadi, and everybody, there is a driving force behind it. Plus, it is our responsibility to contain or reverse it, *As It Pleases God*, bringing more to the table than just our pleasurable goodies.

Now, on the other hand, if pleasurable goodies are all we have going for ourselves, then it is time to step into the Spiritual Classroom for charactorial development, Mentally, Physically, Emotionally, and Spiritually.

Why is character development so important in the Eye of God, especially when contending with *The Spirit of Delilah*? Once again, if we take a look around, it is obvious that *The Spirit of Delilah* knows more about Spiritual Laws, Principles, and Protocols than we do. If we do not update our mind and

The Pitfalls of Manipulative Spirits

heart postures and our charactorial fruits to Kingdom Standards, we may come into agreement with *The Spirit of Delilah* while not knowing or recognizing it for what it is or what it is not.

Picturesquely, suppose we are not toxic, and we settle or commit to someone who is extremely toxic. In this case, something is definitely wrong, even if we attempt to rationalize or justify our actions, thoughts, desires, or beliefs. Here is what 2 Corinthians 6:14 says about this matter: *"Do not be unequally yoked together with unbelievers. For what fellowship has righteousness with lawlessness? And what communion has light with darkness?"*

In our Spiritual Journey through the Vicissitudes, Seasons, and Cycles of Life, each of us will face our share of challenges, triumphs, and everything in between. If not, then live a little longer. Life is designed to expose areas where we need further development, and sometimes, it will use the cycle of déjà vu with *The Spirit of Delilah*, forcing us to confront what we are denying or lying about.

In cultivating self-awareness, I am not saying we will not have our moments of weakness, nor am I saying that we will not make mistakes. All I am saying is that amid our pursuit of excellence, personal growth, maturity, meaningful relationships, and holding ourselves to high standards, we must exercise wisdom without feeling defeated, overwhelmed, embarrassed, ashamed, or helpless.

Listen, in the grand tapestry of dealing with *The Spirit of Delilah*, if a mistake is made, according to *Divine Dominion: As It Pleases God*®, here are a few tips on what to do, but not limited to such:

- ☐ When dealing with *The Spirit of Delilah*, we must remember that we are human, and the Blood of Jesus still WORKS and COVERS us as Spiritual Atonement.

The Pitfalls of Manipulative Spirits

Regardless of what we have going on or with whom, it is wise to COVER ourselves (Mind, Body, Soul, and Spirit), the situation, the circumstance, or the event with the Blood of Jesus, allowing Him to become the Mediator for us. 1 John 1:7 says, *"But if we walk in the light as He is in the light, we have fellowship with one another, and the blood of Jesus Christ His Son cleanses us from all sin."*

☐ When dealing with *The Spirit of Delilah*, we need to ASK the Holy Spirit to TEACH us what we need to know or understand about the situation, circumstance, or event. Here is the Spiritual Seal to stand on, according to John 14:26: *"But the Helper, the Holy Spirit, whom the Father will send in My name, He will teach you all things, and bring to your remembrance all things that I said to you."*

☐ When dealing with *The Spirit of Delilah*, we must DOCUMENT the answer or information, ensuring we do not forget what the Holy Spirit said or unveiled. When dealing with *The Spirit of Delilah*, He does not like constantly repeating Himself, especially when manipulative deception is involved. Why? Our Spiritual Wires can easily get crossed with undocumented information or when going on memory alone. Plus, from much experience, it takes less energy to take notes than to be Spiritually Chastised. Revelation 1:19 says, *"Write the things which you have seen, and the things which are, and the things which will take place after this."*

☐ When dealing with *The Spirit of Delilah*, we need to REPENT and FORGIVE, regardless of who is at fault. Acts 3:19 says, *"Repent therefore and be converted, that your*

The Pitfalls of Manipulative Spirits

sins may be blotted out, so that times of refreshing may come from the presence of the Lord." In addition, 1 John 1:9 says, "*If we confess our sins, He is faithful and just to forgive us our sins and to cleanse us from all unrighteousness.*"

- ☐ When dealing with *The Spirit of Delilah*, we must give THANKS in all things. 1 Thessalonians 5:16-18 says, "*Rejoice always, pray without ceasing, in everything give thanks; for this is the will of God in Christ Jesus for you.*"

- ☐ When dealing with *The Spirit of Delilah*, we need to HUMBLY use the Fruits of the Spirit and behave Christlike, even if we mess up royally. Colossians 1:10 says, "*That you may walk worthy of the Lord, fully pleasing Him, being fruitful in every good work and increasing in the knowledge of God.*"

- ☐ When dealing with *The Spirit of Delilah*, we must ACTIVATE the Law of Reciprocity, sowing our teachable lessons and experiences back into the Kingdom to feed God's sheep, *As It Pleases Him*. Revelation 12:11 says, "*And they overcame him by the blood of the Lamb and by the word of their testimony, and they did not love their lives to the death.*"

- ☐ When dealing with *The Spirit of Delilah*, we need to STAY in our own lanes, doing what we were called to do, according to our Predestined Blueprint. Now, if one does not know it, then it is time to get in the know. Here is what John 15:5 wants us to remember: "*I am the vine, you are the branches. He who abides in Me, and I in him, bears much fruit; for without Me you can do nothing.*"

The Pitfalls of Manipulative Spirits

In the Eye of God, mistakes are an intrinsic part of the learning process, and a moment of weakness does not make us a failure if we learn from it or if we reverse it to create a win-win. Nevertheless, with a work-in-progress mindset, we should not remain in such a condition, regardless of where we are, what we have been through, or the decisions we have made...there is always HOPE.

Even if our challenges or issues feel overwhelming, pray, repent, forgive, and keep it moving in the Spirit of Excellence. Clearly, we cannot change others, but we can change ourselves for the Greater Good without indulging in *The Spirit of Delilah's* antics or strongholds. Doing so helps us weed out *The Spirit of Jezebel, Delilah, and Haman*. Plus, it assists in preventing these negative Spirits of malice, jealousy, deceit, and the desire to undermine others from sideswiping us due to our relational humanness.

The Spirit of Haman

In the Book of Esther, *The Spirit of Haman's* plotting is a perfect illustration of how personal vendettas and feuds can escalate into widespread tyranny and genocide, affecting countless innocent lives.

In the Biblical narrative, Haman was deemed as an affluent, high-ranking official in the Persian Empire with an uncontainable ego. As King Xerxes' prime minister, he enjoyed considerable authority while getting a kick out of people bowing down to him. Frankly, *The Spirit of Haman* desired to compete with no one for the spotlight until Mordecai came into the picture.

Mordecai, a Jewish leader known for his unwavering Spiritual Principles and devotion to his Faith in God, refused to bow down to Haman. As a result, *The Spirit of Haman* plotted

The Pitfalls of Manipulative Spirits

a heinous scheme to annihilate not just Mordecai, but all the Jewish people across the Persian Empire.

The demonic influence behind Haman was not only violent, hateful, and discriminatory. It also unveils the dangerous consequences of unchecked or abusive power fueled by his personal grievances with those who believed that God was in control. Once his heinous schemes and intentions were made known by Queen Esther to King Xerxes, his plan backfired. In reckoning for his disloyalty, Haman was executed on the gallows he had prepared for Mordecai.

The Spirit of Haman is rooted in a demonic influence that operates through oppression, antisemitism, and schemes against God's people with plotted wickedness and debaucherous acts of unkindness. While at the same time seeking to undermine our Justice System and our right to have Divine Dominion. By degrading the hard work and gut-wrenching labor of our Forefathers, *The Spirit of Haman*, strategically tries to rewrite the law to benefit his agenda and to override the Will of God with betrayal, deceit, verbal abuse, or hostility.

In today's day and age, *The Spirit of Haman* is hidden within the ranks of political maneuvering with an attempt to silence or destroy those who stand for righteousness. All of which require Divine Intervention to break this yoke of deception, oppression, and unjustified opposition. In a world filled with challenges, ulterior motives, wishful thinking, and disdaining uncertainties, here is what we need to do to break *The Spirit of Haman*, but not limited to such:

- ☐ To break *The Spirit of Haman*, we must PRAY for **Divine Protection**. Here is a sample prayer: *"Father, my God, in the Name of Jesus, I ask for Your Divine Shield of Protection to cover me from any manipulative hurt, harm, danger, or disgrace that may come my way. Protect my Mind, Body, Soul, and Spirit,*

The Pitfalls of Manipulative Spirits

as well as my name and reputation. My Lord, Grant me the Divine Wisdom to navigate through challenging situations with grace, strength, and honor, As It Pleases You. In Jesus' Name, I pray. Amen." **READ**: Psalms 91.

☐ To break *The Spirit of Haman*, we must PRAY for **Divine Discernment**. Here is a sample prayer: *"Father, my God, in the Name of Jesus, grant me the Divine Insight to comprehend not only my own heart but also the hearts of those around me. Please help me to recognize the struggles and joys woven into the fabric of our shared existence with Divine Clarity. My Lord, teach me to listen with compassion and understanding. In addition, please teach me how to discern and empathize with others properly, offering genuine support rooted in understanding rather than judgment. To You, My Heavenly Father, I give thanks. In Jesus' Name, I pray. Amen."* **READ**: Psalms 119.

☐ To break *The Spirit of Haman*, we must PRAY for **Divine Wisdom** and **Understanding**. Here is a sample prayer: *"Father, my God, in the Name of Jesus, I come before You with a humble heart, seeking Your Divine Wisdom and Understanding. As I gather my thoughts and intentions, As It Pleases You, open my Mind, Body, Soul, and Spirit to Your Divine Light, leading the way in Spirit and Truth. So speak, Lord, Your servant is listening. To You, My Heavenly Father, I give thanks. In Jesus' Name, I pray. Amen."* **READ**: Psalms 25.

☐ To break *The Spirit of Haman*, we must PRAY for **Divine Justice**. Here is a sample prayer: *"Father, my God, in the Name of Jesus, I come before You today with a heart full of trust, faith, and hope, seeking Your Divine Protection and Guidance. Lord, You are my refuge and strength, a fortress in times of*

The Pitfalls of Manipulative Spirits

trouble; therefore, I seek Divine Justice for every wicked plot that has been schemed against me. May it be overturned in the Name of Jesus. For I know that no weapon formed against me shall prosper, for You are my Heavenly Defender as the Holy Ghost Fire covers me. To You, My Heavenly Father, I give thanks. In Jesus' Name, I pray. Amen." **READ**: Psalms 7.

☐ To break *The Spirit of Haman*, we must PRAY for **Divine Favor**. Here is a sample prayer: *"Father, my God, in the Name of Jesus, as I come before You today, I thank You for Your unwavering love, grace, and mercy that surrounds my life. I acknowledge that You are the Divine Source of all my BLESSINGS and the giver of every GOOD GIFT. Lord, I humbly seek Your Divine Favor in my life, trusting that Your plans for me are good and full of hope, according to my Predestined Blueprinted Purpose. To You, My Heavenly Father, I give thanks while asking that Your Supernatural Favor rests upon every area of my life for the Greater Good. In Jesus' Name, I pray. Amen."* **READ**: Psalms 5.

☐ To break *The Spirit of Haman*, we must PRAY for **Divine Exposure of Evil Plans or Hidden Agendas**. Here is a sample prayer: *"Father, my God, in the Name of Jesus, as I come into Your presence, I acknowledge that You see all things—both light and darkness, good and evil, right and wrong. Therefore, I humbly ask for Your guidance for Divine Revelation, revealing the plots of the enemy that are concealed in the shadows of the night. My Lord, let Your Divine Light shine upon every hidden agenda that stands against Your Divine Will and Purpose for my life, my community, and my nation. Lord, my protector, and shield, let Your Spirit rise up in me, dismantling anything that is not of You, my Heavenly Father. With Divine Dominion:*

The Pitfalls of Manipulative Spirits

As It Pleases You, I pray for those who are unaware of the evil lurking beneath the surface. Please have mercy on us all. In Jesus' Name, I pray. Amen." **READ**: Psalms 140.

- [ ] To break *The Spirit of Haman*, we must PRAY for **Divine Strength** and **Courage**. Here is a sample prayer: *"Father, my God, in the Name of Jesus, in the stillness of this moment, I come before You, Spirit to Spirit, with an open heart and mind, yearning for the courage to stand firm in righteousness amid the winds of opposition and injustice. Fill me with Your Divine Strength and Boldness with the Spirit of Truth on HIGH. Help me to approach adversity with unwavering faith, trusting that You will guide my words, thoughts, and actions. In every situation, I will be filled with Your Loving Spirit and Divine Courage as I stand firm in righteousness with the boldness, mercy, and grace needed to move in the Spirit of Excellence. To You, My Heavenly Father, I give thanks. In Jesus' Name, I pray. Amen."* **READ**: Psalms 35.

- [ ] To break *The Spirit of Haman*, we must PRAY for **Divine Reversal**. Here is a sample prayer: *"Father, my God, in the Name of Jesus, with Divine Authority, As It Pleases You, I nullify any and all plans that are not of You, My Heavenly Father. Lord, I acknowledge that there are forces that seek to undermine, deceive, and destroy the goodness that You have instilled in my life and the lives of Your sheep. For this reason, I lift up to You the schemes of those who wish to bring chaos and confusion, and I ask for Your mighty hand to move in ways that only You can. Lord, I am reminded in Your Word that no weapon formed against us shall prosper. As I stand on this promise today, believing that You, O God, are a God of Divine Reversals, I trust You...We trust You. My Lord, it is You who have the power to*

The Pitfalls of Manipulative Spirits

turn the darkest situations around, bringing light where there is darkness and shadows. I ask that You dismantle every plot and plan the enemy has orchestrated against us and, in its place, bring forth Your Divine Will and Purpose, which is good and pleasing to You, My Heavenly Father. I give thanks for this. In Jesus' Name, I pray. Amen." **READ**: Psalms 126.

- [ ] To break *The Spirit of Haman*, we must PRAY for **Divine Victory.** Here is a sample prayer: *"Father, my God, in the Name of Jesus, I come before You today with a heart full of hope, love, and a desire for UNITY. I am seeking Your Divine Guidance and Intervention in all things. I acknowledge the challenges I face, both personally and as part of my nation. So, I turn to You, my Heavenly Father, the Divine Source of all strength and wisdom, for help. I pray for healing and reconciliation within my home, my community, and my country as we are all connected in Christ Jesus and united under Your Divine Love. Lord, I lift up my leaders to You. Fill them with Your Divine Wisdom and Discernment on how to become Divinely Victorious for us as ONE people. May every step I take be a TESTAMENT to Your Divine Glory and a free-will offering of my love for others. To You, My Heavenly Father, I give thanks. In Jesus' Name, I pray. Amen."* **READ**: Psalms 108.

Will these prayers work for Believers? Absolutely! As a personal communicative lifeline, *Spirit to Spirit*, prayer, in itself, changes things. Through fervent supplication, it has a knack for going *Beyond the Church Walls* to unmistakably seek to *Pull Back The Curtains* on us or them, especially when dealing with *The Spirit of Haman*.

The Pitfalls of Manipulative Spirits

When believers gather to pray, we can move mountains. Matthew 18:19-20 says, *"Again I say to you that if two of you agree on earth concerning anything that they ask, it will be done for them by My Father in heaven. For where two or three are gathered together in My name, I am there in the midst of them."*

Chapter Four
Beyond the Church Walls

When going *Beyond the Church Walls*, my ear has been to the ground long enough to hear those proclaiming Holiness, and their attitude, behaviors, character, and demeanor represent a mirror image of unrighteousness while thinking they are righteous and justified. Yet, they have a trail of rotten fruits, traumatized victims, unmended bridges, hateful actions, broken relationships, a history of debauchery, and so on. If one has not experienced this yet, just live a little longer.

As we take this a step further, the Heavenly of Heaven's call to action is designed to Awaken us from our Spiritual Slumber. How do we know when we are Spiritually Awakened? When we take the focus off of ourselves, placing it on the Will of God and our Divine Blueprint, *As It Pleases Him*, we will know the change has occurred.

But as long as selfishness is clouding our sense of good judgment, we still have work to do. Selfishness does not make us bad people; it simply means we must do a little more work to unravel the worldly knots that have us entangled in a web of deception. Why must we remove the knots? Humility helps us to obtain our Birthrights and Blessings without having shame or ungratefulness attached.

Bringing shame to the Kingdom due to some form of recklessness, negligence, debauchery, or ungratefulness are a few ways to become detached from the Holy Spirit, causing Him to go into a state of dormancy until we come to ourselves.

Can the Holy Spirit depart from us? Of course. God will allow His Spirit to depart while allowing a distressing one to take His place, primarily when we are in a state of willful disobedience. In addition, this will also happen when we begin to use Him as a form of manipulative leverage to get what we want, or when we outright pimp Him out, similar to the King Saul experience in 1 Samuel 15 and 16.

Now, on the other hand, He will come upon us to intervene as well, preventing us from destroying ourselves or His Chosen Vessels of Conveyance. By far, this is similar to how the Spirit of God came upon Balaam in Numbers 24:1-2. *"Now when Balaam saw that it pleased the LORD to bless Israel, he did not go as at other times, to seek to use sorcery, but he set his face toward the wilderness. And Balaam raised his eyes, and saw Israel encamped according to their tribes; and the Spirit of God came upon him."*

How do we begin to operate with a Heavenly Perspective while having the Holy Spirit remain in our favor? *Beyond the Church Walls*, we must first wholeheartedly desire the unveiling of Divine Mysteries from the Heavenly of Heavens, Spirit to Spirit. Here is how I know about this: Ephesians 3:1-7 says, *"For this reason I, Paul, the prisoner of Christ Jesus for you Gentiles—if indeed you have heard of the dispensation of the grace of God which was given to me for you, how that by revelation He made known to me the mystery (as I have briefly written already, by which, when you read, you may understand my knowledge in the mystery of Christ), which in other ages was not made known to the sons of men, as it has now been revealed by the Spirit to His holy apostles and prophets: that the Gentiles*

Beyond the Church Walls

should be fellow heirs, of the same body, and partakers of His promise in Christ through the gospel, of which I became a minister according to the gift of the grace of God given to me by the effective working of His power."

Secondly, *Beyond the Church Walls*, we must begin with RESPECT for God's Divine Order, *As It Pleases Him*. When we disrespect what He has set forth from the Beginning, we will begin to digress on the respective disposition cycle. Once this occurs, the human psyche must use other means of appearing as if we are respectful, such as making excuses about why we deserve it or playing the victim for not receiving it.

In all simplicity, we will either fake respect or demand respect without realizing free-willed respect gets the job done, *As It Pleases God*. From a Divine Perspective, when it comes to Divine Dominion, listed below are a few items to RESPECT, but not limited to such:

- ☐ We must RESPECT our Creator. He is the Beginning and the End; therefore, we are somewhere in between, so Respect the process of Divine Conveyance. *"In the beginning God created the heavens and the earth. The earth was without form, and void; and darkness was on the face of the deep. And the Spirit of God was hovering over the face of the waters."* Genesis 1:1-2.

- ☐ We must RESPECT the Light and Darkness and the timetable governing it. Therefore, we should give thanks for both because they create balance and understanding, allowing us to know and experience the difference between the two. In addition, it gives us a way to measure our days based on a simulation of the light of day and the dark of night, depending upon where we are located. And, regardless of where we are, it provides a 24-hour cycle of an inclusive timetable of measurement. *"And God saw the light, that it was good; and*

God divided the light from the darkness. God called the light Day, and the darkness He called Night. So, the evening and the morning were the first day." Genesis 1:4-5.

- ☐ We must RESPECT the Universal Laws set in motion by our Heavenly Father, while putting everything in its proper perspective. For example, the Law of Gravity keeps us pulled to the Earth's core, ensuring we do not float around from pillar to post. Although this does not include the Higher Laws, it is one that we can all understand and relate to outside of the Laws governing the travel of Light and Sound or the Law of Oneness, Energy, Action, Cause and Effect, Reciprocity, Attraction, Correspondence, Relativity, Polarity, Rhythm, and so on. The key is to RESPECT them all. *"Then God said, 'Let there be a firmament in the midst of the waters, and let it divide the waters from the waters.' Thus, God made the firmament, and divided the waters which were under the firmament from the waters which were above the firmament; and it was so. And God called the firmament Heaven. So, the evening and the morning were the second day."* Genesis 1:6-8.

- ☐ We must RESPECT the elements of water because it is indeed a sustaining force to life and the cleansing process therein. *"Then God said, Let the waters under the heavens be gathered together into one place, and let the dry land appear; and it was so. And God called the dry land Earth, and the gathering together of the waters He called Seas. And God saw that it was good."* Genesis 1:9-10.

- ☐ We must RESPECT the SEEDS and FRUITS of all things, knowing that Seedtime and Harvest will produce after their own kind. *"Then God said, Let the earth*

Beyond the Church Walls

bring forth grass, the herb that yields seed, and the fruit tree that yields fruit according to its kind, whose seed is in itself, on the earth; and it was so. And the earth brought forth grass, the herb that yields seed according to its kind, and the tree that yields fruit, whose seed is in itself according to its kind. And God saw that it was good." Genesis 1:11-12.

- ☐ We must RESPECT the Seasons we are in or the Seasons of another. We must also Respect Mother Nature, even if we do not understand the cycles. What is the point of respecting Mother Nature, especially when she is not God? First and foremost, Mother Nature is not a deity, but it can be affected by one! Secondly, it is designed to take care of itself and us, especially when we develop a bond with it, knowing that it is designed to serve us as we do our part in protecting it. *"Then God said, Let there be lights in the firmament of the heavens to divide the day from the night; and let them be for signs and seasons, and for days and years; and let them be for lights in the firmament of the heavens to give light on the earth; and it was so."* Genesis 1:14-15.

- ☐ We must RESPECT the Greater and Lesser Lights, good and evil, right and wrong, just and unjust, and so on. Spiritual Duality is the process of growing, regrafting, and restoration; plus, it brings everything into or puts things out of BALANCE in due time, according to the Will of God. *"Then God made two great lights: the greater light to rule the day, and the lesser light to rule the night. He made the stars also. God set them in the firmament of the heavens to give light on the earth, and to rule over the day and over the night, and to divide the light from the darkness. And God saw that it was good."* Genesis 1:16-18.

- ☐ We must RESPECT Nature's Living Things and their Way of Multiplying as they do what they are called to do, reproducing after their own kind. *"Then God said, 'Let the waters abound with an abundance of living creatures, and let birds fly above the earth across the face of the firmament of the heavens.' So, God created great sea creatures and every living thing that moves, with which the waters abounded, according to their kind, and every winged bird according to its kind. And God saw that it was good. And God blessed them, saying, 'Be fruitful and multiply, and fill the waters in the seas, and let birds multiply on the earth.'"* Genesis 1:20-22.

- ☐ We must RESPECT Animals. Every animal serves a purpose, regardless of whether we understand them or not. Or, whether they creep us out, they still have a Divine Role to play according to their Blueprint. *"Then God said, 'Let the earth bring forth the living creature according to its kind: cattle and creeping thing and beast of the earth, each according to its kind;' and it was so. And God made the beast of the earth according to its kind, cattle according to its kind, and everything that creeps on the earth according to its kind. And God saw that it was good."* Genesis 1:24-25.

- ☐ We must RESPECT all Human Life. *"Then God said, 'Let Us make man in Our image, according to Our likeness; let them have dominion over the fish of the sea, over the birds of the air, and over the cattle, over all the earth and over every creeping thing that creeps on the earth.' So, God created man in His own image; in the image of God, He created him; male and female He created them."* Genesis 1:26-27.

Beyond the Church Walls

- We must RESPECT the Giftings, Callings, Talents, Creativity, and Purpose of each person, place, or thing without coveting. *"Then God blessed them, and God said to them, Be fruitful and multiply; fill the earth and subdue it; have dominion over the fish of the sea, over the birds of the air, and over every living thing that moves on the earth."* Genesis 1:28.

- We must RESPECT the Seed hidden in all things. Why the SEED of all things? Everything has its own place under the Sun. If we respect the process, it will respect us, causing the natural elements of life to favor us. *"And God said, 'See, I have given you every herb that yields seed which is on the face of all the earth, and every tree whose fruit yields seed; to you it shall be for food. Also, to every beast of the earth, to every bird of the air, and to everything that creeps on the earth, in which there is life, I have given every green herb for food;' and it was so."* Genesis 1:29-30.

- We must RESPECT the Good in all things. Once we do, it becomes easier to pinpoint the win-win. *"Then God saw everything that He had made, and indeed it was very good. So the evening and the morning were the sixth day."* Genesis 1:31.

- We must RESPECT the Ending of all things. Doing so helps us to be at peace with people, places, and things that are not a part of our Divine Design or when their time is up in a particular chapter of our lives. *"Thus, the heavens and the earth, and all the host of them, were finished."* Genesis 2:1.

- We must RESPECT the Day of Rest for all things. For we all need a day of rest and restoration, Mentally,

Physically, Emotionally, Spiritually, and Relationally. *"And on the seventh day God ended His work which He had done, and He rested on the seventh day from all His work which He had done. Then God blessed the seventh day and sanctified it, because in it He rested from all His work which God had created and made." Genesis 2:2-3.*

- ☐ We must RESPECT the Divine History of Creation. God does not ask us to agree, but He demands Respect in this area of the Ancientness of Days and His Divine Order. *"This is the history of the heavens and the earth when they were created, in the day that the LORD God made the earth and the heavens, before any plant of the field was in the earth and before any herb of the field had grown. For the LORD God had not caused it to rain on the earth, and there was no man to till the ground; but a mist went up from the earth and watered the whole face of the ground." Genesis 2:4-6.*

- ☐ We must RESPECT how we were created while not taking anything for granted, especially the Breath of Life. *"And the LORD God formed man of the dust of the ground, and breathed into his nostrils the breath of life; and man became a living being." Genesis 2:7.*

What does Respect have to do with our Heavenly Perspective? In our Heaven on Earth Experiences, if we are not able to respect the simple things, we will not appreciate the Heavenly Treasures, Wisdom, or Secrets. Instead, we will find a reason to discount, second-guess, doubt, scatter, fault-find, or nitpick everything, including the Blessings of the Kingdom and the living embodiments of God's Divine Purpose.

Beyond the Church Walls

According to the Ancient of Days, before engaging or disengaging, dealing with *The Calculations of Men*, within or *Beyond the Church Walls*, it is always wise to repeat Ephesians 3:20-21, "*Now to Him who is able to do exceedingly abundantly above all that we ask or think, according to the power that works in us, to Him be glory in the church by Christ Jesus to all generations, forever and ever. Amen.*"

The Calculations of Men

As the embodiments of the Kingdom, to become and remain Blessed in the Eye of God, we must first recognize and agree that we are. If we fail to recognize this one fact, we will begin to player hate when we should be celebrating. The last thing the Kingdom wants is a party pooper raining on our parade or that of another.

Why are party poopers frowned upon in the Eye of God? There is a Spiritual Calculation involved in all things, and if we fail to become grateful, we will begin to make a lot of avoidable mistakes. If we violate the Spiritual Calculations or the Spiritual Principles governing a person, place, or thing, we will have some form of accident or incidental episode from within, spreading outwardly.

For example, when driving a vehicle with our natural eyes, we feel as if we are just driving, and that is it. However, from a Spiritual Perspective, we cannot see the behind-the-scenes calculations involved in stopping, turning, reversing, parking, driving, changing lanes, and so on. Therefore, we take this privilege for granted, becoming irresponsible in our approach. The more we disrespect the laws and the calculations associated with driving, the more we will eventually have an accident.

On the other hand, if we respect the laws and calculations, they are more apt to help us avoid having an accident or becoming a victim while working on our behalf and not against us. Let us take this a step further; humans are the only sector of Creation having this privilege. Yes, driving is a privilege! And, we have the nerve to become ungrateful, especially when the birds of the air are on a wing and a prayer. The beasts of the field are still on their feet, trotting to and fro, getting blisters, tackling thorns, and searching for food with a level of uncertainty.

All in all, everything according to the Heavenly of Heavens is calculated. It does not matter if we understand it, how we feel, or what we think; the Processes of God must be respected, regardless of how they appear to our naked eyes. Once we *Pull Back The Curtains*, we will begin to see the Kingdom differently. By Divine Default, when doing so, *As It Pleases God*, we will start viewing people, places, and things with our Spiritual Eye or from a Heavenly Perspective instead of succumbing to a human or worldly perspective.

Pulling Back The Curtains

As we *Pull Back The Curtains* of life, we must know that our outlook is based upon our in-look (view from within). How we see ourselves from within determines how we perceive life, even if we have been conditioned to behave, react, or communicate a certain way. Though we can mask our perceptions and perspectives, the moment we are placed under pressure, what is within comes out.

How is it possible to explode, especially when our self-control is up to par? First and foremost, we are not robots. We are human beings having the ability to deal with people, places, and things Mentally, Physically, Emotionally, and Spiritually, so we must know what to control. Secondly, no one is exempt from having a moment when triggered; it is knowing what to do when it happens that makes the difference between self-control and being out of control.

Beyond the Church Walls

When *Pulling Back The Curtains* on self-control, we are able to step into action, freeze up, go into hiding, go into fight mode, go into negative habit-forming mode to cope, break down, act a fool, remain calm, plead the fifth, and so on. As a result, we must become cautious in all of our sayings, doings, and becomings. Why must we exercise caution in this area? It may cause Spiritual Blindness, Deafness, or Muteness, depending on our motives, including our heart and mind postures.

To maximize *Divine Dominion: As It Pleases God®*, it is imperative to clear our Spiritual Vision, unclog our Spiritual Ears, and develop our Spiritual Language from the Heavenly of Heavens. By doing so, our perceptions will begin to merge with the Heavenly Perception of the Kingdom to eventually become ONE. However, to complete the merging process, we must Spiritually See, Hear, and Speak clearly without having worldly static clouding our sense of good judgment.

Believe it or not, our survival instincts are predicated on our perceptions, determining what we will or will not do to sustain life as we see it from a Worldly or Kingdomly Perspective. A Worldly Perspective can be derived from a few phrases, but not limited to such:

- ☐ 'By any means necessary.'
- ☐ 'Get them before they get me.'
- ☐ 'My way or no way.'
- ☐ 'Whatever it takes.'
- ☐ 'Everything is about me.'
- ☐ 'What is mine is mine.'
- ☐ 'Any cup is mine as long as I have one.'
- ☐ 'Me, Me, Me.'
- ☐ 'I always get my way.'
- ☐ 'I will fight until the end.'

Beyond the Church Walls

- ☐ 'I have tricks in my bag' or 'I have tricks up my sleeve.'
- ☐ 'My god is better than yours' or 'I am the god over my own life.'

Clearly, we have the free will to believe what we so desire, yet all of the above statements can become negative or positive based on our perceptions. As we synergize with the Heavenly of Heavens, by changing the trajectory of how we think, we can open up the Gates of Heaven on our behalf. When it comes down to our perceptions, if we intertwine the Divine Synergy of the Kingdom, we empower ourselves by default.

At first, it may feel a little weird, but once we become accustomed to having a Kingdom Mindset, it will trump anything known to man, breaking Spiritual Blindness, Deafness, and Muteness to the core. Plus, it shatters negative, deflective mirrors designed to rehash our past to blind our future. Really? Yes, really! A Kingdom Perspective can be derived from a few expressions, but not limited to such:

- ☐ 'By any means necessary according to the Will of God.'
- ☐ 'Let me put on the Whole Armor of God before they attack me.'
- ☐ 'God's way or no way.'
- ☐ 'Whatever it takes to allow God's Will to be done.'
- ☐ 'As It Pleases God.'
- ☐ 'Everything is about the Kingdom according to my Divine Blueprint.'
- ☐ 'What belongs to me is already according to my Divine Blueprint.'
- ☐ 'My cup runneth over according to my Divine Blueprint.'
- ☐ 'It is between Us and Them' or 'We are ONE.'
- ☐ 'The Will of God must be fulfilled according to my Divine Blueprint.'
- ☐ 'The Fight is Finished' or 'God has already provided.'

Beyond the Church Walls

- ☐ 'No weapon formed against me shall prosper.'
- ☐ 'My God, who art in Heaven, is my Way, my Truth, and my Life.'
- ☐ 'My God provides my daily Bread according to His riches and glory in Christ Jesus.'

When we redirect our wants, needs, and desires back to the Kingdom to affirm our STANCE or as a positive affirmation, we allow our plans to have an opportunity to become corrected, redirected, regrafted, or adjusted according to our Divine Blueprint.

Why must Believers take a stand to affirm themselves? Once again, God did not create us as robots; He wants us involved as relational beings. Secondly, He does not give us all the details upfront because we have to want whatever He has in mind, *As It Pleases Him*, while developing our focus. As a word of caution, if we are constantly consumed with distractions without setting some form of Spiritual Guards or Limitations, we may NOT be ready to be in Purpose on purpose as of yet. Thirdly, it also trains our Spiritual Muscles to instinctively know what is for us and what is not, based on our internal components through our senses, instincts, or conscience.

When *Pulling Back the Curtains*, we must put away our selfishness, pride, coveting, competitiveness, jealousy, envy, or greed to get our full portion. Unbeknown to most, while in or out of the Will of God, we are often operating on a fraction or a portion of our Divine Blueprint. In my opinion, this is similar to a faucet leaking or dripping water, and to get it to flow fully, we must increase the pressure.

Now, this fraction depends upon us, on the timing, the amount of training required, the appropriate season, the amount of healing needed, the level of trauma endured, and so on. Fortunately, or unfortunately for some, this is why we feel a void, longing, internal drive, or tugging from within, letting us know there is MORE. Yet, due to our lack of understanding in this area, we are unable to figure out what is wrong or why we are feeling the way we do. So, we suppress it, hoping we will have an 'Aha' moment. Well, this is it! That 'Aha' moment has come and is NOW!

According to the Heavenly of Heavens, our Positive Mental Mindset depends upon us to have a want, work for, or place a demand on it. Simply put, we are waiting for the 'Aha' moment, but it is already prewired into our DNA. Yes, it is already in our system; we just need to become AWARE of it to unveil it. By Divine Design, it is hidden under layers of negative debris; therefore, we must do a clean sweep of all negative characteristics, behaviors, thoughts, actions, desires, habits, and so on, *Pulling Back the Curtains*. When doing so, do not worry about the residue left behind.

Why should we not worry about negative residues? First, we have the Holy Spirit to help in the clean-up process to correct the correctable through the Fruits of the Spirit and Christlike Character. Secondly, we have the Blood of Jesus to cover the menial quirks we have through our ability to pray, repent, and fast on occasion to enforce the Heavenly Contract of grace, mercy, and forgiveness.

By *Pulling Back the Curtains* and reinforcing our lives with the Word of God and positive affirmations, we can steer our lives back to the right path, mainly when we get off course, lost, distracted, distressed, or confused. What is the right path? Regardless of how we attempt to complicate life, there are only two paths leading to all things or any form of pitstop along the way, which are:

- ☐ The Path of Righteousness.
- ☐ The Path of Unrighteousness.

Beyond the Church Walls

Keeping the Kingdom uncomplicated can streamline our character into good or bad, right or wrong, just or unjust, positive or negative quickly, without anyone calling us out or pointing the finger. We do not need anyone to tell us when we are right or wrong; we already know! However, the complications come into play when we attempt to rationalize or justify whatever or with whomever.

When *Pulling Back the Curtains*, querying ourselves with a self-analysis, self-awareness, or self-mirror of righteousness vs. unrighteousness will help us in ways beyond human understanding. In addition, it will also automatically put our human psyche in self-correct mode using our conscience and senses.

Once the psyche is trained to become ONE with the Holy Spirit, due to our Spiritual Awareness, if it knows it is right, our conscience will peacefully move forward. Conversely, if it is wrong, our conscience will kick in, and it is questioned in the *What, When, Where, Why, How,* and with *Whom* formation. And, being that the human psyche does not like to be questioned constantly, it will do the right thing naturally, putting our conscience on high alert to avoid being called out.

Unbeknown to most, the human psyche does not like to be put on display for corrective action to occur, nor does it like any red flags to alert the Holy Spirit of miscalculations or misdirection. For this reason, when delving into any known or unknown unrighteousness, it will seek to control us Mentally, Physically, and Emotionally by any means necessary while negatively governing our thoughts, emotions, feelings, perceptions, and so on, similar to having a temper tantrum.

To add insult to injury, when we become Spiritually Blind, Deaf, or Mute, the negative will appear positive. How is this possible when negative is negative and positive is positive? Frankly, this is when we think we are right in our own eyes or

Beyond the Church Walls

we are in denial, but all so wrong in the Eye of God based upon our fruits or characteristics. What does this mean? It simply means that we went about doing something the wrong way, or our intentions were unrighteous. For this reason, it is best to query ourselves with the Fruits of the Spirit in or out of our moments of unsurety.

More importantly, once the thermostat of our psyche is set on righteousness, *As It Pleases God*, it governs our motives to ensure the gauge is set correctly, even amid hiccups woven into our daily lives. Also, if something wrong happens based upon the erring of another, a mistake of uncommonness happens, when our worthiness is underhandedly being tested, or we are intentionally set up to err to bring shame to our names, our conscience will alert us. Despite being in this state, if our intentions were righteous, we would not be penalized severely for any wrongdoings due to having the correct and sincere heart posture, *As It Pleases Him*.

Do we get a free pass? Unfortunately, this is not my call. The level of Divine Grace and Mercy and free passes are between God, the offender, and the offendee. Moreover, we do not know what He is using to train, mold, or provoke us. Clearly, there are times when we can set the record straight when such a hiccup happens, but there are times when we must leave well enough alone while continuing to move forward in the Spirit of Righteousness and Excellence, *As It Pleases Him*.

In the Union of Oneness, it is imperative to understand that we are Vessels of God, regardless of how we feel about our relationship with Him, our past mistakes, the issues we are facing, and so on. However, our *Divine Dominion: As It Pleases God*® positions us to embrace our Divine Blueprint according to our Heavenly Intents of being in Purpose on purpose.

Beyond the Church Walls

Triggering Seeds

According to the Heavenly of Heavens, we must prove and establish our worthiness based on our actions, reactions, desires, motives, character, and willingness. We cannot do whatever we want, whenever we desire, however we decide, and with whomever, without accounting for the cost positively or negatively. So, it behooves us to take responsibility without becoming reckless Mentally, Physically, Emotionally, or Spiritually.

What does recklessness have to do with our *Divine Dominion*? Recklessness has Spiritual Repercussions, bringing about yokes, bondages, generational curses, or the Wrath of God. For instance, and with all due respect, some preach that we do not have to do anything to be in the Will of God or to pursue Purpose, but this is the biggest form of deception known to mankind. From a Spiritual Perspective, this is like telling us that we do not need a SEED to reproduce or we do not need oxygen to live.

Listen to me, and listen to me well; according to the Cycle of Life, there must be a TRIGGER of a SEED to receive the proper instructions causing growth, movement, or reaction. If there is no trigger or provocation of some sort, there is no reaction or a jumpstart for the Law of Causation. Without some form of action, it contributes to stagnancy, death, or some form of phantom symptom of falseness, deception, masks, or, better yet, what we call in today's day and age, a false sense of worth.

According to the Heavenly of Heavens, being that fakeness does not have a seedful trigger of growth or maturity, the Cycle of Life will return whatever it is back to the earth by taking out the weakest, unproductive link. Why would this happen, especially when we have *Divine Dominion: As It Pleases God*®? Fakeness is manmade and cannot be reproduced naturally without the help of the originator who created the synthesis.

Inopportunely, this is why we get a lot of individuals faking their Spiritual Astuteness, creating an illusion for onlookers. Once the mask is removed, they are exhausted or fall into a state of depression instantly. How can we resolve this? Do not pretend! In the Kingdom, transparency is a must, and if something is fake, admit it!

Building Kingdom Authenticity is best done by looking and tilling for the Seed, Trigger, or Susceptibility hidden in our Spiritual Gifts. What does all of this mean for us in layman's terms? Based upon the Spiritual Decree set forth in the Garden of Eden, mainly with the Adam and Eve Experience in the Book of Genesis, we must put in the work, becoming a work-in-progress from the inside out. How do we make this make sense? In all simplicity, the Seed or Trigger will reside in something or someone.

Now, based on our *Divine Dominion: As It Pleases God*®, we must take out the shovel and dig deep within the human psyche to extract the Divine Treasures we possess, which are hidden in a weakness, vice, habit, or the negative. From experience, this is accomplished by TILLING it until it becomes a win-win or a positive manifestation without settling for defeat or deception.

How do we Spiritually Till? Spiritually Tilling our own ground is accomplished by asking the right fact-finding questions in the *What, When, Where, Why, How,* and with *Whom* formation to become better at whatever or with whomever. We must also learn, train, understand, educate ourselves, and document consistently, taking notes without fail.

What is the purpose of going through the Spiritual Tilling process for a weakness? Our Divine Fruitfulness or Provisions will most often reside in a Seed that must be broken, nurtured, and watered to produce. In addition, it also teaches

Beyond the Church Walls

gratefulness, gives us experience, develops obedience, and helps us become merciful, compassionate, forgiving, and understanding.

In *Pulling Back The Curtains*, by missing the developmental process or refusing to put in the work, we deprive ourselves of specific lessons, experiences, cleansings, or uprooting processes that can only come from us. Why can this process only come from us? Just as no two fingerprints, footprints, eye prints, or mind prints are the same, this also applies to our blueprinted experiences. By Divine Design, this allows us to have intricate details that no one else is privy to have access to except the Holy Spirit.

The bottom line is that everyone is different, having different issues, traumas, stories, playbooks, and upsets in need of regrafting, making our weaknesses our greatest strengths. Based on the consequential workable punishment of mankind from Genesis 3:18, *"Both thorns and thistles it shall bring forth for you, and you shall eat the herb of the field."* Due to Adam and Eve's acts of disobedience, all mankind must put in the work to gain Divine Access to the fruits of our labor.

If we do not put in the work, we will have real developmental or growth issues. Unfortunately, no one can stand in proxy for us; we must Spiritually Till our own grounds. To be clear, we can have someone help or pinpoint the areas in need of reckoning, but the 'sweat of our brow' must come from us. Please allow me to Spiritually Align, *"In the sweat of your face you shall eat bread Till you return to the ground, For out of it you were taken; For dust you are, And to dust you shall return."* Genesis 3:19.

For example, if I had refused to listen, learn, understand, regraft, uproot, prune, cast down, usher in, take notes, and so on, I would not be able to write on this Spiritual Level with such conviction, clarity, and astuteness. Although my Spiritual Journey was not easy, and I would not wish this upon my worst enemy, it was necessary for my Commissioning Process for such a time as this.

Yet, with outright humility, I do not pull any punches, nor do I back down from doing what I have been called to do, regardless of the opinionated thoughts or biases of others. Why? I respect the fact that everyone is entitled to their opinion. If they are not receiving Divine Instructions from the Heavenly of Heavens, then their time is being misgoverned in some way, which means deception is amid the opinion.

I am here to provide Spiritual Understanding, Tools, How-To, and Know-How to build the Kingdom of Heaven, *As It Pleases God*. Thus, I cannot put in the work for anyone or change their opinionated thoughts. So, in order to stay focused and gather the necessary information to help those who are willing to put in the work to help themselves, I will ILLUMINATE the way, guiding them toward the Light without violating their free will.

In the Eye of God, the *Tilling Process* is up to us, especially if we want to maximize our Spiritual Gifts. If we choose not to, then we cannot lay the blame elsewhere, and we have no right to become jealous, envious, or covetous of another person who makes it their business to put in the work to till their Fields of Greatness. Do we not have free will to do whatever we like, especially when *Triggering Seeds*? Yes, we do, but exhibiting this sort of negative behavior to someone who is putting in the work will cause God to allow the Vicissitudes of Life to smite us, tossing us to and fro.

In my opinion, if we want to exhibit negative behaviors or characteristics, we should exhibit them around those who are in the same category of negativity. Why? Negative plus negative equals negative...If we wallow with our equal, then the Spiritual Penalties are much less because both are in AGREEMENT.

Beyond the Church Walls

On the other hand, suppose we exhibit negative fruits or characteristics to unjustifiably afflict the person who is putting in the work from the inside out, doing the Will of God, *As It Pleases Him*. In this case, we will become the ENEMY of God. Why would we become His enemy as Believers? The two are not in AGREEMENT, creating conflicting vibes. Then again, if the positive person is operating in the Spirit of Righteousness with the Fruits of the Spirit and Christlike Character, *As It Pleases Him*, we will inadvertently create a ditch for ourselves as well. Blasphemy, right? Unfortunately, wrong again.

Spiritual Cluelessness is how we get caught up, become yoked, or unawaringly create generational curses affecting our Bloodline. Please allow me to align this accordingly: "*Behold, the wicked brings forth iniquity; Yes, he conceives trouble and brings forth falsehood. He made a pit and dug it out, and has fallen into the ditch which he made. His trouble shall return upon his own head, and his violent dealing shall come down on his own crown. I will praise the LORD according to His righteousness, and will sing praise to the name of the LORD Most High.*" Psalm 7:14-17.

Our *Divine Dominion: As It Pleases God*® is not predicated on taking the easy way out, opting to pass the buck, or blocking those who are in Purpose on purpose. Listen, we have stored information within the human psyche that we need to gain access to, and we need the Holy Spirit to do so. Why do we need Him? We need experience and understanding about ourselves, righteousness, and access to the mysteries associated with our Divine Blueprint or our Heaven on Earth Experiences that only He has Divine Access to. Plus, with His guidance, we can boldly walk in the Spirit and in Truth with no regrets and *As It Pleases God*.

On the other hand, if we opt to remain Spiritually Asleep, we become limited, subjecting ourselves to Spiritual Ignorance or Deprivation. How is this possible, especially when we are sitting pretty? Regardless of what we think, how much we have accomplished, our status, or whatever is associated with our worldly means of operation, without the Holy Trinity, we subject ourselves to psychological invasion. How so? We will become consumed from within with the lust of the eyes, the lust of the flesh, and the pride of life, leading to chaos, negativity, ungratefulness, jealousy, pride, envy, coveting, debauchery, and so on.

Spiritual Giftings

Now, let us take this a step further: If we decide NOT to walk in our Spiritual Giftings, we simply prolong the process until we eventually surrender. Unfortunately, we inadvertently kick-start the Cycle of Déjà vu instead of the Cycle of Change according to our Divine Blueprint. In my opinion, repeating the same cycle over and over is exhausting and time-consuming, especially when it takes the same amount of energy or less to unveil our authentic selves.

When it comes down to our Divine Blueprint or our *Divine Dominion: As It Pleases God*®, we are indeed a Genius in this area. Ethically, it cannot come forth if we do not surrender to it or become distracted by killing the dream of another. Yet, all is not lost if we work diligently on the Fruits of the Spirit and building Christlike Character. By doing so in the Spirit of Excellence and Righteousness, there is no limit on what we can achieve, nor can anyone put a cap on our Level of Impact. Really? Yes, really!

Unbeknown to most, when we surrender to our Divine Blueprint, the Floodgates of Wisdom will yield on our behalf and that of our Bloodline, GUARANTEED! Therefore, once we align ourselves accordingly, we will no longer have to question our worthiness; it becomes established in the Kingdom among the Heavenly of Heavens.

Beyond the Church Walls

All of our Spiritual Resources from the Heavenly of Heavens are properly positioned to complete the Mission of the Kingdom, period! As a word of caution, once we get to this Spiritual Level, we are the only person who can hinder this process. For this reason, we must MAKE SURE of a few things, but not limited to such:

- ☐ We must make sure the Holy Trinity is at the forefront of our lives.
- ☐ We need to make sure that our Fruits of the Spirit are up to par.
- ☐ We must make sure that our Christlike Character is coming forth as pure gold.
- ☐ We need to make sure we are a work-in-progress in a constant State of Repentance.
- ☐ We must make sure we give thanks in all things while creating a win-win out of everything with a Positive Mental Mindset.
- ☐ We need to make sure we document our *Spirit to Spirit* Encounters.
- ☐ We must make sure we forgive with no strings attached.
- ☐ We need to make sure we remain calm.
- ☐ We must make sure we share.
- ☐ We need to make sure we govern our tongues.
- ☐ We must make sure we cancel negative thoughts, words, emotions, or desires and replace them with positive ones.
- ☐ We need to make sure we approach everything, *As It Pleases God*.

Lastly, if we do not limit ourselves to the earthly realm, we become Spiritually Unstoppable in our Heaven on Earth

Beyond the Church Walls

Experiences. So, today marks a new beginning. Pick up your CROWN, and grow GREAT in *Divine Purpose*!

Divine Purpose

Beyond the Church Walls, when we are out of Divine Purpose or the Will of God, our bodies will react accordingly, even if we do not understand what is taking place. All the psyche knows is that something is missing, and it will sometimes overcompensate in other areas, such as materialism, gold-digging, portraying a certain image, obsession with titles, status, fame, and so on. Conversely, if we embark upon our Divine Purpose, all of this will fade away, allowing us to evolve into our authentic selves.

Normal purpose is often described as what drives individuals to pursue goals, cultivate relationships, and strive for personal growth. Our Divine Purpose, on the other hand, is the reason for one's existence, according to our Predestined Blueprint. In addition, it is the key to unlocking our Divine Authenticity and Dominion from the Heavenly of Heavens.

Our purpose, passions, talents, or Divine Purpose could be the same or totally different based on what God is using to train, nudge, or correct us. Then again, it could be tied into what we do in exchange for the Higher Calling of Christ Jesus. How can this possibly work in a real-life situation? Hypothetically speaking, I have a perfect example: Due to the influence of our parents' aspirations or societal expectations, we pursue a prestigious law degree, only to feel a deeper yearning for a vocation in the medical field as a doctor.

As the whispers of our Divine Purpose grow more deafening, the tugging from within becomes undeniable. Once we come to the crossroads between personal ambition and our Divine Calling with an unmistakable nudge from the Heavenly of Heavens, we must make a decision. Based on the scenario from above, in surrendering to the Will of God, we

Beyond the Church Walls

become a doctor, *As It Pleases Him*. And, being that we are already lawyers, He allows us to do both simultaneously in the Spirit of Duality.

How does the Spirit of Duality work from an occupational change? Just because a change is made does not negate the tools, skills, and knowledge gained from the lawyer-to-doctor transition. Here is how it works: First, we have the intellect and persuasive skills of legal counsel as a lawyer. Secondly, with the healing ingenuity, emotional skills, and ethics of a doctor, to save lives while providing wise counsel to healthcare professionals. Thirdly, we have the backing of the Kingdom for being *In Purpose on Purpose*.

Most often, we think the Spirit of Duality applies to good and evil, right and wrong, just and unjust, and so on. Fortunately, it also applies to our wants, needs, and desires, as well as our Dual Purposes, Talents, and Gifts. In bridging gaps in our lives with the tapestry of experiences, it is only wise to add God into the equation of all things, even when we do not understand what is going on or why. Rest assured, when we give it to God, *As It Pleases Him*, He will work that thing out...whatever it is or is not.

By giving God what He wants, *As It Pleases Him*, He allows us to use the tools we already have, making us better, stronger, useful, and wiser for the Kingdom while turning us into an ultimate POWERHOUSE with a strategic edge. Just know that Divine Purpose supersedes our self-made purposes, reasonings, passions, and desires for personal satisfaction or instant gratification. Above all, know this: Surrendering to the Will of God does not mean relinquishing our dreams, desires, or goals but rather embracing the understanding of our reasons for being, removing selfishness, ungratefulness, and pompousness from the equation.

Why does Divine Purpose come before all else? It is connected to our sense of being, designed to guide and protect us for its use for the Greater Good. If omitted or overlooked, feelings of aimlessness, dissatisfaction, ungratefulness, and unease will come forth, even if we think we have it going on and are the best thing since sliced bread. One thing is for sure: We will lack peace, harmony, and fulfillment.

Our Divine Purpose acts as a Spiritual Compass, illuminating our Spiritual Journey. It also provides us with Supernatural Direction and Assistance to align our actions, thoughts, and choices amidst the chaos and confusion of everyday life. Cultivating a sense of openness, obedience, and awareness to become a work-in-progress for the Kingdom of God gives us the upper hand in being placed on the leading edge of Divine Wisdom and Spiritual Revelation.

When seeking to be *In Purpose on Purpose*, we may not know how Divine Purpose will unveil itself in our lives. Still, we must remain open and receptive to God's Divine Ingenuity, do what needs to be done, learn what must be learned, understand what needs to be understood, heal what needs healing, and overcome what is in our power to do so.

The common denominator in our Divine Purpose is to uplift, inspire, multiply, or bring healing and restoration to others. When we align our self-made purposes with our Divine Purpose, *As It Pleases God*, this is often where the Supernatural happens. When God is in the equation of all things, and when developing our *Heart and Mind Postures* for the Greater Good, the obstacles we encounter may serve as opportunities for growth rather than roadblocks, especially when using the Fruits of the Spirit and the Law of Reciprocity. In a Spiritual Flow as such, this is also where seemingly lose-loses become win-wins for the Kingdom of God.

Chapter Five
The Heart and Mind Posture

Let us begin this chapter with the question, 'How is your heart?' It is a seemingly simple inquiry, yet it invites deep introspection. Now, I am going to ask another question, 'How is your mind?' In a fast-paced get-up-and-go world, the answers we provide often reflect a mere surface-level assessment of our emotional and mental state of being. Customarily, we might instinctively respond with a casual, 'It is okay,' but what does that really mean? Are we truly okay, or are we concealing layers of complexity beneath our superficial facades?

Actually, a prompt reply of 'It is okay' should raise a red flag for us because that is a silent but very loud signal that we might be brushing aside our true feelings. But what if we are really okay with both? Then congratulations. Nonetheless, in delving a little deeper into the Eye of God, *The Heart and Mind Posture* of mankind must be constantly renewed.

Why is renewal required for Believers? *'For as a man thinks in his heart, so is he.'* Proverbs 23:7. For this very reason, Romans 12:2 warns, *"Do not be conformed to this world, but be transformed by*

Heart and Mind Posture

the renewing of your mind, that you may prove what is that good and acceptable and perfect will of God."

Have you ever wondered why God tests *The Heart and Mind Postures* of mankind? Well, Proverbs 4:23 has the answer: *"Keep your heart with all diligence, for out of it spring the issues of life."* Do the issues of life really come from the heart of mankind? Absolutely! Our heart represents our innermost thoughts, intentions, desires, traumas, and emotions that reveal our character. At the same time, the mind is the arena where we bounce around thoughts to lubricate our reasoning faculties.

According to the Heavenly of Heavens, testing is designed to help us build a *Spirit to Spirit* Relationship with God, *As It Pleases Him*. Secondly, it is designed to purify, purge, and prepare us for our Heaven on Earth Experiences. Just as gold is refined by fire, so are we! Matthew 6:21 tells us, *"For where your treasure is, there your heart will be also."* Thirdly, it is designed to help us build our faith, trust, and hope IN HIM without equating busyness with our worth.

When life is lifing, to preserve our sanity and overcome our weaknesses, we must MASTER the ability to cast down all forms of negativity and debauchery to ensure it does not affect our *Heart and Mind Postures*. Here are the Divine Instructions from 2 Corinthians 10:4-5. *"For the weapons of our warfare are not carnal but mighty in God for pulling down strongholds, Casting down arguments and every high thing that exalts itself against the knowledge of God, bringing every thought into captivity to the obedience of Christ."*

The goal is to present Divinely Composed and Poshed interior and exterior characteristics of authenticity to ensure we can pass *The Good Enough Test* in or out of the Kingdom. What is the purpose of this? It embodies a sense of balance, fulfillment, clarity, and peace that only God, our Heavenly Father, can provide. If one has never possessed this, then it is easily overlooked; however, if they have...they do not take this

Heart and Mind Posture

state of being lightly. How do we know if we are not there yet? The most viable indication is...Nothing is ever good enough for us!

The Good Enough Test

Is anything ever enough for us? When do we draw the line in the sand with our ungratefulness? Or better yet, when will we deal with the quicksand hidden in our psyche? The sinking feeling that nothing is enough has a grip on our Divine Destiny, sucking the life out of it, out of us, and anyone we come in contact with. More importantly, if we do not gird up our loins to do something about it, our gratefulness will disappear under layers of debris into the elements of the unseen.

Unbeknown to most, those who are ungrateful most often do not realize they are being ungrateful. Once we become accustomed to this characteristic, it causes us to adapt to its conditions. So much so to the point where we want what we want, when we want it, how we want it, where we want it, and with whom we desire it. In essence, this is indeed what we call human nature, hidden under layers of something else!

When ungratefulness becomes our norm, our psyche will block our conscience from alerting us of any form of unappreciativeness. As a result of this negative oversight, our psyche sucks in the negativity as a form of nutrition, feeding, nurturing, and growing until it snowballs into a full-blown case of worldly materialism at its best. Then, once we are consumed, we pass this negative character trait into our Bloodline, not realizing the manifestation is growing bigger and bigger as time passes.

When we talk about ungratefulness, it has a wide range of attributes leading up to a downfall or building up for an eruption of our Bloodline. In so many words, ungratefulness becomes like a plague, consuming all who are in our path

Heart and Mind Posture

without us realizing it. Frankly, this plague is so silently potent to the point where we do not even realize it is generated from us. As a matter of fact, we will think everyone else has the issue without ever once thinking to examine ourselves.

Well, dear heart, or better yet, dear mind, the buck stops here! We must regraft this negative character trait, keeping us bound to not appreciating the simple things in life, such as Love, Joy, Peace, Patience, Kindness, Goodness, Faithfulness, Gentleness, and Self-Control. Why do we need them, especially when they are not putting food on the table? In my opinion, they help to keep food on the table, Mentally, Physically, Emotionally, and Spiritually.

Plus, they keep us from getting caught up in a web of deception based on our overzealous wants, needs, and desires, or outright selling our souls for material things associated with power, money, sex, status, likes, and clicks. Moreover, they help us combat jealousy, envy, pride, coveting, and competitiveness that lead to all other forms of inner debauchery and rotten fruits.

As we take this a step further, negative characteristics contaminate the food we bring to the table on any level and with anyone. How is this possible, especially when we are Believers? No one is exempt from the effects of negativity, nor are we exempt from becoming a victim unless it is counteracted with positivity and gratefulness.

When our lives become fed with hate, misery, chaos, unkindness, rudeness, deceit, harshness, and recklessness, we inadvertently become susceptible to the Gravitational Pull of ungratefulness. This is why the Bible says, *"Do not eat the bread of a miser, nor desire his delicacies; for as he thinks in his heart, so is he. 'Eat and drink!' he says to you, but his heart is not with you. The morsel you have eaten, you will vomit up, and waste your pleasant words."* Proverbs 23:6-8. For the most part, we think life is all fun and

Heart and Mind Posture

games, and we should overlook certain things as long as we get what we want; yet, when we become ensnared, then we are left to wonder how it happened. Well, this is how it happens; we ignore the Nuggets of Wisdom and red flags forewarning us about things to come based on certain character traits or defects.

The Quinternity Effect

In the hustle and bustle of daily life, when life is lifing, we often forget to bring our bodies into the equation of what is taking place from within. Our bodies are constantly providing signals that reflect our Mental, Physical, Emotional, and Spiritual states through our senses, conscience, and bodily functions. Often enough, they are presented through fatigue, tension, headaches, discomfort, sleep disruptions, digestive problems, stress, anxiety, or even cravings.

Once we learn to engage with our bodies, we become empowered to live healthier, more fulfilling lives, *As It Pleases God*. Ephesians 5:29-30 says, *"For no one ever hated his own flesh, but nourishes and cherishes it, just as the Lord does the church. For we are members of His body, of His flesh and of His bones."*

How do we get our bodies to speak to us? We must begin asking it questions. Unbeknown to most, the body has a voice, but unfortunately, this is the one voice that is ignored by most. Of course, we pray to God to send us a sign, not realizing the body is one of the best ways in which He communicates with us. Really? Yes, really! The body will tell us everything we need to know if only we listen to it.

The Mind-Body Connection is POWERFUL. How do I know? I use it faithfully, and this is why I share this Divine Information, leading the way, *As It Pleases God*. According to the Heavenly of Heavens, this is not new information.

Heart and Mind Posture

Actually, it is ANCIENT. We have somehow forgotten or lost touch with it until now.

We often look to communicate with God, our Heavenly Father, outside of ourselves. However, in the Eye of God, when communicating, *As It Pleases Him*, we are looking the wrong way. The Divine Communication Tools are already within our bodies; therefore, with *The Commitment*, we need to know this. We do not need to dive into anything spooky or cultic to Divinely Connect to our Heavenly Father, nor should we become brainwashed about Him. Whatever we need to connect to Him, *Spirit to Spirit*, is already within us, ready, willing, and able to assist.

For starters, here are FIVE things we need to get the ball rolling with the Quinternity of getting the body to speak to us in ways that will trump human reasoning:

- ☐ Willingness.
- ☐ Obedience.
- ☐ Querying.
- ☐ Listening.
- ☐ Documenting.

If we opt out of these five things, the body will withhold information from us, even if we feel entitled. Above all, our Spiritual Discerning faculties will not work as they should, clouding our sense of clarity. As a result, the psyche will begin to speak louder than our Spirit Man, preventing us from waking up from our slumber. Is this real? It is as real as the oxygen we are breathing!

We are a Divine System in the Eye of God; thus, we have the Divine Right to connect to it, *As It Pleases Him*. Now, if we opt out, then we must depend on another man's system to tell us what we should already know, but have overlooked. The

Heart and Mind Posture

wealth of information is already hidden within our loins, and it is our responsibility to EXTRACT and CONVERT it.

How do we extract and convert information, especially when we feel clueless? Feeling clueless does not mean that we are. All we need to do is tap into the Divine Reservoir of information by getting the body to speak. In my opinion, if you take the time to watch the news, watch television, engage in social media, talk on the phone, and so on...you do have time.

From my perspective, the lack of time is an excuse! Here is why I believe what I believe: Matthew 6:22-23 says, *"The lamp of the body is the eye. If therefore your eye is good, your whole body will be full of light. But if your eye is bad, your whole body will be full of darkness. If therefore the light that is in you is darkness, how great is that darkness!"*

The impact of our inner lives really makes a difference in our well-being, determining a guided or misguided vision. With an uplifting perspective, *As It Pleases God*, we will find that the body speaks to us in ways that will trump human reasoning.

The Difference

The Quinternity is not the same as Quaternity. Here is the deal: Quaternity deals with the Mind, Body, Soul, and Spirit. In contrast, Quinternity deals with the concept or system consisting of five parts or elements. The five essential elements of Quinternity regarding any system are:

- ☐ Inputs.
- ☐ Processes.
- ☐ Outputs.
- ☐ Feedback.
- ☐ Environment.

Heart and Mind Posture

In the Eye of God, Quinternity applies to Biological Systems, Business or Operational Systems, Social Sciences or Social Systems, Technology or Automation Systems, and the Body of Christ. In understanding any system for our Heaven on Earth Experiences, whether it be in the context of technology, biology, sociology, or Spirituality, it is crucial to identify and analyze the core components that make it function.

Although not limited, the five functions cater to our bodily systems, human connections, and relationship conduciveness or configuration to create BALANCE. They are connected to the Cornerstone of our thoughts, desires, emotions, words, and actions.

The geniuses of yesteryear used this Divine Concept and the Power hidden within Quinternity, and so can you. With the correct *Heart and Mind Posture*, you no longer need to wait on trendsetters; you have the power hidden within your loins to become one, *As It Pleases God*.

By paying close attention to the Quinternity associated with elements, individuals, and organizations can optimize varying systems for greater efficiency and effectiveness. All of which have a way of leading to better outcomes and increased adaptability or productivity. Also, when Quinternity is understood, *As It Pleases God*, it helps us blend science, philosophy, and imagination together, opening the four dimensions of Quaternity of the Mind, Body, Soul, and Spirit beyond measure.

How do we make Quinternity make sense? For example, for the Divine System of the hand to work properly in relation to our bodies, we have five fingers on each hand in a normal setting. Then again, we have five toes in a normal setting to support each foot. If we miss one toe or finger, an imbalance will occur. Even if we somehow have an extra finger or toe, an imbalance will still occur as well. Nevertheless, when the

Heart and Mind Posture

body feels balanced, *As It Pleases God*, it will speak louder than it would for those who do not include Him at all.

Speak and Document

When our commitment is in full effect to our Heavenly Father, *Spirit to Spirit*, the conscience will speak, the senses will speak, the psyche will speak, the mind will speak, and most of all, energy will speak to us through our bodily senses, urges, and demeanor. In the same way that the Body of Christ speaks, with the correct *Heart and Mind Posture*, we are required to listen, learn, document, and share. If not, then what are we really doing here? So, as we navigate our personal journeys, we must learn how to listen effectively, regardless of whether we are in or out of the Kingdom of God.

In the *Speaking and Documenting* Process, we do not need to overcomplicate things; keep it simple, and it will work as it should. Just use the Quinternity example of the hand with any system, using a five-finger countdown of what, when, where, how, and why for questioning and imaginative exploration. Does it work? I have a stamp of guarantee on it, especially if documentation occurs, whether or not the Voice of God is speaking.

Why do we need to document information? It opens the Floodgate of Wisdom, Divine Wisdom, to be exact. When God can trust us to become the portal of information to help ourselves and others, He will trust us with more. If we do not document, He will not trust us to become a conduit with the transfer of information.

For instance, when someone attempts to impress me with how much they know about God or convince me of their Divine Eliteness, I take into account what is documented. Here is the deal: Revelation 12:11 says, "*And they overcame him by the blood of the Lamb and by the word of their testimony, and they did not*

Heart and Mind Posture

love their lives to the death." With the information we are entrusted with, Isaiah 30:8 tells us what to do with it: *"Now go, write it before them on a tablet, and note it on a scroll, that it may be for time to come, forever and ever."*

In addition, the importance of visions, systems, plans, and Testimonies, writing them down and acting upon them with faith and diligence, is required of us. We may not be able to write a book, but still, as Vessels of God, there is no reason not to take notes. Here is what Habakkuk 2:2-3 says about this matter: *"Then the Lord answered me and said: 'Write the vision and make it plain on tablets, that he may run who reads it. For the vision is yet for an appointed time; but at the end it will speak, and it will not lie. Though it tarries, wait for it; because it will surely come, it will not tarry.'"*

What if we have a photographic memory? Photographic memories do not impress God. Is it not He who gave it? More importantly, if we use our photographic memories for our benefit only, unfortunately, in the Eye of God, it is a misuse of the GIFT. Plus, when we consume our own fruits without sharing, *As It Pleases God*, the body will begin to withhold information from us or do weird stuff as the hole from within becomes a pit.

Our Spiritual Gifts are not for our benefit only; they are designed to feed God's sheep to benefit the Kingdom. Please allow me to Spiritually Align this: 1 Corinthians 12:4-7 says, *"There are diversities of gifts, but the same Spirit. There are differences of ministries, but the same Lord. And there are diversities of activities, but it is the same God who works all in all. But the manifestation of the Spirit is given to each one for the profit of all."*

We must leave a trail of information for the next in line, and if we are not doing so, it is time to get busy. It is time to *Speak and Document*, taking the necessary actions to put pen to paper about our trials, successes, failures, and experiences.

Heart and Mind Posture

Remember, knowledge becomes our weapon of power, building bridges when it is properly shared to feed God's sheep, *As It Pleases Him.*

When building a repertoire of knowledge and wisdom, we must begin building from the ground up when we are dealing with *The Heart and Mind Posture*. According to the Heavenly of Heavens, it is not wise to build from the highest common denominator; we must build from the lowest to the highest, creating a stable foundation. If not, ungratefulness, imbalance, disorder, frailty, and disrespect are added to our equational efforts.

When looking from the top down, there will always be a different perspective or view involved than there would be from the ground up. Plus, if we start building a building from the top down, we are in big trouble. Thus, when Building Upward with what we have in our hands with Divine Creativity, we must begin with a solid foundation, focusing on BALANCE and STABILITY.

The lowest common denominator represents the most basic, universally accessible level of understanding, training, authentication, or appreciation to develop genuineness. On the other hand, striving for the highest common denominator will challenge creators to aim for the most elevated, multifaceted, professional, and sophisticated expressions of doing what they do best. As a result, it brings about perfectionists, idealists, and realists who may crumble under pressure.

Why would some crumble over creative pressure? It happens all too often; it is just that most do not discuss it openly. Unfortunately, when we have little or no experience in getting our hands dirty (putting in the real work that no one wants to do), we tend to turn up our noses at those appearing beneath us or having less than us. But most often,

Heart and Mind Posture

the hidden creativity will lie within those who are considered to be the lowest common denominator.

For example, I ran into someone who made a statement: 'No one making less than them or having less than them could not tell them anything.' I shook my head in dismay while holding my tongue because he was a pastor. I asked myself, 'How did we get to this point of being deceived beyond measure by human standards and reasonings, especially when God is Spirit?'

This man was preaching from the Holy Bible. He had the nerve to make a statement as such, especially when God's Divine Call is open to all, regardless of our social status, financial status, articulation, degrees, job, or human knowledgeable wisdom. Let me repeat: NO ONE is exempt from becoming usable, according to their Predestined Blueprinted Mission! God will use anything or anyone to accomplish His Divine Purpose.

Here is the deal: The Bible this man uses, better yet, the one we all use, is written by our Forefathers, who had less than us, who still did more, and were used more for the Kingdom of God. Yet, this man was secretly gleaning information from those appearing as the lowest common denominator, deceiving people left and right. Yet he did not realize he was dealing with one of the highest common denominators, built from the ground up with zero fluff.

Unfortunately, he did not realize to whom he was speaking. How can he not know as a Believer? He lacked Spiritual Discernment, allowing his tongue to write checks that his soul could not cash. With outright humility, I did not utter a mumbling word, attempt to defend myself, or debate the Word of God. Why? I had to get this story. The only way to do so is to zip my lips, allowing my tongue to become the pen of a ready writer, allowing my *Character and Worthiness* to get busy doing what I do best.

Chapter Six
Character and Worthiness

According to the Ancient of Days, beforehand, Kingdom Poshness was not for all to understand due to certain Spiritual Seals. Nevertheless, the AWAKENING is here and now with the concealed Sacred Truths, along with a Divine Roll Call containing a Spiritual Filter, sifting through our *Character and Worthiness*.

The Greater Truths veiled beneath the surface are no longer being veiled to those who have a willing ear to hear. Basically, the time has come to open the doors of Divine Wisdom for all who are willing and characteristically worthy to enter.

Why is God filtering through our character traits and worthiness? First, in the Spiritual Vetting Process, a *Spirit to Spirit* Relationship with our Heavenly Father and Wisdom goes hand-in-hand. Secondly, He does not want Divine Wisdom to become misused, abused, or distorted. Thirdly, even when He is silent, when we feel unusable, when we are searching for meaning, or when we cannot feel His Divine Touch, it does not change the information readily available at our fingertips.

Character and Worthiness

We can tiptoe around the appearance of what we perceive to be the desired lifestyle of the Kingdom. However, it looks for what we possess from within and how we handle people, places, and things outwardly when it comes down to the Kingdom, especially when no one is looking. In simplicity, we must possess the qualities and characteristics money cannot buy. Why? According to the Heavenly of Heavens, they contribute to our Heaven on Earth Experiences, primarily when receiving Divine Secrets, Mysteries, and Treasures, enabling us to stay instinctually in the Spiritual Know.

The Ancient of Ancients is not playing around when it comes down to reaping Kingdom Benefits without us accounting for the cost, Mentally, Physically, Emotionally, or Spiritually. How does cost counting relate to Believers? Respectfully speaking, in the quest for success, prosperity, glitz and glamour, immediate rewards, and all else in between, we want the BENEFITS of the Kingdom for free while remaining the same. Then, as a slap in God's face, we sell half-truths of manipulation to others for a fee without telling them the truth about the Operative Efforts of the Kingdom, preventing them from finishing their race, *As It Pleases Him*.

Instead, we hype them up with worldliness, materialism, and title-baiting to boost our egotistical status while pretending to be humble. Really? Yes, really! In reality, we are bombarded with overnight success stories, massive wealth accumulation, and the easy acquisition or transition of power. However, we are not often informed about the cost...the deeper reality or the sacrifice!

The bottom line is that it costs a person to be who they are. As a matter of fact, it has cost me deeply to be who I am, yet the GREATER PURPOSE is what keeps me in the Spiritual Game, doing what I am called to do. In addition, if it costs you nothing whatsoever, then one must question what you are working with! Matthew 16:24, "*Then Jesus said to His disciples, 'If*

Character and Worthiness

anyone desires to come after Me, let him deny himself, and take up his cross, and follow Me.'"

Remember, easy is not always good, wise, or Godly; we must account for the FRUITS surrounding it, or them. If not, we can easily slip into a USER mentality or heart posture, drawn away by all manner of doctrine. Here is what God desires for us according to Ephesians 4:14, *"That we should no longer be children, tossed to and fro and carried about with every wind of doctrine, by the trickery of men, in the cunning craftiness of deceitful plotting."*

Picturesquely, it is heartwrenching to see a so-called Shepherd just as messy as the flock in which they lead, milking them with the Word while leaving the Spiritual Meat on the table. Is this really happening? It is happening in real-time, and God is not too happy about the way in which we carry on in His Divine Name.

Is this not a little insensitive? Maybe or maybe not, but the Divine Message is clear...step up or step down! *"For though by this time you ought to be teachers, you need someone to teach you again the first principles of the oracles of God; and you have come to need milk and not solid food. For everyone who partakes only of milk is unskilled in the word of righteousness, for he is a babe."* Hebrews 5:12-13.

We must equip ourselves to make the hard decisions with ease instead of making the easy decisions complicated or hard while becoming a real SERVANT of the Kingdom. Please understand that Matthew 7:14 says, *"Narrow is the gate and difficult is the way which leads to life, and there are few who find it."* Why is it so difficult? The difficulty lies in developing our character and nurturing our fruits. If we do not work on them or do not know absolutely anything about them, *As It Pleases God*, it deflates our worthiness by default because we are designed to grow positively in Spirit and Truth from the *Inside Out*.

Character and Worthiness

According to God's Divine Principles and Cultivating Virtues, here are the prerequisites regarding the sought-after charactorial traits from the Heavenly of Heavens. *"Therefore, as the elect of God, holy and beloved, put on tender mercies, kindness, humility, meekness, longsuffering; bearing with one another, and forgiving one another, if anyone has a complaint against another; even as Christ forgave you, so you also must do. But above all these things put on love, which is the bond of perfection. And let the peace of God rule in your hearts, to which also you were called in one body; and be thankful. Let the word of Christ dwell in you richly in all wisdom, teaching and admonishing one another in psalms and hymns and spiritual songs, singing with grace in your hearts to the Lord. And whatever you do in word or deed, do all in the name of the Lord Jesus, giving thanks to God the Father through Him."* Colossians 3:12-17.

Inside Out

Our character is who we are from the inside out, and regardless of whether we are negatively flawed or positively enhanced, it will manifest outwardly in due time. Moreover, here is why it is so crucial for us to say, *Enough is Enough* on ungratefulness, *"For the wrath of God is revealed from heaven against all ungodliness and unrighteousness of men, who suppress the truth in unrighteousness, because what may be known of God is manifest in them, for God has shown it to them. For since the creation of the world His invisible attributes are clearly seen, being understood by the things that are made, even His eternal power and Godhead, so that they are without excuse, because, although they knew God, they did not glorify Him as God, nor were thankful, but became futile in their thoughts, and their foolish hearts were darkened."* Romans 1:18-21.

According to the Heavenly of Heavens, we must work on ourselves consistently to become better, stronger, wiser, and more astute, taking the higher road of Spiritual Redemption.

Character and Worthiness

How does taking the higher road become applied redemption when living real life as Believers? We can be kind to others amid their debaucherous efforts without expecting to get something out of it based on good and ethical principles alone. Nevertheless, when we add God, *As It Pleases Him*, into our equational efforts, regardless of whether we take the high, low, or no road, everything will work out for our good. Here is the Spiritual Seal that we can enforce: *"But love your enemies, do good, and lend, hoping for nothing in return; and your reward will be great, and you will be sons of the Most High. For He is kind to the unthankful and evil. Therefore, be merciful, just as your Father also is merciful."* Luke 6:35-36.

To be clear, the act of doing good starts as an inner manifestation first, making itself outward. For the record, just because we are merciful does not mean we have to subject ourselves to provocation, abuse, or become a doormat. There are times we must love, forgive, and have mercy while pleading the 5th or peacefully walking away with clean hands and a pure heart, shaking the dust off our feet. Here is what Matthew 10:14 shares with us: *"And whoever will not receive you nor hear your words, when you depart from that house or city, shake off the dust from your feet."*

If people do not like you...shift. If people do not want you...shift. If people degrade you...shift. If you are a thorn in someone's flesh...shift. What if we cannot shift? Unbeknown to most, if we cannot shift our bodies, we can definitely shift the mind, and the body will soon follow when the time and conditions are right.

According to the Heavenly of Heavens, in Earthen Vessels, our job is to exhibit the Fruits of the Spirit and Christlike Character, not to wallow or entertain the gravitational pull of rotten fruits designed to demagnetize our *Unlimited Potential*.

Based on the Spiritual Law of Free Will, we do not need to force anything on anyone, especially if they are not our

Character and Worthiness

children. Whether we are in our limited or unlimited state of being, if people reject us or what we have to offer, here is what Matthew 7:6 says about this matter: *"Do not give what is holy to the dogs; nor cast your pearls before swine, lest they trample them under their feet, and turn and tear you in pieces."* Once again, SHIFT!

Unlimited Potential

The *Unlimited Potential* we are seeking is already locked up within our loins...all we need to do is use the Heavenly Keys provided as a GIFT to mankind to gain Divine Access. To truly harness the benefits, forming a *Spirit to Spirit* Connection with our Heavenly Father helps to facilitate this process in Earthen Vessel.

In recognizing and accepting this Divine Assistance, *As It Pleases God*, it is imperative to work on our character traits to ensure they become Christlike. If not, we will become Spiritually Blocked to avoid the misuse of our Spiritual Gifts.

How do we work on our charactorial behaviors, *As It Pleases God*? The Spiritual Cheatsheet is wrapped in using the Fruits of the Spirit. Once we perfect them, it is a wrap! God will move Heaven and Earth with Divine Favor for those who become a work-in-progress using the Fruits of the Spirit consistently in the Spirit of Excellence. By embracing this perspective, we do not need to be perfect...just willing and usable, and all else will take care of itself while helping us to self-correct at the drop of a dime.

We must become aware of three components of releasing our *Unlimited Potential* into the earth. We need:

- ☐ Divine Omnipotence.
- ☐ Divine Omniscience.
- ☐ Divine Omnipresence.

Character and Worthiness

The Divine Omnipotence (All-Encompassing Power) from the Heavenly of Heavens is here to assist us with unlimited power. All we need is faith and hope in Divine Assistance from the Holy Spirit while developing good character traits, *As It Pleases God*. Whether we are living real life or a superficial one, with God's Divine Omnipotency, we must confidently know and acknowledge that we are reinforced and maintained by the Holy Trinity, which is greater than ourselves.

Divine Omniscience is available to give us the knowledge and Infinite Awareness (The Foresight) needed to move forward in the Spirit of Excellence. For those who are not in the know, the Divine Omnipresence (The All-Knowing God) is with us, transcending physical boundaries to provide unity and the interconnectedness we need among the brethren to feed His sheep.

As God governs all things, including us, with wisdom and love, knowing all things, we cannot hide anything from Him. The moment we think we have one up on Him, we will suffer some form of breakdown, Mentally, Physically, Emotionally, Spiritually, or Financially. To be clear and with all sincerity, I do not wish a breakdown upon anyone. I am only the Divine Messenger, helping you to help yourself and to help you grab hold of the *Unlimited Potential* lying dormant inside of you.

In *Navigating Life's Challenges* concerning human free will, the goal is to pay attention to what is taking place within your psyche to understand your next move better. It also helps us determine the scripture that needs applying, what must be reversed or counteracted, the forgiveness or repentance that needs to occur, or what we must seek the Lord regarding.

What if we do not pay attention, especially as Born-Again Believers? By not paying attention to the obvious, we can definitely 'get got' with the inconspicuous wiles of the enemy.

Character and Worthiness

Actually, here is what Proverbs 12:1 says, *"Whoever loves instruction loves knowledge, But he who hates correction is stupid."*

When dealing with *Unlimited Potential* in the Eye of God, we must place Him first, especially if we desire for it to be authentic. How do I know? According to Proverbs 1:7, *"The fear of the Lord is the beginning of knowledge, But fools despise wisdom and instruction."* Placing Him a the forefront of all things helps to bring balance into whatever, whenever, however, and with whomever without overdoing it or doing too much.

When I run into someone who is doing absolutely too much, all types of red flags go up. Why would this happen, especially when dealing with all types of personalities in the Kingdom? In the Eye of God, it is a sign of insecurity and limited potential, even if they are appearing to do great things. How so? Most often, there is a team behind them putting in the work while they gloat, allowing their ego to float off into la-la land. In addition, we will also find this individual criticizing others severely or projecting their insecurities onto others to keep this negative cycle in motion. Here is what Ecclesiastes 7:16-17 says, *"Do not be overly righteous, Nor be overly wise; Why should you destroy yourself? Do not be overly wicked, Nor be foolish; Why should you die before your time?"*

When engaging in the authenticity of *Unlimited Potential*, there is no need to talk a good game when you have the same opportunity to become a game changer in the Eye of God. The choice is on the TABLE...eat from the Divine Table, *As It Pleases Him*, or remove yourself and stop blocking the next person from taking their seat.

Chapter Seven
Navigating Life's Challenges

When *Navigating Life's Challenges*, it is astounding how some of us know everything about God or what the Bible says. Yet, we know very little about ourselves, the way we were created, our reason for being, or our Predestined Blueprint. To add insult to injury, most of us lie about knowing who we are all together while putting on a show to entertain without empowering.

In dealing with the issues of *Navigating Life's Challenges*, for sure, I am not here to point the finger. Surely, this was indeed the previous me prior to my Spiritual Makeover; I mean, I was from the bottom of the pit, grunge. Was it that bad? It was so bad that I needed a charactorial overhaul. You see, I am from the country, the real backwoods country...We knew nothing about character building whatsoever. All we knew about was SURVIVAL.

It was through many experiences such as these that have enabled me to write, extract, and convey with clarity, efficiency, and effectiveness. All of which are designed to lift, build, and guide God's precious sheep in the Spirit of

Navigating Life's Challenges

Excellence, Love, and Mercy. Above all, I teach others how to do likewise for the Greater Good of mankind in the Spirit of Oneness.

Let me say this before moving on: Many people still laugh and make fun of my countryness or where I am from until I open my mouth with Divine Wisdom and Astuteness, making their baby leap from within. It is often said, 'Do not judge a book by its cover until you read its content.' Well, the same applies to everyone because if we are breathing the Breath of Life, it means God is not finished with us yet.

One thing is for sure in *Navigating Life's Challenges*: If God can do it for me, He can do likewise and more with you. How so? I have Battle Scars, and you do not! I have Battle Wounds, and you do not! Simply put, I had to go to war for this Divine Unveiling, and you do not! As I pass the Divine Mantle of Informative WISDOM to the Kingdom's NEXT, if you follow instructions, *As It Pleases God*, you can become better than the TEACHER. Really? Yes, really! Proverbs 9:9 says, "*Give instruction to a wise man, and he will be still wiser; teach a just man, and he will increase in learning.*"

Believe it or not, negativity feeds upon positivity for temporary energy, similar to a solar panel. Once we feel the drain or the zap of energy, we need to back up or move on, period! Plus, when the Holy Spirit leads us, we will receive instinctual nudges when to hold, fold, or walk away, but we must be Spiritually Awake to receive our cues.

Unbeknown to most, we are confusing staying WOKE with being Spiritually AWAKE. Here is the deal: Woke is in reference to worldly things based upon human perception, biases, conditioning, and so on, with a specific target in mind. Meanwhile, being Spiritually Awake or Woke is derived from our Spiritual Instincts back by the UNCTION of the Holy Spirit, dealing with our psyche and spreading outwardly.

Navigating Life's Challenges

When being Spiritually Awake or Woke, we must understand our *What, When, Where, Why, How,* and with *Whom* self-analysis first, ensuring our outer manifestations are in alignment with building the Kingdom, the Fruits of the Spirit, and Christlike Character. Unfortunately, it is not based upon tearing down, belittling, disrespecting, or pointing the finger; it is predicated on becoming Spiritually Aware of what God is expecting from us regarding our Heaven on Earth Experience.

How do we know if we are consumed with ungratefulness? First, it appears in our relationship with God, ourselves, and others, in this order. Secondly, it is evident in our thoughts, character, words, deeds, demeanor, behaviors, and so on. Thirdly, it is also determined by the *Gravitational Pull* of whatever is spinning our cycle or who is stimulating or attempting to defrag our Divine Blueprint, positively or negatively.

2 Timothy 3:1-7 says, *"But know this, that in the last days perilous times will come: For men will be lovers of themselves, lovers of money, boasters, proud, blasphemers, disobedient to parents, unthankful, unholy, unloving, unforgiving, slanderers, without self-control, brutal, despisers of good, traitors, headstrong, haughty, lovers of pleasure rather than lovers of God, having a form of godliness but denying its power. And from such people turn away! For of this sort are those who creep into households and make captives of gullible women loaded down with sins, led away by various lusts, always learning and never able to come to the knowledge of the truth."* If we are plagued by any of this now, all hope is not lost. What must we do? Let us go deeper into the *Spirit of Gratefulness* to extract what we need to *Navigate Life's Challenges* that are PLEASING in the Eye of God.

Spirit of Gratefulness

Gratefulness, or gratitude, from a Divine Perspective, is more than just a polite acknowledgment of thankfulness. It is a profound appreciation for the experiences, people, places, things, and moments that shape our lives. While at the same time recognizing the good hidden within them, no matter how small it may be. In my opinion, this is how we can determine our individualized setbacks or opportunities. Moreover, we can only choose one of them...so it is wiser to opt for the opportunities instead of the setbacks. Why? It is a MINDSET!

A mindset that is dialed in on opportunities must learn how to REPENT and FORGIVE quickly to create a win-win out of everything, regardless of how it appears to the naked eye. The goal is to focus our energy on the Eye of God, bringing forth the Fruits of the Spirit while exhibiting Christlike Character to all we come in contact with. Does it work? Of course! Once again, I am living proof. Plus, when operating in such a manner enhances our people skills to a level the enemy cannot contend with. Here is the *Spiritual Seal* bridging the gap to all, *"But I say to you, love your enemies, bless those who curse you, do good to those who hate you, and pray for those who spitefully use you and persecute you, that you may be sons of your Father in heaven; for He makes His sun rise on the evil and on the good, and sends rain on the just and on the unjust."* Matthew 5:44-45.

God is the Creator of it all, and if we operate in the Spirit of Righteousness, He will make all things work for our good, especially when the Spirit of Love is involved. What is the benefit of loving those who hate, use, abuse, or despise us? It helps us maintain the bonds of love within our human psyche, preventing an uprising from within and allowing us to proactively help ourselves and others.

In the Kingdom, it does not benefit us to hate, abuse, misuse, or engage in debauched behaviors. Instead, it creates Spiritual Taboos and generational curses; therefore, it behooves us to use the Fruits of the Spirit to change the trajectory of our Bloodline, especially if we have fallen short.

Navigating Life's Challenges

According to scripture, it says, *"But above all these things put on love, which is the bond of perfection. And let the peace of God rule in your hearts, to which also you were called in one body; and be thankful. Let the word of Christ dwell in you richly in all wisdom, teaching and admonishing one another in psalms and hymns and spiritual songs, singing with grace in your hearts to the Lord. And whatever you do in word or deed, do all in the name of the Lord Jesus, giving thanks to God the Father through Him."* Colossians 3:14-17.

Spirit to Spirit, there is no need to player-hate or second-guess ourselves or others. The goal is to become thankful for all things while creating a win-win by reversing our negatives into positives through our words, affirmations, scriptures, behaviors, thoughts, and so on. So, get out of the quicksand, *Enough is Enough*, and step up to your rightful place in the Kingdom. *"For in it the righteousness of God is revealed from faith to faith; as it is written, 'The just shall live by faith.'"* Romans 1:17.

Representing the Kingdom

As a *Representative of the Kingdom*, in our Earthen Vessels, we must work on ourselves from the inside out, bringing forth Spiritual Truths. To be clear, God does provide handsomely for those who are in Purpose on purpose. He also makes Provisions for His Vision and orchestrates a comfortable lifestyle for His Representatives. However, He requires us to do our part in upholding the Fruits of the Spirit and exhibiting Christlike Character, becoming the Fountain of Wisdom for His sheep while setting an example for them to follow.

What if God does not provide for us? It may be the wrong Blueprint, our understanding of our Blueprint needs regrafting, our fruits or character are not aligning with Kingdom Expectations, or our *Spirit to Spirit* Relationship is not connecting properly amid prayer, meditating, or repenting.

Regardless of where we are on our Spiritual Journey, He does not want us to give way to the Spirit of Lack. Why? Operating in the Spirit of Lack is not a desired Mindset of the Kingdom due to the gravitational pull associated with being disadvantaged. By far, this negative connotation of deception invokes jealousy, envy, greed, coveting, competitiveness, and so on, zapping our Divine Wisdom or sense of reasoning.

What type of Mindset should we have? When *Representing the Kingdom*, in the regrafting phase from negative to positive, we should say this until it becomes our Bedrock of Hope: "*My God shall supply all my needs according to His riches in glory by Christ Jesus.*" Philippians 4:19.

In the Kingdom, our Spiritual Nature is not hiding from us; in all actuality, we are hiding from it. Why would our true nature go into hiding? The human psyche knows it must up the ante on its attitude, behaviors, and thoughts while Kingdom Proofing its efforts. What does this mean? We are held to a higher standard, and we are accountable for what we are or are not doing in or out of Kingdom Formality.

In all-knowing from the Heavenly of Heavens, WISDOM is the most prized possession known to man and the Ancient of Days. When *Representing the Kingdom*, wisdom can get us stuff, but stuff cannot bring us Divine Wisdom; therefore, we are required to change our Mindsets to that of the Kingdom.

Wisdom from the Ancient of Days is ready to open on our behalf, giving us the Spiritual Unction to function according to the standards set forth from the BEGINNING of time. We can pretend this information does not apply to us, only to find it does. How? Everything we need is already! Our Blueprint is already set in motion, and the only person blocking it from coming forth is the one who does not recognize the Greatness from within.

Navigating Life's Challenges

Divine Wisdom

Everyone is born a Genius; we simply forget this fact once we get a taste of worldliness in its rarest form, casting layers of debris on our Divine Wisdom to create a disconnect from the Kingdom. So much so, to the point where we think Wisdom is encapsulated in what we know, a strategy, goals, reasoning, and so on, when it is not. However, we can indeed incorporate Wisdom in them, but it is a Spiritual Standalone or Absolute, needing no help from anyone or anything; yet, it offers help to all who are justified in their efforts. What does this mean? We cannot use Divine Wisdom to conduct evil practices.

Why should we NOT use Divine Wisdom in our debaucherous efforts? It is Divine, and it is intellectually beyond our knowing capacity, training, and conditioning. The misuse of Divine Wisdom comes with a sacrificial price tag NOT covered by the Blood of Jesus. So, when attempting to misuse what is Divine or wanting a higher capacity to know things outside of their Spiritual League, one must go to the dark side to conduct this sort of folly. The moment we dare to use it in such a manner, it creates snares within the human psyche, called voids, yokes, strongholds, contention, oppression, thirsts, and fits of hunger with a BULLSEYE on our esteem and credibility.

All forms of Spiritual Disengagement are formed through the lust of the eyes, the lust of the flesh, and the pride of life. These three portals take us from a Kingdom Genius to the average worldly status. Unfortunately, this turns our inherited Wisdom into unrecognizable sources of insecurities, weaknesses, powerlessness, and negativity while we think we are on top of the world.

Yet, the enemy is laughing in the face of those who do not know or understand who they are in the Kingdom. By failing to realize this bullseye, they fall for the okey doke with little or no self-control, surrounded by rotten fruits and atrocious character traits! While, at the same time, yoking those who falsify their *Divine Wisdom*, making them power-hungry, money-hungry, or sexually hungry.

When all is said and done, WISDOM is a GIFT that is not for sale. We will never find it packaged on a shelf, regardless of how manipulative we have become in our approach to selling it. According to the Heavenly of Heavens, this is why a lot of Spiritual Potentials or Elites get in trouble with God.

Selling or pimping God, selling or pimping Divine Wisdom, selling or pimping Spiritual Healing, selling or pimping Divine Blueprints, selling or pimping Blessings, or selling or pimping Kingdom Entry will cause us to sell our souls short. Why do we sell ourselves short in the Eye of God? These things are FREE. I will say it again: These things are FREE!

Unbeknown to most, selling these things outside of the Divine Will of God or pimping Him is a form of witchcraft. What is more, when going to the dark side to obtain them, we must proceed at our own risk because the Blood of Jesus cannot be used in our folly. Really? Yes, really!

With all due respect, this is the reason why worldly individuals appear to be more prosperous than those who are Believers. How do we make this make sense? Selling or prostituting God is a big no-no! Meanwhile, unbelievers are clear about their intents; they work on their charactorial behaviors and treat people better than so-called Believers do while exercising more self-control and helping each other. As a result, God uses them based on standard principles, while the Believers are clueless about any principles, let alone Biblical Ones. Blasphemy, right? Wrong.

How is it that we know more scriptures in the Bible and do not know the Fruits of the Spirit? How is it that we do not know what God hates? Wait, wait, wait, do not answer this yet...How is it that we do not know the power of a seed?

Navigating Life's Challenges

How would we make money then? I am so glad you asked. The key is hidden in the withholding or serving process. Here are a few sample questions, but not limited to such:

- ☐ If someone really needed HELP, would you withhold your ability to help them if they had no money? *"Assuredly, I say to you, inasmuch as you did it to one of the least of these My brethren, you did it to Me."* Matthew 25:40.

- ☐ If someone is ready to receive DIVINE WISDOM, would you withhold the information if they had no money? *"Let your light so shine before men, that they may see your good works and glorify your Father in heaven."* Matthew 5:16.

- ☐ If someone needed SPIRITUAL HEALING, Mentally, Physically, Emotionally, or Spiritually, would you withhold the healing from them if they had no money? *"I have shown you in every way, by laboring like this, that you must support the weak. And remember the words of the Lord Jesus, that He said, 'It is more blessed to give than to receive.' "* Acts 20:35.

- ☐ If someone is ready, willing, and able, who really needs help with their DIVINE BLUEPRINT, would you withhold the ability to help them if they had no money? *"Let each of you look out not only for his own interests, but also for the interests of others."* Philippians 2:4.

- ☐ If someone desperately needed a BLESSING, would you withhold it from them if they had no money? *"He who has pity on the poor lends to the Lord, and He will pay back what he has given."* Proverbs 19:17.

Navigating Life's Challenges

You see, when dealing with Divine Wisdom, it wants to know if you will give freely in the same way that you receive freely. If so, God will grant us PROVISIONS designed to flow to us and through us, like what we call currency. I love the way Luke 6:38 puts it: *"Give, and it will be given to you: good measure, pressed down, shaken together, and running over will be put into your bosom. For with the same measure that you use, it will be measured back to you."*

Divine Wisdom contains a free-flowing currency similar to an electrical current. The moment we block the flow, someone is going to get shocked. From my perspective, it is our cue to clean up our act, but it can also mean that we are barking up the wrong tree, and this is where Spiritual Discernment comes into play. Nevertheless, as a result of monopolizing and capitalizing on God for our SELFISH wants, needs, desires, and benefits, our souls go up for the highest bidder. Here is what 1 John 3:17 says, *"But whoever has this world's goods, and sees his brother in need, and shuts up his heart from him, how does the love of God abide in him?"*

Some would say, 'I would not sell my soul.' When it should be, 'I will never resell my soul.' Let me explain: If we are clueless about the psyche of mankind or our kind (our human nature), then we do not know if we have sold our soul or not unless the Spirit of the Lord exposes it. With this being said, we all have something to work on or work at... Romans 3:23 even says, *"For all have sinned and fall short of the glory of God."* *"If we say that we have no sin, we deceive ourselves, and the truth is not in us."* 1 John 1:8.

In reality, if we are behaving in a way that is UNPLEASING to God, who knows where our loyalty lies, especially when selfishness is involved, right? Therefore, when *Navigating Life's Challenges*, we need to stop lying to ourselves and own our truth. In following this process of obtaining Divine Wisdom, we should take the time to get to know ourselves from the

Navigating Life's Challenges

inside out, for real, for real. At the same time, making our best attempts to use the Fruits of the Spirit and behave Christlike without being spiteful. If this does not occur, Divine Wisdom will take a back seat until we are ready for Her to appear.

In the Kingdom, we operate on SELFLESSNESS and FREE WILL. Why is it a problem when Believers are selfish and violate the free will of others intentionally? Regardless of whether we are Believers or not, our INTERNAL FACTORS, such as our charactorial traits, desires, obedience, heart or mind posture, and discipline, are crucial elements to determine our level of wisdom. But of course, to get to the Divine Status, *As It Pleases God*, we must put in the work.

What do we need to do to regain our Spiritual Access to Divine Wisdom? According to scripture, the *Wisdom of the Ancients* is readily available with specific conditions, but not limited to such:

☐ The *Wisdom of the Ancients* will question us according to our situation, ensuring we get an understanding of our 'Why.' *"Does not wisdom cry out, and understanding lift up her voice?"* Proverbs 8:1.

☐ The *Wisdom of the Ancients* requires a planned meeting place for instructions. In the beginning, this can become challenging if we are not accustomed to sitting still or taking notes. But with time, we will recognize the importance of doing so. *"She takes her stand on the top of the high hill, beside the way, where the paths meet."* Proverbs 8:2.

☐ The *Wisdom of the Ancients* wants us to realize the importance of sharing Divine Wisdom with others when it is called upon. In so many words, we cannot become selfish with the Wisdom given. Why?

Navigating Life's Challenges

Wisdom is designed to Bless the receiver as they become a giver, activating the Law of Reciprocity, which keeps the Floodgates open on our behalf and that of another. *"She cries out by the gates, at the entry of the city, at the entrance of the doors: To you, O men, I call, and my voice is to the sons of men."* Proverbs 8:3-4.

☐ The *Wisdom of the Ancients* wants us to become compassionate and understanding of all. Why? We are all a work-in-progress, having something to work on or at. *"O you simple ones, understand prudence, and you fools, be of an understanding heart."* Proverbs 8:5.

☐ The *Wisdom of the Ancients* requires us to present ourselves with well-governed *People Skills*, effectively communicating in the Spirit of Excellence without allowing anything and everything to flow out of the gateway of our mouths. *"Listen, for I will speak of excellent things, and from the opening of my lips will come right things."* Proverbs 8:6.

☐ The *Wisdom of the Ancients* wants us to speak the truth in the Spirit of Love, Righteousness, and Kindness. *"For my mouth will speak truth; wickedness is an abomination to my lips. All the words of my mouth are with righteousness; nothing crooked or perverse is in them."* Proverbs 8:7-8.

☐ The *Wisdom of the Ancients* declares that once we understand the Systematic Processes of the Kingdom, the information needed will find us. *"They are all plain to him who understands, and right to those who find knowledge."* Proverbs 8:9.

Navigating Life's Challenges

- The *Wisdom of the Ancients* does not want us to misuse this Spiritual Reservoir, putting worldliness or materialism above it. We should never take this invaluable commodity for granted. Why? If our Divine Flow of Wisdom is cut off, we are left to our own devices. Personally, I would not risk it. *"Receive my instruction, and not silver, and knowledge rather than choice gold; for wisdom is better than rubies, and all the things one may desire cannot be compared with her."* Proverbs 8:10-11.

- The *Wisdom of the Ancients* does not want us to become arrogant and prideful, engaging in all types of evil practices. *"I, wisdom, dwell with prudence, and find out knowledge and discretion. The fear of the LORD is to hate evil; pride and arrogance and the evil way and the perverse mouth I hate."* Proverbs 8:12-13.

- The *Wisdom of the Ancients* wants us to gain Spiritual Counsel in our developmental process or Spiritual Classroom, building our strength from the inside out. *"Counsel is mine, and sound wisdom; I am understanding, I have strength."* Proverbs 8:14.

- The *Wisdom of the Ancients* foretells that any form of Royal Priesthood is governed by the Spirit of Wisdom to judge and rule, establishing Divine Order. *"By me kings reign, And rulers decree justice. By me Princes' rule, and nobles, all the judges of the earth."* Proverbs 8:15-16.

- The *Wisdom of the Ancients* advocates that Love and Righteousness go a lot further than what we could ever imagine, giving us the ability to call upon Divine Wisdom to assist us at the drop of a dime with Divine

Provisions. *"I love those who love me, and those who seek me diligently will find me. Riches and honor are with me, enduring riches and righteousness."* Proverbs 8:17-18.

Why do we need to know about the *Wisdom of the Ancients*? Divine Wisdom helps us develop Kingdom Poshness, perfect the Fruits of the Spirit, and operate with Christlike Character naturally and authentically. In addition, it aids in putting the finishing touches on our level of impact with our Divine Blessings and Dominion, making us the Crème de la Crème.

The bottom line is that if we give God what He wants, *As It Pleases Him,* He will give us what we need and some of what we desire. Here is what the Bible says, *"My fruit is better than gold, yes, than fine gold, and my revenue than choice silver. I traverse the way of righteousness, in the midst of the paths of justice, that I may cause those who love me to inherit wealth, that I may fill their treasuries."* Proverbs 8:19-21.

Chapter Eight
The Cost of Emotional Infections

In the Eye of God, *Emotional Infections* are very costly. If we do not choose the Path of Righteousness, then we will revert to a path of unrighteousness by default, and the Holy Spirit will lie dormant when our motives are wrong or when we are attempting to pimp God or desecrate the Blood of Jesus. As a result, we pick up a Like-Spirit that allows us to engage in wrongdoings, evil practices, negativity, and so on.

According to the Heavenly of Heavens, here is the catch with *Emotional Infections* as such: When going to the dark side to get the illusional appearance of purpose, we cannot use the Blood of Jesus to cover us; we must use our own sacrifices. Even if we are clueless about what we are doing, it does not exempt us from counting the cost of what we are doing or with whom.

Why must we use our own sacrifices as Believers, having the right to use the Blood of Jesus for Spiritual Atonement? Unrighteousness and contempt disqualify us from using the Blood of Jesus to cover practices of ill will, debauchery, or witchcraft behaviors until repentance occurs. If we continue

The Cost of Emotional Infections

in our folly in such a manner, whatever Spiritual Principality is governing that particular sacrifice, we will open ourselves up to that particular entity or entities. Keep in mind, once open to such, they do not play fair, and they most often do not come alone. Is this real? Absolutely.

Here is what Matthew 12:43-45 says about Spiritual Takeovers: *"When an unclean spirit goes out of a man, he goes through dry places, seeking rest and finds none. Then he says, 'I will return to my house from which I came.' And when he comes, he finds it empty, swept, and put in order. Then he goes and takes with him seven other spirits more wicked than himself, and they enter and dwell there; and the last state of that man is worse than the first."*

As a result of our self-induced or willful participation in these yokes, we will find ourselves settling or falling under the purpose of another or outright building upon another man's foundation. Really? Yes, really! For this reason, they are called dream killers, appearing Heaven Sent, but designed to lead us straight into the Pit with a one-way ticket. Plus, this is not what the Kingdom is about. *"Therefore, do not let your good be spoken of as evil; for the Kingdom of God is not eating and drinking, but righteousness and peace and joy in the Holy Spirit. For he who serves Christ in these things is acceptable to God and approved by men. Therefore, let us pursue the things which make for peace and the things by which one may edify another."* Romans 14:16-19.

What can we do to safeguard ourselves from the path of unrighteousness or *Emotional Infections*? Ephesians 4:22-24 says, *"That you put off, concerning your former conduct, the old man which grows corrupt according to the deceitful lusts, and be renewed in the spirit of your mind, and that you put on the new man which was created according to God, in true righteousness and holiness."*

The Cost of Emotional Infections

Ace In The Hole

What is the big deal about putting off the old man, especially when we have free will to do whatever we like and whenever we want? Of course, we all have the right to live on our own terms; however, when doing so, is it fair to call on the Holy Spirit when we have not put in the time to build that relationship?

For example, this is like having a fake friend who only calls when they need something, spitting in our face as if we are a nobody, talking about us like a junk-yard dog behind our backs, and kicking dirt on us when they do not need us. Yet, when the table turns in our favor, they want to take the credit for standing by us. When, in all actuality, the truth is, they were one step away from burning the bridges on us, then a need presented itself, and they remembered us as the *Ace In The Hole*.

Can one imagine using the Holy Trinity as their *Ace In The Hole*? Although this example is sad, it is all too true. After all, this is why *"The Spirit searches all things, yes, the deep things of God."* 1 Corinthians 2:10.

Why would the Holy Spirit search within? According to scripture, *"For what man knows the things of a man except the spirit of the man which is in him? Even so no one knows the things of God except the Spirit of God."* 1 Corinthians 2:11. Hands down, we need the Divine Presence of the Holy Spirit to search the human psyche for hidden things of the heart. We can tiptoe around, bragging about how powerful we are; however, our power is indeed limited without the Holy Spirit. How can I say such a thing, right? Well, the truth is revealed behind closed doors, with our fruits, and in our character...and they do not lie on us. They may lie to us, but once again, they do not lie on us!

In all actuality, if we are NOT aligning ourselves with Spiritual Principles, we are NOT in a Spiritual Classroom, we are doing our own thing without a conscience, and we are engaging in all sorts of debauchery. We must question whether or not the Holy Spirit is dwelling from within or if it is a Spirit of another kind.

Carnality vs. Spirit Man

What is the difference between carnality vs. Spirit Man? One is worldly, and the other is Spiritual. But let us take this a step further with scripture, which says, "*Now we have received, not the spirit of the world, but the Spirit who is from God, that we might know the things that have been freely given to us by God. These things we also speak, not in words which man's wisdom teaches but which the Holy Spirit teaches, comparing spiritual things with spiritual. But the natural man does not receive the things of the Spirit of God, for they are foolishness to him; nor can he know them, because they are spiritually discerned. But he who is spiritual judges all things, yet he himself is rightly judged by no one. For 'who has known the mind of the LORD that he may instruct Him?' But we have the mind of Christ.*" 1 Corinthians 2:12-16.

As discussed earlier, we are Spiritual Beings having a human experience. When we undercut or undermine our innate ability to make a *Spirit to Spirit* Connection back to the Source, we create a disservice to ourselves, weakening our Spiritual Bonds or Spiritual Advantages by default.

How do we know if we are struggling with carnality? The most prominent signs are when we have a battle with any form of envy, strife, or division, which leads to all other negative character traits, keeping us in the milking stages of our Spirituality.

Is the Holy Spirit biased? Of course not. We all have the same opportunity to receive the solid foods of the Holy Spirit, but we must do our part in receiving Divine Assistance. Here is the decree associated with the 'Why' of the Holy Spirit. "*And I, brethren, could not speak to you as to Spiritual people but as to carnal,*

The Cost of Emotional Infections

as to babes in Christ. I fed you with milk and not with solid food; for until now you were not able to receive it, and even now you are still not able; for you are still carnal. For where there are envy, strife, and divisions among you, are you not carnal and behaving like mere men?" 1 Corinthians 3:1-3.

Regardless of where we are from, what we are doing, or how we have been conditioned, the Fruits of the Spirit and Christlike Character are needed to receive the fullness of what God has to offer. So, it behooves us to engage *Spirit to Spirit* with our Heavenly Father and step into the Spiritual Classroom for the regrafting process of the Kingdom.

What makes the Spiritual Classroom so important? Unbeknown to most, it helps us to maximize our Seedtime and Harvest phase of living, causing all things to work in our favor. Once we understand and respect the fact that God is our SOURCE for all things, we can better discipline ourselves accordingly, even if the Vicissitudes of Life are pressing us to the max or we are yoked to the core. Simply put, we are able to learn, grow, and sow back into the Kingdom without having a pity party, feeling like a victim, or seeking revenge. While at the same time, knowing if God allowed it, it is designed for our growth, benefit, and training process, all orchestrated for our good with the Spiritual Intent of Blessing us to become a Blessing.

According to the Heavenly of Heavens, the Kingdom is looking for willful usability and moldability. As it relates to the Heavenly of Heavens, here is the team-playing mindset we should develop, *"I planted, Apollos watered, but God gave the increase. So then neither he who plants is anything, nor he who waters, but God who gives the increase. Now he who plants and he who waters are one, and each one will receive his own reward according to his own labor. For we are God's fellow workers; you are God's field, you are God's building. According to the grace of God which was given to me, as a wise master builder I have laid the foundation, and another builds on it. But let each*

The Cost of Emotional Infections

one take heed how he builds on it. For no other foundation can anyone lay than that which is laid, which is Jesus Christ." 1 Corinthians 3:6-11.

We must be willing to do our part in the Kingdom, ensuring our Heaven on Earth involvement is experienced inwardly and spread outwardly. However, to do so, we cannot become selfish in our attempts. *"Therefore, judge nothing before the time, until the Lord comes, who will both bring to light the hidden things of darkness and reveal the counsels of the hearts. Then each one's praise will come from God."* 1 Corinthians 4:5.

God uses us to carry out the Missions of the Kingdom; however, we must believe in Him, ourselves, and others, extending love and hope to all regardless of our condition or the condition of another, *As It Pleases Him*. By far, this gives the Holy Spirit the common ground to mentor us according to Kingdom Standards, amid whatever or with whomever, making us a work-in-progress according to the Heavenly of Heavens.

In my opinion, life is by far the best Spiritual Classroom known to mankind because we learn as we go, getting hands-on experience. However, it may not feel good when we are going through it. In the end, when we win, we have first-hand knowledge, *Spirit to Spirit*, on how to position ourselves to cause things to work in our favor. More importantly, with this Spiritual Relationship, we do not have to deal with the unsurety of second-hand information with zero experience, going with the flow of the *'anything goes'* way of life.

According to the Heavenly of Heavens, God will open the Curtains of Holiness on our behalf if we dare to step outside of our comfort zone to receive what He has to offer.

Victim No More

In our redemptive efforts, God is a God of second, third, fourth, fifth, sixth, seventh chances, and so on. So, if we are

The Cost of Emotional Infections

forgiven, why are we not forgiving others? Or, better yet, why should we forgive those who have warped motives? God must judge the motives of all; however, it is our responsibility to keep the negative debris from forming by simply forgiving, moving on, and bearing no grudges. For this reason, let us deal with forgiveness first: *"Then Peter came to Him and said, 'Lord, how often shall my brother sin against me, and I forgive him? Up to seven times?' Jesus said to him, I do not say to you, up to seven times, but up to seventy times seven."* Matthew 18:21-22. Secondly, *"You shall not hate your brother in your heart. You shall surely rebuke your neighbor, and not bear sin because of him. You shall not take vengeance, nor bear any grudge against the children of your people, but you shall love your neighbor as yourself: I am the LORD."* Leviticus 19:17-18.

Truthfully, to maximize our highest and greatest potential amid being a *Victim No More*, we must put our differences and biases away, dealing with the issues at hand in the Spirit of Righteousness, even when people spit in our face, use, mock, talk about, or disrespect us. If not, the same hang-ups we have with others, we will eventually knowingly or unknowingly yoke ourselves.

Here is what Job 17:3-9 says about this: *"Now put down a pledge for me with Yourself. Who is he who will shake hands with me? For You have hidden their heart from understanding; therefore, You will not exalt them. He who speaks flattery to his friends, even the eyes of his children will fail. But He has made me a byword of the people, and I have become one in whose face men spit. My eye has also grown dim because of sorrow, and all my members are like shadows. Upright men are astonished at this, and the innocent stirs himself up against the hypocrite. Yet the righteous will hold to his way, and he who has clean hands will be stronger and stronger."*

According to the Heavenly of Heavens, it is in our best interest to do a clean sweep of all negativity, unforgiveness, and resentment. Why should we do such a thing, especially

The Cost of Emotional Infections

when we are hurt? Our Blessings are tied to overcoming the undesirable characteristics that easily beset us, and it is also associated with the intimacy we will have with God. Really? Yes, really. Here is what Psalm 24:3-5 says: *"Who may ascend into the hill of the LORD? Or who may stand in His holy place? He who has clean hands and a pure heart, who has not lifted up his soul to an idol, nor sworn deceitfully. He shall receive Blessings from the LORD, and righteousness from the God of his salvation."*

Clearly, no one is immune to negative feelings; our responsibility is to deal with them accordingly, ensuring they do not infect our fruits with toxins or disobediently warp our character. For this reason, it is imperative to use the Fruits of the Spirit to develop Christlike Character, warding off the provocation to further decline our Earthen Vessels, affecting our relationships and people skills.

In being a *Victim No More* of our past, present, and future, we do not want to position ourselves to have a temper tantrum or meltdown amid the Vicissitudes of Life. Nor do we want others to cringe when they see us coming or running for cover when we appear. According to the Heavenly of Heavens, we must consistently work on ourselves to become better without having the negative characteristics of envy, jealousy, pride, coveting, anger, hatred, resentment, competitiveness, outbursts, vindictiveness, or slander overshadowing our ability to effectively communicate or cause us to run away from dealing with the inevitable.

Unfortunately, people will more than likely NOT tell us when we are repulsive. They will usually allow us to continue in our folly, hiding in the bush like a roaring lion waiting for us to trip up, then letting loose their vengeful wrath to see what we are really made of. Now, for the sake of this book, *Divine Dominion: As It Pleases God*®, we do not want it to get to this point, so let us go a little deeper.

The Cost of Emotional Infections

Regardless of who we are and why, when faced with negative character traits, emotions, behaviors, thoughts, and so on, we must eventually deal with them to avoid the cycle of déjà vu, exhausting us, or our Bloodline. When aligning ourselves with the Heavenly of Heavens, we must *Repent* in order to *Redeem*. At the same time, most would want *Redemption* alone without getting to the root cause of the issue, trauma, condition, mindset, or whatever.

In *Divine Dominion*, we cannot overlook the Tilling Process, lifting the generational curse from the Garden of Eden. Once again, we must put in the work, Spiritually Tilling our own ground from the inside out and becoming our Brother's Keeper once done. If not, we will find a history of time not being on our side, including the mismanagement of it while pretending to be on top of our game. When, in all actuality, our game is on top of us with a yoke intertwined in the core of our being, disguised as something else. Listed below are a few examples of yokes, but not limited to such:

- ☐ When we exclude God and are constantly missing the mark, it produces a yoke.

- ☐ When we procrastinate, delaying people, places, and things unnecessarily, it initiates a yoke.

- ☐ When we become content with unfinished projects, it indicates a yoke.

- ☐ When we have a problem multitasking and planning, it forms a yoke.

- ☐ When we remain confused about what we must do, it is due to a yoke.

The Cost of Emotional Infections

- When we have a history of unhealthy or fallible relationships turning us into enemies, it is facilitated by a yoke.

- When we are always a *'Day late and a dollar short'* in life, it is a sign of a yoke.

- When we leave people worse off than when we met them, it is orchestrated by a yoke.

- When we overcommit ourselves, becoming easily overwhelmed and burned out with a yoke attached.

- When we have issues communicating and are easily distracted, it reveals a yoke.

- When we are very indecisive and spend too much time on unhealthy activities, it feeds our yoke or ego.

- When we spend too much time complicating things instead of simplifying, it ties the yoke tighter.

Yokes, or no yokes…they are real and are self-created, self-induced, and self-contained. A yoke, soul tie, and bondage contain the power we give them based on the leverage, environment, or access we provide. If we exclude God from our lives' equation, we become destined to please ourselves to our detriment, thinking we are right or justified. Moreover, if we have a desire to be redeemed, *As It Pleases God*, we must know what they are and why they are holding on for dear life within the psyche. For the record, they do not hang around for no reason; they must be fed. Now, if we are feeding them,

The Cost of Emotional Infections

it is our responsibility to cease engagement with it, that, or them, and stop pretending!

How do we prevent ourselves from becoming a victim? First, the *Victim No More* begins with a mindset. Secondly, we must make a decision not to become one. Thirdly, we must choose VICTORY over all else, regardless of how anything appears to the naked eye. Here are a few things to know about breaking the victim mentality, but not limited to such:

- ☐ We must pride ourselves on making good, sound decisions without exhibiting recklessness, making excuses, or engaging in defiant debauchery.

- ☐ We must make our best attempts not to judge because we do not know what Spirit is behind whatever or whomever. Still, we must understand or recognize the FRUITS of another or character traits having the potential to affect us or our Bloodline. Meanwhile, exhibiting the Fruits of the Spirit and Christlike Character to deflect negativity. Is this not judging? When we redirect the Spiritual Checklist toward ourselves, it is not judging; it is called Spiritual Awareness, especially when we must pinpoint the areas in which we need to set an example or proactively offer help. If we do not know what we are dealing with, then we do not know what to do, what to counteract, or why.

    On the other hand, if we are pointing the finger, attempting to degrade, demean, or dismantle, assassinating the character or fruits of another, while making fun of them or talking about them in a negative demeanor, then this is judging.

The Cost of Emotional Infections

- We must respect another person's opinion or faith. Everyone has a right to believe whatever they like as a part of our free will; however, it is our responsibility to set an example for them by using our people skills. We all have our own Spiritual Journey, and no one is 100% right or wrong. There is always an element of truth; it is only a matter of right vs. wrong, good vs. bad, positive vs. negative, just vs. unjust, Kingdom vs. worldly, and so on. So, even if we disagree, we should never mistreat someone or show an unkind face in the Name of God. Frankly, it is not the Spirit of God behaving in such a manner! From experience, He will take the least likely and make them likely!

- We must get rid of our hidden or open biases and conditioning. Our personal perspectives may not be God's Perspective, *As It Pleases Him*. Therefore, we must align ourselves with the Word of God, ensuring we understand what He is expecting from us.

- We must become selfless in the Eye of God. He frowns upon selfishness because it makes us self-centered, wanting to keep everything for ourselves while breaking the flow. For example, if God is feeding us Divine Wisdom, and it stops at us or we use it to manipulate, then Divine Wisdom will break us or our flow by default. As a result, we become UNUSABLE in the Kingdom.

- We must become transparent, owning our truth. Hidden matters of deception keep the human psyche from healing as it should. Instead, we contribute to the walls erected to block our inner selves, developing all sorts of masks. Whereas, the moment we open

The Cost of Emotional Infections

ourselves up to our truth, we are better able to heal within the imperials of our freedom.

- [ ] We must be willing to become an expert in our Gifts, Calling, Talents, Purpose, or Creativity, working on them daily with one day of rest. Why do we need to rest? According to the Heavenly of Heavens, it gives God, our Gifts, Calling, Talents, Purpose, or Creativity rest, respect, and rejuvenation. In addition, it helps us to understand our Blueprint a little better, keeping us from running around trying to do everything that does NOT fit into the Divine Plan, *As It Pleases God*.

   What if we feel the urge to do something on the one day of rest? There are times when we will get a Spiritual Urge on this one day. There is no need for alarm, especially when obedience is required of us from our Heavenly Father. All it means is that God is saving someone's life, or someone needs what we have to offer due to its time sensitivity. For this reason, we need to have the *Spirit to Spirit* Connection, understanding when to stand up or stand down when called upon by the Heavenly of Heavens. Just as we have respect for God, He has respect for us as well; therefore, this will not be a continuous process.

   Rest, respect, and rejuvenation are prerequisites of the Kingdom, giving us time to build relations with our family and solidifying our foundation. What does this mean? To keep our homes from falling apart, we need at least one day of family bonding without worldly distractions. Still, this one day is not set in stone as long as it is done and everyone understands the meaning of Restful Bonding.

The Cost of Emotional Infections

- [ ] We must become steadfast in righteousness while not being moved by negativity or succumbing to breaking under pressure. We must be able to think positively on our feet while exhibiting the Fruits of the Spirit and Christlike Character without deviation.

- [ ] We must pride ourselves in taming the lust of the eyes, the lust of the flesh, and the pride of life, ensuring they do not become our impending kryptonite amid our peak performance. It causes us to play ourselves short or block our own Blessings. When we are at our best, our hidden or open habits linking to these three portals open the door to sifting, yoking, or oppression.

    In order to genuinely become the best of the best in or out of the Kingdom, we must close the door on these negative portals. By doing so, it levels the playing field. What if it does not? Listen, the *'Cream of the Crop'* will always rise to the top in due season, especially if they continue to work on themselves, Spiritually Tilling their own ground, stepping up their game positively, and putting the Will of God at the forefront, *As It Pleases Him.*

- [ ] We cannot ignore or talk down on Divine Wisdom. According to the *Ancient of Ancients*, we do not want to reject Wisdom. Why? Wisdom has a way of speaking to us, guiding us in the right direction, or becoming deafly silent, allowing us to give way to our own folly, dire consequences, and constant defeat.

- [ ] We must develop a private and intimate relationship with the Holy Trinity, becoming rooted and grounded in the Word of God. We do not want to become swayed by worldliness, causing us to second-guess

The Cost of Emotional Infections

God, the power or guidance of the Holy Spirit, and the Blood of Jesus. Plus, we need to be able to call upon Spiritual Backup at the drop of a dime, knowing beyond a shadow of a doubt that Divine Intervention will show up on our behalf in full Spiritual Armor.

☐ We must willfully use the Fruits of the Spirit and Christlike Character to become better daily without settling for defeat. When gaining our Spiritual Keys to the Kingdom of Heaven, it chooses who gains Spiritual Access and who will not, based on our heart's contents.

We can tiptoe around these Spiritual Principles, as well as the inner chatter surrounding us or taking place from within; yet, when it comes down to the Kingdom, the negativity from within must be corrected to positivity, creating a win-win out of everything. If not, with all due respect, we will become an undercover hypocritical shyster, appearing right in our own eyes.

How can I say such a thing, right? If I do not tell the truth, then who will? I will not sit back and allow us to humiliate ourselves in the Name of God while behaving with such putridness, misrepresenting the Kingdom of Heaven. If we do not believe this to be true, all we need to do is check our thoughts, actions, beliefs, feelings, reactions, and most of all, what we are secretly saying to ourselves, especially when we do not get what we want, we are betrayed, or someone offends us. We will find out whether or not Divine Wisdom can reside, ushering us into Greatness or the abyss.

The Cost of Emotional Infections

When Triggered

In alignment with *Divine Dominion: As It Pleases God*®, the goal is to become better, making the lives of others better as well. Nevertheless, if we find ourselves on the decline from the inside out, causing a decline in the lives of others, we have work to do. To be clear, simply because we have work to do, it does not make us bad people. Remember that we all have good and bad inside of us in need of redirection; we just need to know what to do, why we are doing so, and what our triggers are.

Most would never admit to turning into someone else that they do not recognize, *When Triggered*, nor would they admit to becoming triumphantly aggressive in their approach. But, behind closed doors, it happens all too often, mainly when we do not get what we want or our expectations are shattered. In all reality, the other person from within is really our psyche releasing itself for human display or consumption. So, we must be cautious, especially when we are negatively unleashing the wrath hidden in the lust of the eyes, the lust of the flesh, and the pride of life.

Why do we need to be careful about our triggers? It means self-control is not present, and our rooted trauma has not been dealt with accordingly, or *As It Pleases God*. If any of the three elements (the lust of the eyes, the lust of the flesh, and the pride of life) are present, we can yolk ourselves without batting an eye or giving it a second thought.

In the Kingdom, being stuck on the negative creates a great disservice to ourselves and others. Why? It leads to some form of obstructive Mental, Physical, and Emotional violence or trauma, where we knowingly or unknowingly inflict this upon those looking up to us for answers, help, guidance, or who need what we have to offer.

As a part of *Divine Dominion*, the Heavenly of Heavens is bringing this form of soulful lapse to our attention. Why is

The Cost of Emotional Infections

the attention of the Believers required? If we look around, we are in a state of mass dilemma, and we cannot see that we are in such a state. Plus, it has become the norm to be disrespectful, rude, unkind, and biased with zero to no repercussions. Nevertheless, in the Kingdom, it does not go unnoticed in the Eye of God. Moreover, if He has me documenting it, *As It Pleases Him*, it is a BIG issue!

According to the Heavenly of Heavens, as we address this issue, we must know that we all have a trigger, sore spot, or something to work on, at, or through, but we do not have to lose our cool or play dirty. If we do, we can openly regain our composure, self-correct, or reverse it at that moment. We do not have to wait until we get home or into our prayer closet; we can use the Fruits of the Spirit at that very moment. If we do not know what they are, we should keep a flashcard of them in our pockets until we are well-versed in them.

So, when our psyche has a temper tantrum, attempting to embarrass or oust us, we need to put it in check by correcting it instantly, without waiting or playing clean up. By doing so, we will train ourselves to exhibit the Fruits of the Spirit and Christlike Character from the jumpstart and to think on our feet.

All in all, when making sense of our lives or when redeeming ourselves, we can better make sense of what is happening around us without allowing it to affect or get into us. How is this possible? Our Divine Blueprint is already. All we need to do is align ourselves accordingly, getting in Purpose on purpose, and the Cycle of Life will filter in or out what we need or do not need. In addition, it will also place us in a Passover Covering. In light of our faithfulness, this is when we cover ourselves with the Blood of Jesus, allowing the Holy Spirit to do what needs to be done in the delivering phase for the completion of our Divine Mission, ushering us into *Divine Dominion*.

The Cost of Emotional Infections

Privilege vs. Underprivileged

According to the Heavenly of Heavens, everyone desires a 'Better Lifestyle,' even if we cannot see our better amid living our best life due to selfishness, conditioning, ungratefulness, biases, jealousy, envy, coveting, or competitiveness. How can we make this make sense? If we are born into a particular environment, it is all we know until we learn something different or get a complete understanding of our lifestyle.

For example, if a child is born into poverty, they will never know they are poor if they do not surround themselves with children who are NOT impoverished. Yet, when they are exposed to another environment, appearing better than what they are accustomed to, they will begin to experience negative feelings, emotions, and thoughts. If they are NOT taught otherwise or do not understand their 'Why' in life, these feelings will fester negatively due to the illusion of deprivation.

On the other hand, if we have a child of privilege, most often, they do not understand how to deal with lack, and they feel as if they should have the desires of their heart, whether good, bad, or indifferent. I understand we all want the best for ourselves and our children; however, according to the Kingdom, we must choose a straight, narrow, and positive path for all. Why? We have those who are conditioning themselves and their children that they are better than others, as opposed to learning how to RELATE to those who are different or less fortunate, how to become GRATEFUL in all things, and how to develop confidence from the inside out, not from the outside in.

As a result of being taught privileged pompousness or the lack of self-control as a child, if they do not get what they want and when, they experience the same negative attributes of an impoverished child, inadvertently putting them in the same category without realizing the implications of doing so. Now,

The Cost of Emotional Infections

according to the Heavenly of Heavens, due to the lack of understanding, they learn how to cover negative attributes up by bragging, bullying, temper tantrums, and manipulating those who appear underprivileged unless they are taught otherwise.

All in all, positive or negative characteristics begin in our childhood, snowballing throughout time, intensifying or justifying traumas, thirsts, or pangs of hunger. Suppose negativity is left uncorrected with truth and positivity. In this case, it overlaps into adulthood, embedding negative roots into our psyche so deep, that it will take the Holy Trinity to help us to uproot and regraft the negative to positive with the Fruits of the Spirit.

As it relates to *Privilege vs. Underprivileged*, the main difference in all things, be it worldly or Spiritual, and our true level of Status in or out of the Kingdom is *Self-Control*. It leads us, our children, or our Bloodline into our Heaven on Earth Experience or the Abyss with a one-way ticket. We can blame it on everything else in life or make excuses, but when it comes down to the human psyche, the *Control of Self* bridges the gap to the three portals ensnaring all mankind: the lust of the eye, the lust of the flesh, and the pride of life.

In perfecting our routines, habits, or regimen, we must govern ourselves accordingly, *As It Pleases God*, to get to the ROOT of our control or the lack of it to partake of the *Grandfather Clause*. Why? It is our God-Given right to have and become the best of the best, *As It Pleases Him*. Then again, if we do not want to do what it takes to get it, we also have the free will right to pass the Spiritual Mantle to the next person or settle for mediocrity. However, if we forfeit it, we have no reason to complain to God about anything or anyone, especially when He has given us the Spiritual Information, Tools, and Principles on a SILVER PLATTER.

The Cost of Emotional Infections

For Show vs. For Sure

In the Kingdom, we deal with two types of *Lifestyles*: the 'For Show' or the 'For Sure.' When we are moved to put on a *Show* to impress, persuade, or show status, we have God all wrong. He is looking for those who are *Sure* about their Blessings, Favor, Provisions, or Blueprint, possessing the courage to move forward in His Will and Ways without distractions from those who are hung up on material gain.

If one has not noticed by now, those who are money-hungry or lovers of money will sell their souls at the drop of a dime. According to the Heavenly of Heavens, they are the most conniving, scheming, using, and unfaithful individuals known to man due to their inherent yoking factors related to the lust of the eyes, the lust of the flesh, and the pride of life.

In addition, without pointing the finger, they also possess character flaws, driving a wedge in the heart of the righteous, hanging the innocent out to dry without offering a helping hand, or kicking people when they are down for a feeling of superiority or control. All in all, it is reflected in their fruits and character traits by default, regardless of the type of mask they assume.

Hence, God, our Heavenly Father, is interjecting Divine Wisdom into our lives to save the human psyche from self-destructing, giving us hope and another chance to get whatever it is right. How do we recognize a destructive type of individual? Listed below are a few recognizable factors, but not limited to such:

- ☐ We must pay attention to their *Fruits*. Beyond a shadow of a doubt, our fruits have a way of ratting us out without us realizing what it is doing until it is done. What is the purpose of this? Unbeknown to most, there is a big difference in attempting to clean up, prune, or do something about our fruits as opposed to

The Cost of Emotional Infections

allowing them to remain As-Is, denied, downplayed, or outright hidden.

- ☐ We must pay attention to negative or condescending actions, beliefs, behaviors, desires, words, or responses. Besides, from much experience, these are usually the ones who forget where God brought or delivered them from. So, if we ask the right fact-finding questions, we can narrow down the root of their fruit without clueing them in on what we are doing or becoming fooled by their lifestyle.

- ☐ We must pay attention to their people skills. Communication is everything; if we fail to communicate effectively, our relationships fall apart by default, be it public, private, exclusive, or workable relations. To be clear, we do not have to agree on all things to be amicable, kind, humble, and patient. Even if people rub us the wrong way, we still do not have to 'Show Out' or 'Put on a Show,' especially when we have the Fruits of the Spirit and Christlike Character at our beckoning call. We cannot go wrong with Kingdom Mannerability.

- ☐ We must pay attention to their *Level of Respect*. Listen, if someone does not respect their elders, authorities, rules, or laws, beware. For example, if a person is trying to woo me and does not respect their parents, I back up, period!

    Frankly, I do not care how much money, status, or fame they have—disrespectfulness is not for me. Is this not judging someone? No, it is called paying attention, becoming astutely aware of the generational curses following a person who does not honor their mother or

The Cost of Emotional Infections

father. Really? Yes, really! Ephesians 6:1-3 clearly says, "*Children, obey your parents in the Lord, for this is right. 'Honor your father and mother,' which is the first commandment with promise: 'that it may be well with you and you may live long on the earth.'*"

Listen, if disrespectfulness is taking place, and repentance is not established or occurs, the curse is set in motion. It cannot be reversed until the person who set it in motion REPENTS and REGRAFTS the root of this behavior. For me, I do not play around with curses of such magnitude. Why? Unbeknown to most, this is a Bloodline Curse, and if a person does not see a problem with their behavior, then self-control is not in place, rotten fruits are already set in motion, disobedience is on the horizon, and history will repeat itself. More importantly, this does not happen from the outside in, but from the inside out, plaguing the human psyche.

- We must take into account the *Level of Tolerance*. If they have little or no tolerance for people, places, and things, this should be a RED FLAG for us. If we violate our conscience, we bring the intolerance to our level of being with a gravitational pull from their psyche to ours. For example, if they are battling with the Spirit of Anger, then we will inherit it if we bond (engage in a Spiritual Transfer) with it through the lust of the eyes, the lust of the flesh, or the pride of life. What does the pride of life have to do with anything? It is usually through our pride that we do not let go of those who are vexing our Spirit.

- We must pay attention to their *Level of Humility*. In the Kingdom, pompousness is a recipe for disaster. It

The Cost of Emotional Infections

brings about the Rod of Correction faster than disobedience. How is this possible? Disobedience should be corrected before pompousness, right? In the worldly means, this would be the case, but when dealing with Kingdom Principles, we deal with the ROOT.

In order for disobedience to take place, most often, it is due to the root of pompousness; therefore, the Bible frowns upon this characteristic. This underlying characteristic leads to all forms of evil. For this one, let us align it with scripture: *"But now you boast in your arrogance. All such boasting is evil. Therefore, to him who knows to do good and does not do it, to him it is sin."* James 4:16-17.

Furthermore, when someone lacks humility, they tend to lose control of their tongue as well, saying things that should not be uttered. What do we need to do? Repent of this behavior, and become humble; but more importantly, here is what the scriptures tell us, *"The fear of the LORD is to hate evil; pride and arrogance and the evil way and the perverse mouth I hate."* Proverbs 8:13.

☐ We must pay attention to their *Lovability*. The *Wisdom of the Ancients* warns us about those who are heartless, conscienceless, and victimizing. If we encounter someone who is hateful, cruel, evil, biased, vindictive, prideful, jealous, envious, competitive, or covetous, we must exercise extreme caution around them.

To be clear, it does not mean they are a bad person; however, it is only a matter of time before we become a victim. If we are not strong enough to handle the trauma, it is best to treat them with a long-handled spoon. When we are able to love God, ourselves, and others with no strings attached, treating everyone with

The Cost of Emotional Infections

outright dignity, we are well on our way to doing great work from the inside out.

- ☐ We must pay attention to their *Consistency*. Those who are all over the place Mentally, Physically, Emotionally, and Spiritually indicate unsurety regarding their Gifts, Calling, Talents, Purpose, or Creativity. By far, these are the ones who have sticky fingers of inconsistency, taking, touching, or manipulating what does not belong to them. Better yet, this form of insecurity can become our kryptonite, especially when left uncorrected, unresolved, unrepentant, or unaddressed.

- ☐ We must pay attention to how well they own their *Truth*. If we encounter someone who does not assume responsibility or always makes excuses, beware. Passing the buck is an automatic sign of recklessness, irresponsibility, or wallowing in untruthfulness. Also, it is symbolically telling the Heavenly of Heavens that we are complete, or we do not have anything to work on or work at. For sure, our internal security begins with being true to ourselves, owning our truth, or repenting of the lies we keep telling ourselves while becoming a work-in-progress.

- ☐ We must pay attention to their *Level of Authenticity*. Faithfulness and trustworthiness go a long way in the Kingdom. If God can trust us, there is no limit on what we can achieve or what He will do for us. However, if we cannot trust a person as far as we can see them, then it is best to save ourselves from heartache. Why? Unrest within the human psyche is traumatizing for anyone dead set on deception; it will lead both into a ditch, similar to the blind leading the blind.

The Cost of Emotional Infections

- We must pay attention to their *Helpfulness*. Suppose a person can sit back, avoid, or watch a person suffer without lending a helping hand. In this case, if it is within their power to do so and avoid helping to make them suffer, something is definitely wrong from within their genetic makeup. Selfishness is not of God, period.

- We must pay attention to their *Words*. What comes out of our mouths tells the world who we are, as well as the contents of our hearts. Therefore, we should set a guard over our mouths, giving thought to every word. Why? They are a direct reflection of who we are, not who we pretend to be; we can only put on a show for so long before our words ensnare us without us knowing.

Once again, keep in mind that we are all different, so we cannot limit ourselves or others; however, we must master the ability to relate to anyone, on any level, and from any background.

Why must we master our relatability as Believers? We will never know WHO or WHAT God is using; therefore, if we fail the test, rejecting *What* or *Who* He sent to Bless us, we may have to hang our heads down in shame because we missed the Spiritual Marking or Cue. How can we miss it? It is often due to some form of Spiritual Blindness, Deafness, or Muteness, predicated upon some form of lust of the eyes, lust of the flesh, or pride of life, dividing us from the inside out. Frankly, this all happens without us realizing what is taking place until the Divine Unveiling, as we appear right in our own eyes and all too wrong in the Eye of God.

The Cost of Emotional Infections

Listen, and listen to me well. With all due respect, we are a diversified people, and if we choose to become divided, Mentally, Physically, Emotionally, and Spiritually due to a superficial lifestyle of worldliness, it will be to our detriment, crushing us to the core in due time. Why would this crush us? Suppose we portray ourselves as a Spiritual Elite, rejecting the Earthen Vessel that God sent due to some form of bias. In this case, we set ourselves up to become symbolically broken until we return to Him in a repentant state of being.

As a Word to the Wise, God will never send what we need packaged the way we envision. Nor will He present it idolistically the way the world would package it.

What is the purpose of God tricking us? He is not tricking us; we trick ourselves based on our thwarted perception of self-gratification without using our Spiritual Intuition or Discernment, *As It Pleases Him.* If we were in a Spiritual Relationship as we ought, the Holy Spirit would have informed us prior to whatever or whomever. So, if we DO NOT get the message from the Heavenly of Heavens, we may miss out, reject, or neglect whatever or whomever. As a result, we cannot lay the blame elsewhere.

Why can we not blame God for NOT informing us about something or someone? First, we should have taken the opportunity to examine the Spiritual Fruits as our secret ONE-UP from the Heavenly of Heavens. Secondly, having a *Spirit to Spirit* Connection would have advised us of the Cornerstone or Stepping Stone we are dealing with, especially when embarking upon *Divine Dominion: As It Pleases God*®. Is this Biblical? Of course, *"Jesus said to them, 'Have you never read in the Scriptures: The stone which the builders rejected has become the Chief Cornerstone. This was the LORD's doing, and it is marvelous in our eyes?' Therefore, I say to you, the Kingdom of God will be taken from you and given to a nation bearing the fruits of it. And whoever falls on this stone*

The Cost of Emotional Infections

will be broken; but on whomever it falls, it will grind him to powder." Matthew 21:42-44.

Why do we need a *Spirit to Spirit* Connection when dealing with *Divine Dominion* or our *Cornerstone*? It helps keep us aligned with our Divine Blueprint, ensuring we do not miss our Spiritual Cue or become a footstool, even if we have a few mishaps along the way. Yet, the moment we begin to pride ourselves on unrepentant or uncorrected worldliness or willful debauchery, we become divided from the Kingdom, regardless of how well we pretend.

Unbeknown to most, inner division is much more invasive than outer division. The hidden impact of what we cannot see packs a more powerful punch than what we can see coming. Unfortunately, we cannot prepare for the unseen, especially when our Spirit is asleep and we are Spiritually Blind, Deaf, Mute, Dull, Lukewarm, or Stiff-Necked.

As a result, we end up fighting against ourselves, not knowing what we are really fighting for unless we involve the Holy Trinity. Here is what we must know: *"So, He called them to Himself and said to them in parables: 'How can Satan cast out Satan?' If a kingdom is divided against itself, that kingdom cannot stand. And if a house is divided against itself, that house cannot stand. And if Satan has risen up against himself, and is divided, he cannot stand, but has an end. No one can enter a strong man's house and plunder his goods, unless he first binds the strong man. And then he will plunder his house."* Mark 3:23-27.

Regardless of whether we are operating in the For *Show or For Sure* state of being, discernment is needed when facing any form of opposition or division to ensure we are not contending with the wrong people, places, and things. Is it possible to wrongfully contend as Believers? It happens all the time, especially when we have not mastered how to examine our fruits and those of another, *As It Pleases God*. Actually, our

The Cost of Emotional Infections

human nature often drives us to assert ourselves and our views without careful examination of our motives or asking fact-finding questions.

As Believers, when dealing with *The Cost of Emotional Infections*, we are called to evaluate not just the actions and beliefs of others but also our own through self-reflection and discernment. All in all, we must ask the tough questions without assuming. Plus, we all know what they say about assuming!

Chapter Nine
Embracing the Fruits of the Spirit

For Divine Unity to come forth as it should in the Eye of God, *Embracing the Fruits of the Spirit* is of the utmost essence of personal and Spiritual Growth and Transformation. What is more astounding is being able to turn obstacles into Christlike Stepping Stones or Cornerstones of Greatness. As we cultivate each fruit, maintaining our Spiritual Lives, *As It Pleases God*, it requires us to focus on the individual fruits of the Spirit, one by one. What is the purpose of using this method? As the pursuit of growth and maturity is a fundamental component of mankind, breaking down our fruits makes it easier for us to pinpoint which ones to work on, which ones we have already mastered, and which ones to use. From my perspective, this allows us to examine our lives closely and discern areas that require our attention.

The Fruits of the Spirit, as outlined in Galatians 5:22-23, include Love, Joy, Peace, Patience, Kindness, Goodness, Faithfulness, Gentleness, and Self-Control. Once again, there is no law against the use of them, but if we do not use them,

Embracing The Fruits of the Spirit

Spiritual Laws, Principles, and Protocols are indeed applicable and enforceable.

When *Embracing the Fruits of the Spirit*, by concentrating on one fruit at a time, they become more palatable to the psyche without shocking or overwhelming it. For example, if we say use the Fruit of the Spirit, then the psyche is asking what fruit because we did not give it the details or instructions. Now, if we say to the psyche, exhibit love...it will begin calculating lovable traits, similar to turning on the signal light in our cars to make a left or right turn.

When dealing with *Divine Dominion: As It Pleases God*®, this same concept applies to each fruit as well. For example, if we are focusing on being patient, we can literally practice intentionally waiting on something or someone. Amazingly, the more we practice, the better we become at being more patient. With time, we can go from normal patience to Divine Patience, *As It Pleases God*.

When living real life, the struggle is real! However, when *Embracing the Fruits of the Spirit*, we have hope. Real hope, to be exact. So, let me break down a few fruits from a charactorial perspective:

- ☐ If we struggle with hatefulness, we can dedicate time to developing the Fruit of Love.

- ☐ If we struggle with inner turmoil, we can dedicate time to developing the Fruit of Joy.

- ☐ If we struggle with chaos, we can dedicate time to developing the Fruit of Peace.

- ☐ If we struggle with unkindness, we can dedicate time to developing the Fruit of Kindness.

Embracing The Fruits of the Spirit

- ☐ If we struggle with rottenness, we can dedicate time to developing the Fruit of Goodness.

- ☐ If we struggle with unfaithfulness, we can dedicate time to developing the Fruit of Faithfulness.

- ☐ If we struggle with abrasiveness, we can dedicate time to developing the Fruit of Gentleness.

- ☐ If we struggle with being all over the place, doing whatever, whenever, however, wherever, and with whomever, we can dedicate time to developing the Fruit of Self-Control.

Most of us talk a good game when it comes to the Fruits of the Spirit...still, in the Eye of God, we must begin using them to stave off the wiles of the enemy and navigate the complexities of life. According to the Heavenly of Heavens, whether we are having a bad day or encounter temptation, doubt, anger, or despair, the Fruits of the Spirit serve as a PROTECTIVE SHIELD, guiding us toward righteous words, actions, beliefs, desires, and thoughts with practical applications and transformative powers.

Are there any guarantees associated with using the Fruits of the Spirit? Yes, the guarantee is that they are loaded with good seeds and seeding conditions. Let me explain: You are the Seed of Abraham and have the right to lay claim to your Divine Inheritance and Dominion. In Genesis, Chapter 15, God promised He would BLESS Abraham and make him a great nation. Believe it or not, you are a part of this Divine Promise, but it comes with Spiritual Conditions.

God did not tell Abraham that the Blessings would fall into his lap. He and his descendants had to work for them, Spiritually Tilling their own ground. Although the Spiritual

Embracing The Fruits of the Spirit

Covenant is everlasting, Abraham and his descendants must uphold their part of the deal. The simple AGREEMENT with God was that they had to pray only to Him, worship Him, listen to Him, obey Him, and follow His will, *As It Pleases Him*. Although the Spiritual Agreement has not changed, we have!

Nevertheless, the GROUNDWORK of our developmental factors has already been laid. If we do not get with the program, we can inadvertently forfeit our Divine Dominion where our Divine Faith, Promise, and Freedom intertwine. What are they intertwining with? They intertwine with the Divine Fulfillment of God's Heavenly Protection and Provisions and His ability to come DOWN to see about us.

In the world in which we live today, when we think about the word down, we do not usually associate it with up unless we are Mentally, Physically, Emotionally, and Spiritually trained to do so. In the Kingdom, to become Divinely Rooted, *As It Pleases God*, we must glean downwardly with an understanding to go up in WISDOM. This Divine Principle allows us to view people, places, and things differently, fine-tuning our perspective. For example, a view from the top will always differ from when we view people, places, and things from the bottom. From both angles of view, regardless of where we are in life or who we are, it behooves us to master the Top-To-Bottom Buildup Techniques and Processes of incorporating the THIRD VIEW.

What is the purpose of seeking the THIRD VIEW? When *Embracing the Fruits of the Spirit*, by adding God's Perspective into our equational maps, thoughts, beliefs, and systems, we can better determine the difference between our illusional vanities and our Kingdom Realities.

As we are confronted with a multiplicity of choices, conflicts, and decisions on a daily basis, we really need that THIRD VIEW to discern, understand, and decide with clarity. This approach goes beyond the binary lens of good

Embracing The Fruits of the Spirit

and bad or right and wrong; it ushers in a Divine Lens of our calculatory efforts with a broader viewpoint that can illuminate paths we might otherwise overlook. However, when using the Holy Trinity as such, we must master *Embracing the Fruits of the Spirit* to ensure we can connect to our Heavenly Father, *Spirit to Spirit*, for relevant and accurate Spiritual Downloads.

What if we opt out of using the THIRD VIEW of the Holy Trinity? Unfortunately, we will NOT discern people, places, and things accurately, or *As It Pleases God*, thrusting us into selfish and biased perspectives. Frankly, this is how we get faithful Believers misjudging others who appear beneath them but may be leading the field in the Eye of God.

For example, I ran into a sincere servant of God who reached out to help me. Now, being that I needed help from them, they ASSUMED that I was beneath them in the Eye of God. To add insult to injury, they also ASSUMED I ranked very, very low on the Spiritual Ranking Chart due to my unwavering humility and kindness while labeling me as being weak. When this was happening in real-time, I was astounded beyond measure, but I had to glean this information to feed God's sheep.

While lending a helping hand, this servant referred to me, Dr. Y. Bur, the WHY Doctor, as being the Blind Man sitting at the pool of Bethesda, along with other sick and disabled people, begging for someone to help him. This story is located in John 5:1-15. It is a great read regarding faith and healing. Now, getting back to the story, the person helping me saw themselves as being a Jesus prototype, as if I were begging for their help or healing.

Here is the deal: Although the need was there, I did not ask for help from them; they insistently offered help, and I accepted it. When they could not control the narrative or bully me, they resorted to insulting me due to their lack of discernment. Not realizing they were setting the Divine Cornerstone for this book, *Divine Dominion: As It Pleases God®*, to be written for a time such as this. The intersecting of two different mindsets (positive and negative) can indeed provide healing properties to those who are frustrated, hopeless, and needy.

The servant of God who openly mocked and judged me did not realize I was Spiritually Notched up from the Heavenly of Heavens to bring forth the *Tree of Life* to those willing to receive. So, you see, as Vessels of the Most High God, we do not know who He is using to TEST us or our fruits. On my watch, one thing is for sure: I am going to get the story! I have been entrusted to do so, and I do not back down from what people think of me; the show must go on, period!

But here is the kicker: this individual was the one outright begging for my help with things they do not have the capacity to do in this lifetime or the next. While at the same time, intentionally searching for a weak spot to target to use against me, to gain control over me, or to outright dominate me. So, the moral of the story...it was all about Projection and Deflection, when it should have been about REFLECTION to gain Divine Direction from the Heavenly of Heavens.

Tree of Life

As a Spiritual Being, whether you understand the process of Divine Dominion metaphorically or realistically, the *Tree of Life* is within you, containing soil, roots, seeds, branches, thorns, leaves, and fruits. In reality, all of these equate to your words, thoughts, beliefs, biases, desires, actions, reactions, attitudes, characteristics, experiences, and traumas. Ultimately, you are held accountable for developing, maintaining, and harvesting your Spiritual Fruits, ensuring they do not cause you to become a Tree of Death.

Embracing The Fruits of the Spirit

In addition, you are also accountable for allowing someone to taint your fruits as well. Romans 14:12 says, *"So then each of us shall give account of himself to God."* And, *"For each one shall bear his own load."* Galatians 6:5. *"But the fruit of the righteous is a tree of life, And he who wins souls is wise."* Proverbs 11:30. So, let us get to work!

Everyone thinks they are mature until they open their mouths, display actionable behaviors, or express their beliefs, biases, and conditioning. Even babies think they are grown, crawling around and acting like bosses. Do we lose this trait from then to now? Unfortunately, we do not...the seed is still there; it must mature and be adequately controlled, *As It Pleases God*. If not, it can become our worst nightmare or downfall.

Our Spiritual Maturity, or the lack thereof, is hidden in our fruits. Really? Yes, really! If our tree becomes diseased, it affects the fruit, causing Spiritual Immaturity and Defiance, even when we are all grown up and appear right in our own eyes. With Spiritual Maturity, the Fruits of the Spirit are the key to one's ability to contend with the enemy, keep both feet ten toes deep in the Kingdom, and have the Heaven on Earth Experience. How is this possible? God gives us the POWER to choose our fruits, so we should choose them wisely.

When bearing fruit, it gives birth to our *Tree of Life*. On the other hand, if we are bringing forth bad fruits, we become tied to the Tree of Death until the generational curse is lifted, reversed, or broken. How do we know the difference? It is noticed in our character and fruits.

We can tiptoe around the value of the *Tree of Life* we possess from within, but if it involves *The Spiritual Seal*, then we must pay attention. Why should we pay attention to this? Unfortunately, the enemy is banking on our ignorance or the denial of the Divine Truth as the Vicissitudes of Life toss us to and fro, trying to wake us up from a Spiritual Slumber. To be clear, even if we are full-fledged Believers of God Almighty, it does not stop the enemy from interjecting or planting negative, debauched, or diseased seeds.

The enemy will shoot his shots, and we must know how to cast them down, uproot, or cancel them while exhibiting self-control without uttering a mumbling word to the shotkeeper. The moment we open our mouths in the enemy's camp, we tell them how to take us down for the count. Listen, if we say nothing, they get nothing, right? Absolutely! If one has an issue in this area, repeat this before saying anything: *"Set a guard, O LORD, over my mouth; Keep watch over the door of my lips."* Psalm 141:3. If we need to repeat it, do so as often as needed until the temptation ceases.

If the *Tree of Life* has power, then where is it? It is hidden in plain sight! The *Tree of Life* is designed to bring about the AWARENESS of its positive or negative characteristics, allowing us to CHOOSE which fruits will dominate. Matthew 7:16 tells us hypothetically, 'A man is known by his fruits, which means the *Tree of Life* is within us.' Let me repeat, 'The *Tree of Life* resides within each and every one of us.'

The *Tree of Life* is designed to serve us from Genesis to Revelation. According to the Heavenly of Heavens, what we root and ground ourselves in determines the Tree, Fruits, Garden, Knowledge, Wisdom, and Level of Dominion.

How can we move in the Spirit of Excellence with good fruits when we are wounded, hurt, or distracted, fighting off the temptation of anger, bitterness, or resentment? Here is a list of tips, but not limited to such:

- ☐ If the desire to complain presents itself, look for the opportunity to respond with compliments. *"Pleasant words are like a honeycomb, sweetness to the soul and health to the bones."* Proverbs 16:24.

Embracing The Fruits of the Spirit

- [ ] The moment an urge to fight piques a desire from within, look for the opportunity to respond peacefully without becoming emotional or combative. Why? *"A soft answer turns away wrath, but a harsh word stirs up anger."* Proverbs 15:1.

- [ ] When someone speaks nasty, disrespectfully, or unruly to us, look for the opportunity to respond kindly without provocation. Why? *"The tongue of the wise uses knowledge rightly, but the mouth of fools pours forth foolishness."* Proverbs 15:2.

- [ ] When we are tempted to do wrong, look for the opportunity to do the right thing or take the high road. Why? *"The eyes of the LORD are in every place, beholding evil and the good."* Proverbs 15:3.

- [ ] When we feel as if we want to fuss, we must look for the opportunity to ask fact-finding, level-headed questions, getting the mental wheels for both parties turning in the right direction of righteousness. Why? *"A wholesome tongue is a Tree of Life, but perverseness in it breaks the Spirit."* Proverbs 15:4.

- [ ] When we feel the need to break someone down to the core, we must look for the opportunity to build them up, Mentally, Physically, Emotionally, and Spiritually. Why? *"There is one who speaks like a piercing of a sword, but the tongue of the wise promotes health."* Proverbs 12:18.

- [ ] When we are tempted to tell a lie or become a talebearer, look for the opportunity to exhibit wholesomeness or outright plead the 5th. Why? *"Better

Embracing The Fruits of the Spirit

is a dry morsel with quietness, than a house full of feasting with strife." Proverbs 17:1.

- [ ] When we are tempted to pay someone back, look for the opportunity to Bless them instead. Why? *"Her ways are ways of pleasantness, and all her paths are peace. She is a Tree of Life to those who take hold of her, and happy are all who retain her."* Proverbs 3:17-18.

- [ ] When we have a desire to become rebellious, we must look for the opportunity and the benefits associated with obedience. Why? *"The ear that hears the rebukes of life will abide among the wise. He who disdains instruction despises his own soul, but he who heeds rebuke gets understanding. The fear of the LORD is the instruction of wisdom, and before honor is humility."* Proverbs 15:31-33.

- [ ] When we begin to develop ulterior motives to violate the will of another, we must look for an opportunity to become an asset and not a liability. Why? *"Every way of a man is right in his own eyes, but the LORD weighs the hearts. To do righteousness and justice is more acceptable to the LORD than sacrifice."* Proverbs 21:2-3.

- [ ] When we feel as if we need to pick on, laugh at, or bully others, look for the opportunity to become a Blessing. Why? We do not know what God is doing in that person's life, nor do we know who they are ordained to become. More importantly, according to scripture, *"He who mocks the poor reproaches his Maker; He who is glad at calamity will not go unpunished."* Proverbs 17:5.

Embracing The Fruits of the Spirit

- ☐ When we encounter negativity, we must positively reverse it, creating a win-win. If we indulge in negativity, we bring it back to ourselves. Is this Biblical? It says, *"Whoever digs a pit will fall into it, and he who rolls a stone will have it roll back on him."* Proverbs 26:27.

With all due respect, it does not take a rocket scientist to simply pay attention. Often enough, we know what and who we are dealing with, but we are in denial because we do not want to know or deal with the truth.

What are the indications that we are in right standing with the *Tree of Life*? Listed below are a few indications, but not limited to such:

- ☐ When the Spirit of God is upon us.

- ☐ When the Anointing of God permeates our lives.

- ☐ When we can share the Word of God with no strings attached, without being ashamed of the Gospel, and not beating others over the head with it.

- ☐ When we can share the Goodness of God, building up those who are down.

- ☐ When we are humble in our approach to healing the broken-hearted, wounded, and abandoned.

- ☐ When we can share the Freedom of the Kingdom, along with the free will liberations we are all entitled to.

- ☐ When we make Spiritual Decrees that carry weight in the Kingdom.

Embracing The Fruits of the Spirit

- ☐ When we do not seek revenge on those who do not believe, while remaining kind, compassionate, understanding, and exhibiting Christlike Character.

- ☐ When we share the Fruits of the Spirit with all we come in contact with.

- ☐ When we can reverse negative outcomes into a win-win, while keeping a Positive Mental Mindset.

- ☐ When we give thanks and praise to God for all things, even when we cannot have our way.

- ☐ When we grow and sow back into the Kingdom, bearing much fruit in the Spirit of Righteousness, ensuring God is glorified.

In putting all things into their proper perspective, here is the scripture we need to know when praying for, ushering in, or regrafting our *Tree of Life*. *"The Spirit of the Lord GOD is upon Me, Because the LORD has anointed Me to preach good tidings to the poor; He has sent Me to heal the brokenhearted, to proclaim liberty to the captives, and the opening of the prison to those who are bound; to proclaim the acceptable year of the LORD, and the day of vengeance of our God; to comfort all who mourn, to console those who mourn in Zion, to give them beauty for ashes, the oil of joy for mourning, the garment of praise for the spirit of heaviness; that they may be called trees of righteousness, the planting of the LORD, that He may be glorified."* Isaiah 61:1-3.

Embracing The Fruits of the Spirit

The Fruitful Prophet

Our soulish psyche, or our soulish nature, tends to hide things from us to remain in charge, causing us to forget who we are in or out of the Kingdom, or downplay the Divine Prophecies over our lives. What if we are not a Prophet? Then my question would be, 'What if we are *The Fruitful Prophet?*' Unbeknown to most, according to our *Divine Dominion: As It Pleases God®*, we are all Prophets over our own lives, spreading outwardly; we are simply Spiritually Blind, Deaf, or Mute to it until we are Spiritually Awakened.

How do we make *The Fruitful Prophet* make sense, especially when we are Believers already? We are Spiritual Beings having a human experience. In short, in *Divine Dominion: As It Pleases God®*, we have the Genetic Blueprinted Prophecy within our DNA, knowing what to do, why to do it, how to do it, where to do it, and with whom. We only need to gain Divine Access, *As It Pleases Him*.

For the record, before going any further, the Kingdom of God, the Word of God, the Holy Spirit, and the Blood of Jesus can take care of themselves because they are ABSOLUTE without any false expectations! Furthermore, they are all crystal clear about their intents, period!

To bring forth *The Fruitful Prophet* or become an authentic REPRESENTATIVE of the Kingdom, we must be able to live by the WORD without wavering, develop Christlike Character, and feed God's sheep using the Fruits of the Spirit, *As It Pleases Him*. Seems easy enough, right? So, why are we not doing it? Could it be the silent acts of idolatry? Could it be that we are proclaiming to be a Prophet while not becoming *The Fruitful Prophet* over our own lives? Could it be...Could it be...

All jokes aside, for the record, God will never give us more information about or into the lives of others than He would give us about ourselves. Simply put, if we know more about others, it says a lot about us. What does it say? For this one, let us take it to Scripture: Matthew 7:3-5 says, *"And why do you look at the speck in your brother's eye, but do not consider the plank in your own eye? Or how can you say to your brother, 'Let me remove the speck from your eye'; and look, a plank is in your own eye? Hypocrite! First remove the plank from your own eye, and then you will see clearly to remove the speck from your brother's eye."*

In the Kingdom, we are required to KNOW THYSELF. Above all, self-examination and awareness of one's own character, motivations, desires, and weaknesses are important to be in Divine Relations with God, *Spirit to Spirit*. If not, we can 'get got' by the enemy's wiles by NOT being able to counteract evil, negativity, and debauchery. Here is what 2 Corinthians 13:5 says, *"Examine yourselves as to whether you are in the faith. Test yourselves. Do you not know yourselves, that Jesus Christ is in you? — unless indeed you are disqualified."*

According to the Heavenly of Heavens, there are many of us walking in the faith, not realizing we are disqualified in the Eye of God. Essentially, disqualification can happen to anyone, even I was once disqualified. Yes, me, Dr. Y. Bur, The WHY Doctor. It was through this phase that I learned the difference between the two. Now, I am not here to point the finger; I just have a few questions for you:

- ☐ Are your motivations pure?
- ☐ What are your thoughts? Are they positive or negative?
- ☐ Are you truly aligned with God's Spiritual Principles?
- ☐ Are you really faithful?
- ☐ Are you authentically loving?
- ☐ Are you behaving kindly?
- ☐ Are you holding a hidden grudge?
- ☐ Are you being hateful or biased?
- ☐ Are you very divisive?

Embracing The Fruits of the Spirit

- ☐ Do you engage in things to manipulate others?
- ☐ Do you lie a lot?
- ☐ How many masks do you put on daily?

These questions give us a lead-in on things that can silently get us disqualified while appearing right in our own eyes and looking beyond surface-level stuff. Furthermore, if we desire to become *The Fruitful Prophet*, we must behave like one. We are held to a higher standard and accountability than most; plus, God is evaluating our heart and mind postures. So do not think for a minute that He does not know what's up...He KNOWS.

In addition, I am appalled by the so-called Prophets who have absolutely zero knowledge about their reason for being or knowing absolutely nothing about their Predestined Blueprint. Yet, they get offended when we say the word, so-called.

What is a so-called Prophet in the Eye of God? It is a person proclaiming to be a Prophet of God (The Messenger of God) with zero Spiritual Fruits to sustain the title, and has misapplied or misinterpreted its meaning. These individuals claim to hold the Prophetic Mantle but often lack the accompanying Spiritual Fruits that should substantiate their title. To be clear, they may not be FALSE PROPHETS, so to speak, because they have good intentions to obey God. But they do not have all the information or the details on the proper Spiritual Protocols, *As It Pleases Him*. So, instead of getting offended, we should want to get it right!

Can God not use anyone? Of course, He can. Still, we cannot make up our own rules, expecting God to obey us...unfortunately, it does not work like that! Here are a few characteristics of a so-called Prophet, but not limited to such:

Embracing The Fruits of the Spirit

- ☐ They lack authenticity.
- ☐ There is an absence of the Fruits of the Spirit.
- ☐ They proclaim authority but lack obedience to it.
- ☐ They possess master manipulation skills.
- ☐ They commercialize Faith for Profit.
- ☐ They capitalize on the weaknesses of others.
- ☐ They will only lead and not follow.
- ☐ They blur the lines between God and mankind.
- ☐ They are very rebellious or hot-headed.
- ☐ They are super pompous.
- ☐ They engage in the exploitation of others.
- ☐ They are extremely unforgiving or unrepentant.
- ☐ They only learn from the people above them while missing the lessons from the people beneath them.

The discrepancy between the CLAIM of a Prophet and the CHARACTER of a Prophet is on the Spiritual Table. And, if they do not match up, *As It Pleases God*, then something has to change, and it begins right now! A True Prophet, in the Eye of God, would ideally exemplify the Fruits of the Spirit, demonstrating their deep FAITH and COMMITMENT through their actions and demeanor.

Listed below are a few step-by-step ways to interact with God to become *The Fruitful Prophet*, but not limited to such, especially when it comes down to exhibiting the Fruits of the Spirit and Christlike Character:

- ☐ '*Speak*' to Him in His Language.
- ☐ Give '*Thanks*' to Him in all things.
- ☐ Acknowledge His '*Goodness.*'
- ☐ Ask and give '*Mercy*' continuously.
- ☐ Petition for Him to '*Save Us.*'
- ☐ Surrender to '*Gatherings*' as a team player.

Embracing The Fruits of the Spirit

- ☐ Ask for *'Deliverance'* from ourselves and others.
- ☐ *'Worship'* Him in Spirit and Truth.
- ☐ Understand and accept the *'Blessings'* to become a Blessing to others.
- ☐ *'Recognize'* the signs of the time.
- ☐ Spiritually Seal our petitions with the word, *'Amen.'*
- ☐ Give Him the *'Praise'* for all things.

Am I pulling for straws here? Absolutely not. Therefore, let us align accordingly, *"Oh, give thanks to the LORD, for He is good! For His mercy endures forever. And say, 'Save us, O God of our salvation; gather us together, and deliver us from the Gentiles, to give thanks to Your holy name, to triumph in Your praise.' Blessed be the LORD God of Israel from everlasting to everlasting! And all the people said, 'Amen!' and praised the LORD."* 1 Chronicles 16:34-36.

How do we deal with ourselves when attempting to become *The Fruitful Prophet*, according to the Heavenly of Heavens? Listed below are a few items to help us, *As It Pleases God*, but not limited to such:

- ☐ When becoming *The Fruitful Prophet*, we must position ourselves in the Blessings of God without wallowing in the negative.

- ☐ When becoming *The Fruitful Prophet*, we must call upon the Spiritual Counsel of the Holy Spirit.

- ☐ When becoming *The Fruitful Prophet*, we must set a guard over our hearts and minds, redirecting any form of darkness into LIGHT.

Embracing The Fruits of the Spirit

- ☐ When becoming *The Fruitful Prophet*, we must understand that the Cycle of Life will work on our behalf if we incorporate God into the equation.

- ☐ When becoming *The Fruitful Prophet*, we must know God avails, unveils, and prevails in all things in alignment with our Divine Blueprint.

- ☐ When becoming *The Fruitful Prophet*, we must position ourselves to sit on the Right Hand of God, with the Fruits of the Spirit and Christlike Character as our Platform of Righteousness.

- ☐ When becoming *The Fruitful Prophet*, we must keep ourselves in a happy state of being from the outside while rejoicing with our inner joy, intentionally spreading outwardly, and making this world a better place to live.

- ☐ When becoming *The Fruitful Prophet*, we must put the lust of the eyes, the lust of the flesh, and the pride of life under the subjection of the Holy Spirit while using the Blood of Jesus as a covering to safeguard our restful elements of hope.

- ☐ When becoming *The Fruitful Prophet*, we must avoid wayward, dubious, or destructive behaviors negatively impacting our attitude, mindset, and demeanor, spoiling our fruits and character.

- ☐ When becoming *The Fruitful Prophet*, we must live by example toward the path of righteousness, correcting the correctable in total transparency.

Embracing The Fruits of the Spirit

- ☐ When becoming *The Fruitful Prophet*, we must represent the Kingdom with our Heaven on Earth Experiences.

- ☐ When becoming *The Fruitful Prophet*, we must be willing to live the Good Life while showing others how to do likewise, with lasting benefits, keeping our Bloodline engulfed with the Divine Provisions of the Kingdom.

According to the Heavenly of Heavens, if we take one step at a time, we can overcome anything; however, before we move on, for the above instructions, here is the scripture: "*I will bless the LORD who has given me counsel; my heart also instructs me in the night seasons. I have set the LORD always before me; because He is at my right hand I shall not be moved. Therefore, my heart is glad, and my glory rejoices; my flesh also will rest in hope. For You will not leave my soul in Sheol, nor will You allow Your Holy One to see corruption. You will show me the path of life; in Your presence is fullness of joy; at Your right hand are pleasures forevermore.*" Psalm 16:7-11.

According to the Heavenly of Heavens, there is Hidden Wisdom in all things, especially in scripture, making it befitting to our situation, understanding, or Kingdom Revelation, *As It Pleases God*. All we need to do is make use of it, *As It Pleases Him*, but no worries, the next chapter will share how to maximize this process from His Divine Perspective.

When Spiritually Engaging in such a manner, in our evolving phase of our *Spirit to Spirit* Relationship and our Developmental Mastery to become *The Fruitful Prophet*, we must incorporate a few items to avoid mediocrity, but not limited to such:

Embracing The Fruits of the Spirit

- ☐ Do not go around babbling or popping off with little or no self-control. *"A serpent may bite when it is not charmed; The babbler is no different."* Ecclesiastes 10:11.

- ☐ Be kind in our words, thoughts, actions, body language, and beliefs. *"The words of a wise man's mouth are gracious, but the lips of a fool shall swallow him up."* Ecclesiastes 10:12.

- ☐ Decline to engage in foolery to destroy the innocent or guilty with an ungoverned tongue. *"The words of his mouth begin with foolishness, and the end of his talk is raving madness."* Ecclesiastes 10:13.

- ☐ Avoid becoming a fast talker, manipulator, shifting the blame, or pointing fingers to avoid taking responsibility for our actions, thoughts, beliefs, corrupt character traits, or debauched fruits. *"A fool also multiplies words. No man knows what is to be; Who can tell him what will be after him?"* Ecclesiastes 10:14.

- ☐ Avoid engaging in vain actions, reactions, thoughts, or beliefs, wasting precious time and energy as a know-it-all. *"The labor of fools wearies them, for they do not even know how to go to the city!"* Ecclesiastes 10:15.

- ☐ We must use our Spiritual Gifts without being lazy, unfruitful, ungrateful, or negatively spilling over with regret. *"Because of laziness the building decays, And through idleness of hands the house leaks."* Ecclesiastes 10:18.

- ☐ We must understand that Divine Provisions are available for the tangibilities of our Heaven on Earth Experience. Yet, we must depend upon our Heavenly

Embracing The Fruits of the Spirit

Father for the Spiritual Intangibilities of the Kingdom for the things money cannot buy, developing a balance between the seen and unseen. *"A feast is made for laughter, and wine makes merry; but money answers everything."* Ecclesiastes 10:19.

- ☐ We must avoid broadcasting known, unknown, or secretive negativity or curses over the lives of others, especially in the Name of Jesus, when it is UNWARRANTED or when operating in the Spirit of Error. *"Do not curse the king, even in your thought; Do not curse the rich, even in your bedroom; for a bird of the air may carry your voice, and a bird in flight may tell the matter."* Ecclesiastes 10:20.

What is the purpose of knowing these Spiritual Principles? According to the Heavenly of Heavens, these are a few of the most unjustifiable and overlooked developmental factors in the Spiritual Classroom of real life, causing the Vicissitudes of Life to put us in a Spiritual Timeout.

Is it not God's job to place us in a Spiritual Timeout? Yes, it is His responsibility. However, He may have already set in motion HIGHER Spiritual or Universal Laws responsible for carrying out their Divine Mission, such as Seedtime and Harvest, the Law of Gravity, the Law of Divine Oneness, and so on, that will not deviate from doing what they are designed to do unless He says so.

Now, unlike mankind, we deviate from our Divine Blueprint, doing whatever, whenever, and however. While at the same time, thinking we can cheat the Divine System without counteracting a Lesser Law with a Higher one, be it Spiritual or Universal. As a result, it returns to teach us a valuable lesson in due time, contributing to our internal,

Embracing The Fruits of the Spirit

external, or hidden dullness, stiffneckness, lukewarmness, or mediocrity. Really? Yes, really. The Spiritual Pushback is no joke; thus, making *Spiritual Maintenance of the Psyche* our best option in the Eye of God!

Can we really cheat the Divine System of God? The answer is NO. However, we can make our best attempts or take shortcuts by going to the dark side. But here again, we have Spiritual Laws, Principles, and Protocols governing it. Of course, we can get a sneak peek into the Spiritual Realm because we are Spiritual Beings having a human experience. If we are not properly equipped, *As It Pleases God*, or we have a desire to override His Divine Will, we can open a door to some sort of possession, obsession, or turmoil for disrupting the Spiritual Balance with unauthorized access. As a result, it can turn *The Fruitful Prophet* into an unprofitable servant really quickly.

Listen to me and listen well. The truth is, the Spirit of Darkness does not play fair; it plays dirty! I mean, really, really dirty, especially with those who are pompous, ignorant, unauthentic, desperate, and disobedient, seeking immediate rewards and personal gain. Realistically, the quest for power, importance, influence, likes, and clicks often drives individuals to explore or engage in the unthinkable when seeking shortcuts to success. If you are dealing with this at this present moment, *Spiritual Maintenance of the Psyche* is calling your name right now. Will you answer?

In *Divine Dominion: As It Pleases God*®, true empowerment, understanding, and growth do not ascend from evading Spiritual Principles, Laws, and Protocols. According to the Heavenly of Heavens, it comes from ALIGNING with them to glean the Divine Wisdom from the Ancient of Days.

Chapter Ten
Spiritual Maintenance of the Psyche

In our Spiritual Journey through real life in real-time, the *Spiritual Maintenance of the Psyche* is a vital aspect that influences our well-being, relationships, mindsets, and sense of purpose. Uncommon to all else, the science of the psyche transcends mere psychological analysis, holding steadfast to the Spiritual Dimensions associated with its manifesto. In the same way that we develop our own personalized plans, the psyche does as well; however, it cannot override our Predestined Blueprinted Mission without our agreement.

As we were created with intention and purpose, we must align ourselves accordingly, even if we fail to understand our reason for being as of yet. When embarking on the *Spiritual Maintenance of the Psyche*, we must understand the psyche from God's Divine Perspective to properly align it with Divine Principles, Laws, and Protocols. Is this real? It is as real as the Breath of Life!

The psyche is the soulish realm or core of man that is comprised of the invisible edifices of the mind, will, desires,

Spiritual Maintenance of the Psyche

and emotions that can be symbolically separated from each other.

For example, the soul is the invisible core or heart of our being, residing within the pit of the belly, similar to a fruit having a seed in the middle. In my opinion, it is more like a file cabinet, storing everything, including our intentions, traumas, hurts, pains, unforgiveness, true feelings, our WHY, and hiding stuff at its whim. In fact, this is where we experience the sinking feeling when shocked or the tenacious butterflies when nervous.

What is the way to differentiate between the soul and the mind? They are not in the same place and have different functions. Plus, it is possible to sell our souls and still be in the right frame of mind. Nevertheless, please allow me to align: *"For what profit is it to a man if he gains the whole world, and loses his own soul? Or what will a man give in exchange for his soul?"* Matthew 16:26. Then again, we can lose our minds and still have our souls intact.

Thus, if we lose the Breath of Life to our souls in the earthly realm, the mind cannot remain. The bottom line is that if we lose our minds and souls simultaneously, we will cease to exist without life support. Without life support or a will to live, according to Spiritual Laws, the body must return to the dust, and the Spirit must return to its MAKER. Blasphemy, right? Wrong. *"Then the dust will return to the earth as it was, And the spirit will return to God who gave it."* Ecclesiastes 12:7. *"For what happens to the sons of men also happens to animals; one thing befalls them: as one dies, so dies the other. Surely, they all have one breath; man has no advantage over animals, for all is vanity. All go to one place: all are from the dust, and all return to dust."* Ecclesiastes 3:19-20.

The Breath of Life connects us to this Heaven on Earth Experience. How is this possible, especially when knowing nothing about this type of connection? Unfortunately, this is how the enemy deceives and prevents us from connecting to

Spiritual Maintenance of the Psyche

the psyche as we should. *"God, who made the world and everything in it, since He is Lord of heaven and earth, does not dwell in temples made with hands. Nor is He worshiped with men's hands, as though He needed anything, since He gives to all life, breath, and all things. For in Him we live and move and have our being."* Acts 17:24-25, 28.

In all reality, the Breath of Life is the most crucial element of the soul that we take for granted. Without it, unfortunately, it means lights out, regardless of who we are, why we are, what we have accomplished, or how much money we have! Know this: *"The Spirit of God has made me, And the breath of the Almighty gives me life."* Job 33:4.

Here is the Divine Decree: *"Let everything that has breath praise the Lord. Praise the Lord!"* Psalm 150:6. If we use the Breath of Life to praise everything besides the MAKER of it, the Cycle of Life will attempt to reset or heal itself by any means necessary. Frankly, it will do what it is designed to do and invoke the VICISSITUDES within the Mind, Body, and Soul. Then again, it may place us in a cycle of déjà vu.

In the Eye of God, we do not have to be tossed around by the enemy for not knowing how we are created from a Divine Perspective. From a Theological Standpoint, even if the enemy tries to paint a narrative of us being mistake-prone or unworthy, we must continue to move forward in the Spirit of Excellence. Why? One of the greatest weapons the enemy will use will surround the elements of deception. If we fall for the okey doke, deceiving ourselves, doubt will begin to plague us with its negative attributes while bringing all of its negative cousins along.

Why must we know about the mind, soul, will, emotions, or the totality of the psyche? If we do not know, we give the enemy an opportunity to get into our heads instead of being able to get them out of it or justifiably flipping the script, *As It Pleases God.*

Spiritual Maintenance of the Psyche

So, let us break the psyche down to ensure we get everything that rightly belongs to us without beating around the bush.

The Mind of Mankind

The mind is a hidden, invisible edifice residing within the core of the brain that cannot be seen, touched, felt, tasted, or traced to preserve the SECRETS of mankind. Why is it hidden, especially as Believers? First, if it were locatable, mankind would attempt to alter or extract the Divine Secrets, overriding God Almighty. Plus, He has to reserve something for Himself.

Secondly, this portal is how we communicate with ourselves through thinking, chatting, analyzing, feeling, seeing, tasting, smelling, touching, calculating, and so on. This process is our way of downloading or rejecting information before inputting it into the soul at our discretion. Pictorially, this is similar to choosing whether we are going to deposit money in the teller machine or not.

Thirdly, it is what we use to EXTRACT and CONVERT information, positively or negatively. In addition, it is through the mind that we counteract negatives into positives or vice versa, creating a win-win or lose-lose situation before making it into reality. Remember, our actions do not make it into reality unless they go through the mind first, through a thought, idea, or contemplation.

Lastly, this is where we embrace PEACEFULNESS before it makes it to the soul based upon the Divine Authority and Blood of Jesus. *"And the peace of God, which surpasses all understanding, will guard your hearts and minds through Christ Jesus."* Philippians 4:7.

In reality, the mind is linked to our consciousness (awareness or alertness) with three main components:

Spiritual Maintenance of the Psyche

- [ ] The conscious mind.
- [ ] The preconscious mind.
- [ ] The unconscious mind.

How do we know the difference? The conscious mind is the part of the mind that is aware of one's thoughts, surroundings, and sensations at any given moment. Frankly, this is how we perceive and interact with the world around us.

The preconscious mind refers to the part of the mind that lies between the conscious mind and the unconscious mind. In all simplicity, this contains thoughts and memories that are not currently at the forefront of our consciousness. Still, it can be easily accessed and brought to the surface when needed with TRIGGERS. In my opinion, this is similar to jogging our memory with pictures, notes, words, calendars, journals, or connecting the dots.

The unconscious mind contains the thoughts, memories, and desires that are not directly accessible to the conscious mind due to repression, denial, trauma, or forgotten information. However, they can still influence our behaviors and emotions because they are filed within the soulish realm or in the Bloodline, shaping our character, thoughts, words, beliefs, biases, and fruits.

In addition, the mind is what the conscience (Spiritual Compass) uses to communicate with us through our senses, giving us glimpses or painting pictures. Unfortunately, this is where most get confused. Being conscious (keeping our memories in place) is not the same as the conscience (keeping our integrity intact).

Plus, this is how God communicates with us from the Heavenly of Heavens, speaking and giving mental playbacks, information, or visions.

Above all, it is through the mind that we HEAR God. Yes, I said it! Do not be deceived; in the Realm of the Spirit, our

Spiritual Maintenance of the Psyche

Spiritual Eye, Ear, and Voice will be filtered through the MIND. Therefore, if our mind is not right, we will receive mixed signals, information, and downloads. To the point where we think it is God, but it is not Him speaking...it is the conscience, the enemy, or deceptiveness trying to gain our agreement. The noise or the frequent chatter of our own thoughts or external influences makes the enemy's job easy. If we do not reel this ruckus in, it will cloud our sense of good judgment and hearing the AUTHENTIC Voice of God, *Spirit to Spirit*.

How is it possible to hear God through the mind? We all have this capacity prewired in the brain, but most often, we do not know how to use it, *As It Pleases Him*. Then again, due to the lack of understanding, we find a way to mystify or make it spooky when it is designed to protect the Spirit Man residing within.

To operate this Spiritual Component of the brain effectively, we must clear the negativity to DISCERN the Voice of God properly. For example, if we are overwhelmed by fear, doubt, anger, unforgiveness, hatefulness, or confusion, we can inadvertently misinterpret the messages we receive. Without proper *Spiritual Maintenance of the Psyche*, it becomes all too easy to confuse our own biased conscience, the whispers of the enemy, or the deceptive seeds from the world with the Voice of God.

Unfortunately, this is God's Genetic Code that cannot be broken...this is why the Bible tells us to guard the MIND and TONGUE. If we do, *As It Pleases Him*, we will always have a WAY OUT without having to say one word! Really? Yes, really! *"No temptation has overtaken you except such as is common to man; but God is faithful, who will not allow you to be tempted beyond what you are able, but with the temptation will also make the way of escape, that you may be able to bear it."* 1 Corinthians 10:13.

Spiritual Maintenance of the Psyche

The One-Up

Now, getting to the will and emotions of man are basically our choosers and feelers that provoke or calm both, making us obedient or disobedient, good or bad, right or wrong, just or unjust, and so on. For this reason, we need the Fruits of the Spirit to guide us before allowing negativity to penetrate the Mind or Soul.

For the record, to eliminate all the confusion among Believers, please allow me to give you a ONE-UP. According to the Heavenly of Heavens, the soul is not the head or brain, nor does it reside there. Thus, the mind is not the soul, nor does it reside in the belly, but they work together in concordance with the soul as the psyche. Pictorially, this is similar to the hand, which has a palm, fingers, and a thumb—they all work together as the hand, with different functions as ONE. Although understanding them can become complex without Spirituality, but for the *As It Pleases God Movement*, I will break it down with downright simplicity.

The psyche of man is nothing to joke around with...it has a vice grip with adjustable jaws that will not release us until we learn how to contend, *As It Pleases God*. The relationship between the psyche and God Almighty is a deeply personal and subjective one, shaped by one's individual beliefs, experiences, traumas, choices, conditioning, biases, environment, actions, thoughts, words, and perspectives.

It is the psyche that warrants us to go back and forth between good and evil, right and wrong, just and unjust, positive and negative, and so on, causing us to become internally confused or exhausted while not knowing or understanding the real difference between them.

How can we not know the difference between right and wrong or good and evil? When we are blocked by jealousy, envy, pride, greed, coveting, competitiveness, ungratefulness, hatefulness, rudeness, and debauchery, we tend to get

Spiritual Maintenance of the Psyche

confused. All of these attributes cover up our something else, allowing the psyche to remain in control of the Mind, Body, and Soul as the Spirit lays dormant. Meanwhile, appearing to have it all together in the public eye, but behind closed doors, we let it all hang out.

In the Eye of God, the psyche of man is an interconnected system of the Mind, Body, and Soul that influences and is influenced by all aspects of our being. Thus, we cannot correct one without the other, and if we break one, it affects the other, requiring BALANCE between them all. Proverbs 23:7 says, *"For as he thinks in his heart, so is he."*

For example, ignoring the body can lead to physical illness, addictions, habits, and lust, which can, in turn, affect the mind and soul. Similarly, disregarding the mind can lead to mental illness, confusion, and scatteredness, which can affect the body and soul. With this DNAtical interconnection of the psyche, it is often misunderstood, misinterpreted, ignored, or underestimated while fighting for its territory.

Why would the psyche fight for territory? It connects us to the SPIRIT. Once the Spirit is AWAKENED, *As It Pleases God*, the psyche can be tamed! *"For the word of God is living and powerful, and sharper than any two-edged sword, piercing even to the division of soul and spirit, and of joints and marrow, and is a discerner of the thoughts and intents of the heart."* Hebrews 4:12. If the Spirit is not AWAKENED to become ONE with the Holy Spirit, then the psyche remains in control, doing whatever, whenever, however, wherever, whyever, and with whomever, lacking self-control or resisting any form of restraints.

To add insult to injury, it is the human psyche that attempts to second-guess God or make Him appear overbearing, defiant, or violent by deflecting. How does the psyche deflect? Through mental chatter, negative thoughts, vile perceptions, player hating, adverse mental playback, rehashing trauma, and so on. There is no one way when it

Spiritual Maintenance of the Psyche

comes to the playing field of the psyche; it will use any and everything to remain in control.

Warring Members

In *Divine Dominion: As It Pleases God*®, it is imperative to know about the Spiritual Duality relating to good and evil, right and wrong, just and unjust, positive and negative, and so on. If we do not know the difference, we can 'get got' and turn on ourselves without knowing it. For this reason, 2 Corinthians 10:5 advises us: *"For the weapons of our warfare are not carnal but mighty in God for pulling down strongholds, casting down arguments and every high thing that exalts itself against the knowledge of God, bringing every thought into captivity to the obedience of Christ, and being ready to punish all disobedience when your obedience is fulfilled."* 2 Corinthians 10:4-6.

Now the question remains, 'Is God violent?' No, but the seed of our psyche is, and He will allow violent things to happen! In the Beginning, God did not create us in violence; it was allowed into the psyche through the Adam and Eve Experience.

Violence is carried out through mankind, and so is Divine Peace. For this reason, we must tame our psyche, *As It Pleases God* and not to please ourselves. If not, the warring of our members is inevitable. Blasphemy, right? Wrong. *"Where do wars and fights come from among you? Do they not come from your desires for pleasure that war in your members? You lust and do not have. You murder and covet and cannot obtain. You fight and war. Yet you do not have because you do not ask. You ask and do not receive, because you ask amiss, that you may spend it on your pleasures. Adulterers and adulteresses! Do you not know that friendship with the world is enmity with God? Whoever therefore wants to be a friend of the world makes himself an enemy of God."* James 4:1-4.

Spiritual Maintenance of the Psyche

How do we recognize a violent psyche or an enemy of God? It varies from person to person, situation to situation, or mindset to mindset. Still, the first indicator will reside in their FRUITS and WORDS. The second is Spiritual Discernment; without it, we will get things wrong or walk around like we have two left shoes. Why? *"But the natural man does not receive the things of the Spirit of God, for they are foolishness to him; nor can he know them, because they are spiritually discerned. But he who is spiritual judges all things, yet he himself is rightly judged by no one."* 1 Corinthians 2:14-15.

But we must pay attention and listen with God at the forefront, preferably with our Blueprint in hand or operating in total obedience to the Will of God. *"And let the peace of God rule in your hearts, to which also you were called in one body; and be thankful."* Colossians 3:15.

Regardless of how we feel about ourselves or the *Spiritual Maintenance of the Psyche*, or whether we understand it or not, we must place the Holy Trinity first. In addition, we must also cover ourselves with the Blood of Jesus, allow the Holy Spirit to guide us, and use the Fruits of the Spirit while praying, repenting, and forgiving in our *Spirit to Spirit* Relations.

What if we are not perfect in our walk? No one is perfect, and we are all on a learning curve and are a work-in-progress. So, *"Do not fear those who kill the body but cannot kill the soul. But rather fear Him who is able to destroy both soul and body in hell."* Matthew 10:28.

In the *Spiritual Maintenance of the Psyche*, now that you know about the Divine Breakdown, please allow the heart and mind posture of obedience and humility to reign with *The Tutor of Mankind* working on your behalf. *"Now may the God of peace Himself sanctify you completely; and may your whole spirit, soul, and body be preserved blameless at the coming of our Lord Jesus Christ."* 1 Thessalonians 5:23.

Spiritual Maintenance of the Psyche

The Tutor of Mankind

When it comes down to the Kingdom, we are not an overnight sensation; we must be trained, equipped, tested, and commissioned. In the Eye of God, what works for one person may not necessarily work for another, so we need *The Tutor of Mankind* to step in on our behalf.

Just as athletes undergo rigorous training to achieve peak performance, we as Believers are required to invest time in Spiritual Discipline and Growth. However, Spiritual Training can take many forms, like reading, studying scripture, documenting, and so on. Still, when we incorporate *The Tutor of Mankind*, which is the Holy Spirit, He brings about a load of Spiritual Benefits. Listed below are a few profound BENEFITS to embrace, but not limited to such:

- ☐ When *The Tutor of Mankind* begins to teach us, we will experience placement growth, becoming fruitful from the inside out.

- ☐ When *The Tutor of Mankind* begins to teach us, we will experience a peaceful rest that is indeed beyond human understanding.

- ☐ When *The Tutor of Mankind* begins to teach us, we will have access to Supernatural Wisdom, gaining access to the Secrets, Mysteries, and Principles of the Kingdom to create a Divine Flow.

- ☐ When *The Tutor of Mankind* begins to teach us, we will have Divine Understanding, keeping us 'In The Spiritual Know.'

Spiritual Maintenance of the Psyche

- ☐ When *The Tutor of Mankind* begins to teach us, we will have the Spirit of Counsel, guiding and advising on all things Spiritual and earthly.

- ☐ When *The Tutor of Mankind* begins to teach us, we will have the Spirit of Knowledge that is teaching, training, and strengthening us on a moment-by-moment basis.

- ☐ When *The Tutor of Mankind* begins to teach us, we will have a fearful reverence of God, keeping us humble, respectful, repenting, and prayerful.

Here is the scripture to align some of the *Stomping Ground* benefits: "*There shall come forth a Rod from the stem of Jesse, and a Branch shall grow out of his roots. The Spirit of the LORD shall rest upon Him, the Spirit of Wisdom and Understanding, the Spirit of Counsel and Might, The Spirit of knowledge and of the fear of the LORD.*" Isaiah 11:1-2. What is the purpose of these benefits? They will help to avoid bringing shame to our names and the Kingdom while polishing our Fruits of the Spirit and Christlike Character to create excellent people skills.

Once again, *The Tutor of Mankind* is the Holy Spirit; however, according to the Heavenly of Heavens, we must first develop a Spiritual Relationship with the Holy Trinity (The Father, Son, and Holy Spirit).

Why are we required to connect to the Holy Trinity? The Holy Spirit is a package deal. If not, we can engage in a Spirit of a different kind, which is unholy or dark in nature. Therefore, we must be specific, and for this book or writings, we are only dealing with the Heavenly of Heavens bringing our Earthen Vessels into the LIGHT, period.

When embarking upon a *Spirit to Spirit* Relationship, we do not have to memorize scriptures; we simply need to know

Spiritual Maintenance of the Psyche

where to gain access to them. Why do we need to know this? Most people shy away from reading or understanding the Word of God because they cannot remember it or how to access scripture. However, on behalf of the Heavenly of Heavens, it is okay not to remember, as long as we are willing to use the Word of God as a Spiritual Compass and document accordingly.

In the same way that we Google everything else, positively or negatively, we are able to Google scriptures as well. It is perfectly okay to research scriptures, especially when it comes down to our Salvation.

In the Kingdom, it is not about what we know; it is about how well we listen, learn, and obey, *Spirit to Spirit*. Additionally, it is also about whether or not we are documenting what we know and what is given to us, *Spirit to Spirit*, to refer back to or share when the time is right.

To be clear, Google cannot save us, nor is it a ticket into Heaven, but it is a tool helping us to help ourselves, giving us the ability to cross-reference what we do not understand or pinpoint the Promises of God. Therefore, it behooves us to use it to Decree the Decreeable or Denounce the Denounceable while *The Tutor of Mankind* trains us in Kingdom Protocols and Principles. Listed below are a few Spiritual Decrees to preface our prayer with, but not limited to such:

- ☐ We must avoid deceitfulness within ourselves and others, or indulging in deceitful measures, while redirecting all things toward righteousness in prayer, using our inside or outside voice. We do not need to be heard while sending up a justifiable prayer amid whatever or whomever. All we need to do is make sure we are not praying amiss, intimidating others, lying to ourselves, or behaving pompously. Here is the Spiritual Decree to preface our prayer: *"Hear a just cause,*

Spiritual Maintenance of the Psyche

O LORD, attend to my cry; give ear to my prayer which is not from deceitful lips." Psalm 17:1.

- ☐ We must avoid seeking revenge, allowing God to take the wheel regarding any form of injustice while redirecting our focus to the positive, productive, and fruitful. Here is the Spiritual Decree to preface our prayer: *"Let my vindication come from Your presence; let Your eyes look on the things that are upright."* Psalm 17:2.

- ☐ We must set a guard over our mouths at all times, exercising great caution about what we are speaking over ourselves and others on a moment-by-moment basis. How is this possible? It is developed through having our *Mindset* locked on doing and becoming righteous in all things, knowing we are being watched. Here is the Spiritual Decree to preface our prayer: *"You have tested my heart; You have visited me in the night; You have tried me and have found nothing; I have purposed that my mouth shall not transgress. Concerning the works of men, By the word of Your lips, I have kept away from the paths of the destroyer."* Psalm 17:3-4.

- ☐ We must stay on course with the Spiritual Blueprint set forth by the Heavenly of Heavens without having all types of distractions causing us to lose focus, jump the track with negativity, or our psyche to become further traumatized. What if we do not know the Blueprint? Then, it is best to get rid of the distractions, set aside some alone time, and focus while developing a Mind Map of the desires of the heart and Awakening our Spirit to become ONE with the Holy Spirit. Here is the Spiritual Decree to preface our prayer: *"Uphold my steps in Your paths, that my footsteps may not slip."* Psalm 17:5.

Spiritual Maintenance of the Psyche

- [ ] We must communicate with God in a *Spirit to Spirit* Connection. How do we go about doing so? The same way we speak to our parents, siblings, friends, husband, wife, children, or whomever, we must communicate as such, but with much reverential respect, involving the Holy Trinity in Unison. Here is the Spiritual Decree to preface our prayer: *"I have called upon You, for You will hear me, O God; incline Your ear to me, and hear my speech."* Psalm 17:6.

- [ ] We must ask for revelation when we are unclear, confused, lack understanding, under attack, and so on. Here is the Spiritual Decree to preface our prayer: *"Show Your marvelous lovingkindness by Your right hand, O You who save those who trust in You From those who rise up against them."* Psalm 17:7.

- [ ] We must ask for Divine Covering. Should we not already have it, especially if we are Believers? Of course, we have a covering to a certain extent, but we must also realize we have free will, and the Spirit cannot violate our will in certain areas. Therefore, we must learn how to invoke the Heavenly of Heavens at the drop of a dime without crying wolf. Here is the Spiritual Decree to preface our prayer: *"Keep me as the apple of Your eye; hide me under the shadow of Your wings, from the wicked who oppress me, from my deadly enemies who surround me."* Psalm 17:8-9.

- [ ] We must become aware of our environment and the people we hang around with. Most often, we become ensnared because we ignore the fruits, especially the loudest person in the room and those who prey upon

Spiritual Maintenance of the Psyche

the weak, vulnerable, and wounded. Here is the Spiritual Decree to preface our prayer: *"They have closed up their fat hearts; with their mouths they speak proudly. They have now surrounded us in our steps; they have set their eyes, crouching down to the earth, as a lion is eager to tear his prey, and like a young lion lurking in secret places. Arise, O LORD, confront him, cast him down; deliver my life from the wicked with Your sword."* Psalm 17:10-13.

- ☐ We must be willing to come boldly to the Throne of God, asking for what rightly belongs to us and being satisfied without becoming jealous, envious, greedy, or covetous. Why? It is not wise to have anyone or anything unlike or contradicting the Kingdom. Here is the Spiritual Decree to preface our prayer: *"With Your hand from men, O LORD, from men of the world who have their portion in this life, and whose belly You fill with Your hidden treasure. They are satisfied with children, and leave the rest of their possession for their babes. As for me, I will see Your face in righteousness; I shall be satisfied when I awake in Your likeness."* Psalm 17:14-15.

- ☐ We must love the Lord with all our hearts without attempting to use or pimp Him for the Benefits of the Kingdom. We need Kingdom Benefactors who receive Blessings to Bless another, keeping the Heavenly Provisions flowing and contributing to our Heaven on Earth Experiences. Here is the Spiritual Decree to preface our prayer: *"I will love You, O LORD, my strength. The LORD is my rock and my fortress and my deliverer; my God, my strength, in whom I will trust; my shield and the horn of my salvation, my stronghold."* Psalm 18:1-2.

Spiritual Maintenance of the Psyche

☐ We must praise God for who He is, not for what He does for us. Blasphemy, right? Wrong. Most often, we interchange praise as a form of thanks without us initially giving or saying thanks, whereas in the Kingdom, praise is praise, and giving thanks is just that. Therefore, amid our praises, we should NOT forget to give thanks. Why? It keeps ungratefulness from settling in our psyche, keeping us focused on the negative and blinded to the positive or win-win. For this reason, we must become thankful for all things while learning the necessary lessons; even if it hurts, something does not appear as we hoped, we have fallen short, and so on. Plus, it keeps us from praising on the one hand and hating our life on another.

Frankly, this feeling gets swept under the rug. But for me, I am here to pull the rug from under this deceptive measure, thwarting our walk with God. Here is the Spiritual Decree to preface our prayer: *"I will call upon the LORD, who is worthy to be praised; so shall I be saved from my enemies."* Psalm 18:3. *"He delivers me from my enemies. You also lift me up above those who rise against me; You have delivered me from the violent man. Therefore, I will give thanks to You, O LORD, among the Gentiles, and sing praises to Your name. Great deliverance He gives to His king, and shows mercy to His anointed, to David and his descendants forevermore."* Psalm 18:48.

☐ We must make our best attempts to keep our hands clean without playing dirty, cleansing our souls continuously. Psalms 19:12 says, *"Who can understand his errors? Cleanse me from secret faults."* Here is the Spiritual Decree to preface our prayer: *"Therefore the LORD has*

Spiritual Maintenance of the Psyche

recompensed me according to my righteousness, according to the cleanness of my hands in His sight." Psalm 18:24.

What is a Spiritual Decree? It means we have the right to quote scripture back to God as Spiritual Leverage, especially if we are in alignment with it to the best of our ability, understanding, or Spiritual Level. And once decreed, the Holy Spirit will do the rest, especially if we are using the Fruits of the Spirit and exhibiting Christlike Character.

What is considered the rest? We are all different; therefore, the correction I would need will not be the same for another. Spiritually, this is why God is graceful and merciful, allowing the Holy Spirit to help us along the way as *The Tutor of Mankind*.

When dealing with all things Spiritual, we cannot pretend to be an amateur when we are a Spiritual Elite, and we cannot pretend to be a Spiritual Elite when we know we are still in the Milking Stages. Why can we not pretend? The Sword of the Spirit is not something we want to play around with; therefore, it is best to humble ourselves in the Ways of God and repent at the drop of a dime. How is this possible, especially when we are being tried to the fullest? Although every situation or circumstance is different in the Eye of God, varying from person to person. Nonetheless, here is what I would say when I do not understand, when lacking full details, or when I need to glean information: *"Let the words of my mouth and the meditation of my heart be acceptable in Your sight, O LORD, my strength and my Redeemer."* Psalm 19:14.

When we use *The Tutor of Mankind*, we can indeed depend on Spiritual Wisdom instead of our own sense of wisdom, shifting us from a worldly perspective to a Kingdom one. What is the purpose of doing so? According to scripture, our Divine Blueprint is equipped with the Spiritual Tools we need, regardless of how it may appear to the naked eye.

Spiritual Maintenance of the Psyche

What is more, if we allow *The Tutor of Mankind* to guide us, we will not miss the mark, especially if we make it our business to do everything in the Spirit of Excellence while using the Fruits of the Spirit and Christlike Character as our Weapon of Warfare. How do we maximize our Weapons in the face of our enemies?

- ☐ We must become understanding and compassionate toward others.

- ☐ We must avoid becoming arrogant, biased, or condescending. Unbeknown to most, humility is our TRUE POWER.

- ☐ We must avoid chaos, deflecting it toward the positive or outright removing ourselves from the environment.

- ☐ We must NOT become a know-it-all or the loudest person in the room. Remember, we are all on a learning curve in some area, and we gain more by effectively listening to become *In-The-Know* than by constantly responding in irrelevancy.

- ☐ We must govern what comes out of our mouths, choosing our words carefully.

- ☐ We must not seek revenge, squashing the enemy from within while invoking the Genius or Giant that is at our beckoning call.

- ☐ We must think, behave, and become positive.

Spiritual Maintenance of the Psyche

- ☐ We must seek peace in all things, especially from the inside out, while learning how to deal with, respond to, or deflect chaos and confusion at the drop of a dime.

- ☐ We must become cautious about how we respond, retaliate, or regraft our lives.

- ☐ We must govern our motives, keeping them aligned with the Kingdom of God.

- ☐ We must help, feed, and Bless others with no strings attached while exhibiting Spiritual Proactiveness.

- ☐ We must do and be good, especially when bad things are happening, while examining ourselves, our fruits, our character, and the root of our issues from the inside out, not from the outside in.

But more importantly, let us align this with scripture, *"Be of the same mind toward one another. Do not set your mind on high things, but associate with the humble. Do not be wise in your own opinion. Repay no one evil for evil. Have regard for good things in the sight of all men. If it is possible, as much as depends on you, live peaceably with all men. Beloved, do not avenge yourselves, but rather give place to wrath; for it is written, 'Vengeance is Mine, I will repay,' says the Lord. Therefore 'If your enemy is hungry, feed him; If he is thirsty, give him a drink; for in so doing you will heap coals of fire on his head.' Do not be overcome by evil, but overcome evil with good."* Romans 12:16-21.

 Our *Spiritual Tutor* is not designed to make us codependent; it is designed to make us interdependent, working together as a Spiritual Team in Oneness. We have a role to play in our *Spirit to Spirit* Relationship, and the Holy Trinity has a responsibility to us as well, similar to a parent-child

Spiritual Maintenance of the Psyche

relationship. All in all, regardless of who we are and why, we must come together in Earthen Vessel to complete the Heaven on Earth Experience according to the Divine Blueprint set in place. If not, we will experience a longing, thirst, hunger, void, or some form of emptiness from within, even if we are conditioned to cover it up or play possum.

In my opinion, we have been beating around the bush for too long, and it is time for us to step up to the plate and take full responsibility for our Divine Mission. What if we do not know what it is? It is time to get *In-The-Spiritual-Know*.

Once we begin to build momentum, here are a few items that we can glean from getting *In-The-Spiritual-Know* with *The Tutor of Mankind*, but not limited to such:

- ☐ We can unlock our full potential.
- ☐ We can confront our limitations.
- ☐ We can become open to new experiences.
- ☐ We can embrace change with a positive mindset.
- ☐ We can create a win-win out of an apparent lose-lose.
- ☐ We will view obstacles as opportunities.
- ☐ We can excel in learning, developing, and pruning.
- ☐ We will master the regrafting process.
- ☐ We can foster a sense of resilience and adaptability.
- ☐ We can focus on ongoing self-improvement.
- ☐ We can master self-correction or self-analysis.
- ☐ We can embrace a proactive approach.
- ☐ We can think on our feet or at the drop of a dime.
- ☐ We will be able to seek and accept feedback.
- ☐ We will know how to bounce back from failures.
- ☐ We will understand that our setbacks are setups.
- ☐ We can embrace the power of *Spiritual Maintenance*.
- ☐ We can develop and master a proactive approach.

Spiritual Maintenance of the Psyche

In the same way that we can master the edifices associated with our likes or dislikes in our worldly affairs, we can also do this with our Kingdom Affairs as well. For example, if we set a goal to achieve something, we will do what it takes to get it unless someone or something stops us. Meanwhile, with our Divine Purpose, the same rules apply, but from a Spiritual Perspective, allowing *The Tutor of Mankind* to guide us or illuminate our path toward righteousness in *The Power of Oneness*.

Chapter Eleven
The Power of Oneness

When operating in the Spirit of Righteousness or *The Power of Oneness*, God will fight for us. As we navigate the complexities of life, we cannot fight evil with evil; we must fight evil with good, especially if we want justification in all of our well-doings. When it relates to *Divine Dominion: As It Pleases God*®, if we stand firm in our commitment to doing good or doing the right things, we can trust that the Heavenly of Heavens will support us in our efforts.

In addition, in *The Power of Oneness*, when we confront the obstacles that threaten to undermine our commitment to goodness and righteousness, we can draw Divine Strength from our Heavenly Father. Frankly, according to our Divine Dominion, Spiritual Interdependence is the way to go when dealing with the enemy's wiles. Most often, when they play dirty, we can say, *Enough is Enough* while playing cleanly with the Spirit of the Lord on our side, without becoming shady, evil, or rude. Here is the scripture to recite in our *Spirit to Spirit* Communal time, "*Through You we will push down our enemies; through Your name we will trample those who rise up against us. For I will not trust in my bow, nor shall my sword save me. But You have saved us from our enemies, and have put to shame those who hated us."* Psalm 44:5-7.

In the Kingdom, we are a family of Oneness based upon two types of relations:

- ☐ Spiritual Relations.
- ☐ Human Relations.

If we miss the mark in the relational department, we will find ourselves failing at our people skills and contradicting the Fruits of the Spirit, causing REVERSE RELATIONS instead.

Reverse Relations are when we are doing everything against or the opposite of the Will of God, predicated on worldliness through our senses, lusts, and selfishness. For example, we are designed to love and be loved. If we are operating in hatefulness, whether within ourselves or with others, we will cause the Cycle of Life to reverse, not working in our favor because we are naturally designed to love.

Most often, amid the reversal, this is when everything falls apart, breaks, goes wrong, or we have a trail of rottenness, chaos, betrayal, debauchery, and confusion. For some, this is their norm, so they do not see a problem with this. Then, from a Spiritual Perspective, there is a problem indeed, and it is within the human psyche, spreading outwardly.

Spiritually Speaking, if we dare to turn the unrepenting Reverse Relations (*worldly to worldly*) into repenting Spiritual (*Spirit to Spirit*) and Human (*Spirit to Man*) Relations predicated on the Fruits of the Spirit and Christlike Character, we will find that a transformation will take place from the inside out.

Our Divine Blueprint is within, and we are naturally designed to exhibit Love, Joy, Peace, Patience, Kindness, Goodness, Faithfulness, Gentleness, and Self-Control;

The Power of Oneness

therefore, we will naturally activate the *Gravitational Pull* of Righteousness by default.

How will the *Gravitational Pull* of Righteousness benefit us? *"As iron sharpens iron, so a man sharpens the countenance of his friend."* Proverbs 27:17. In addition, it also bridges the gap in the transformational process, going from unrighteousness to righteousness, based upon the Spiritual Principles and Laws hidden in the Fruits of the Spirit. Really? Yes, really! Once we repent, the Spiritual Seal is called forgiveness, grace, and mercy through the Sacrificial Lamb who gave His life in ATONEMENT for us.

According to the Heavenly of Heavens, if we go against our Divine Design, the Holy Spirit must lie dormant; therefore, the human psyche takes over, doing whatever it wants and with whomever, especially when it is left ungoverned, untamed, traumatized, or uncorrected. Unbeknown to most, this indeed leads to Spiritual Blindness, Deafness, and Muteness based upon the lust of the eyes, the lust of the flesh, and the pride of life. So, being that we are doing the opposite of our Blueprint, the Cycle, and the Vicissitudes will serve us the opposite of righteousness on a silver platter, as we think we are right in our own eyes but all so wrong in the Eye of God and the Kingdom. Remember, we must account for our motives because *"Every way of a man is right in his own eyes, but the LORD weighs the hearts."* Proverbs 21:2.

The bottom line is that God is watching how we treat others when no one is looking, primarily when we do not need someone, when they appear beneath us, or when they are rough around the edges. Listen, regardless of who is trying to woo us, the question is always:

- ☐ Are we nasty, rude, disrespectful, or unkind?
- ☐ Are we kind, understanding, respectful, and helpful?

The Power of Oneness

When operating in *The Power of Oneness*, our people skills are essential in doing Kingdom Business. If we say we represent the Kingdom and behave like a hellion on wheels, this is not godly! *"Even a child is known by his deeds, whether what he does is pure and right."* Proverbs 20:11.

Yes, we all have our moments, but our moments should be quick enough to repent and apologize amid that moment. If we train ourselves to self-correct immediately, especially when our psyche wants to show out or show its true colors, the incidents or meltdowns will decrease dramatically.

With *The Power of Oneness*, when we align the negative fruit exhibited with the Fruits of the Spirit, or we reverse it into a positive, we can create a win-win from the inside out. Clearly, this reversal technique is not an overnight process, but when used consistently, it will regraft our lives and relations in ways that put our enemies at bay, right before our very eyes.

What is the big deal about regrafting relations with *The Power of Oneness*? We all need them; however, the determining factors are in our healthy or unhealthy relationships. How do we know the difference? It varies from person to person, but if we have a problem being alone, rest assured, we are engaging in unhealthy relations. Is this not judging? Maybe or maybe not, but if there is an underlying issue preventing us from being content with ourselves and our thoughts, we have work to do.

From a Spiritual Perspective, when developing *The Power of Oneness*, we need time alone to hear what is going on between our ears. There are times when we block out the chatter so much that we do not realize it is drowning us in a pool of negativity, spilling over into the lives of others. So, if we do not realize or confront the fact that we are negative, we cannot regraft it into positives. Then again, if we have a hard time taking time out, we will have difficulty analyzing ourselves or doing a checkup from the neck up. As a result, it affects our

The Power of Oneness

people skills, leading to unhealthy relations, even if we are in denial, playing pretend, or outright playing possum. But, behind closed doors, healthy or unhealthy relations are exposed without masks or the superficialities of the public eye. Nevertheless, in *The Power of Oneness*, healthy or unhealthy, *"The first one to plead his cause seems right, until his neighbor comes and examines him."* Proverbs 18:17.

Healthy relations are based upon respect and transparency, while working together to achieve a common goal. Although the divorce rate is at 80%, it does not mean it has to remain this way. In *The Power of Oneness*, how can we change this trajectory? We must get an understanding of how to engage and disengage in and out of relationships. Listed below are a few examples of relational hypotheticals, but not limited to such:

- ☐ If the relationship becomes competitive, where no one listens to each other, it is only a matter of time before conflict and disobedience will arise, affecting all manner of relations. *"Cease listening to instruction, my son, and you will stray from the words of knowledge."* Proverbs 19:27.

- ☐ If we are trying to plot, attempting to change another through manipulation, or violating the will of another without working on ourselves first, this will cause a Spiritual Upset from the inside out. How? We are going to bring strife, anger, debauchery, and resentment into the relationship. *"He who plots to do evil will be called a schemer. The devising of foolishness is sin, and the scoffer is an abomination to men."* Proverbs 24:8-9.

- ☐ If we attempt to put the outside manifestations or appearances of another above the inside man,

The Power of Oneness

disappointment is on the horizon. Why? Our approach must be from the inside out, not the outside in. *"Charm is deceitful and beauty is passing, but a woman who fears the LORD, she shall be praised. Give her of the fruit of her hands, and let her own works praise her in the gates."* Proverbs 31:30-31.

- ☐ If we are pointing the finger or bribing without assuming responsibility, we are going to have issues. *"A gift in secret pacifies anger, and a bribe behind the back, strong wrath."* Proverbs 21:14.

- ☐ If we complain, bicker, fuss, and fight out of envy, drawing others into our folly, we symbolically block out righteousness due to the intents of the heart. *"Do not be envious of evil men, nor desire to be with them; for their heart devises violence, and their lips talk of troublemaking."* Proverbs 24:1-2.

- ☐ If we are a control freak, pouncing upon the weaknesses of another, resentfulness will soon harden the heart of the victim, who may seek revenge in due time. *"Whoever shuts his ears to the cry of the poor will also cry himself and not be heard."* Proverbs 21:13.

- ☐ If we abuse, misuse, or bully in the relationship, we will find the victim will withdraw Mentally, Physically, or Emotionally to protect themselves. *"A brother offended is harder to win than a strong city, and contentions are like the bars of a castle."* Proverbs 18:19.

- ☐ If we player hate or play mind games to exhibit or provoke jealousy, envy, or coveting, the rules of the

The Power of Oneness

game will eventually reverse out of our favor. "*Casting lots causes contentions to cease, and keeps the mighty apart.*" Proverbs 18:18.

- [ ] If we allow our ego to pounce upon or degrade another, we will soon bring inner shame to ourselves in the areas we are nitpicking. "*A man's stomach shall be satisfied from the fruit of his mouth; from the produce of his lips he shall be filled.*" Proverbs 18:20.

- [ ] If we speak down or curse another, we will soon bring this folly back to ourselves. How? This negative manifestation will become unawaringly buried within our psyche. "*Death and life are in the power of the tongue, and those who love it will eat its fruit.*" Proverbs 18:21.

- [ ] If we are consumed with lying and deception, we put all relations at risk. "*A false witness will not go unpunished, and he who speaks lies will not escape.*" Proverbs 19:5.

- [ ] If we do not work on or work at our relationships, they are destined to fall apart. "*A lazy man buries his hand in the bowl, and will not so much as bring it to his mouth again.*" Proverbs 19:24.

In my opinion, with *The Power of Oneness*, Proverbs is the best book in the Bible to develop our people skills. Frankly, this is how I developed mine. *Spirit to Spirit*, I promise it will work for anyone serious about understanding their behaviors from a Spiritual Perspective.

What are the benefits associated with the Book of Proverbs? It teaches us how to behave according to Kingdom

The Power of Oneness

Principles, what characteristics the Kingdom of Heaven is expecting from us, and what to nourish, cherish, pursue, or prune to keep us in an upright, standing position among the Spiritual Elites in Earthen Vessel.

More importantly, in *The Power of Oneness*, our righteousness is not just about our benefits; it is about our Bloodline Blessings. *"The righteous man walks in his integrity; his children are blessed after him."* Proverbs 20:7.

Spirit to Spirit

Our *Spirit to Spirit* Connection from the Heavenly of Heavens should not be taken for granted; not now, and not ever! Our Heaven on Earth Experiences are wrapped in our Level of RESPECT, *As It Pleases God.* We all want the Divine Connection, but in order to truly become Kingdomly Powerful in our *Spirit to Spirit* Connection, respectfulness is a must. If we lack respect, it is best not to pursue a *Spirit to Spirit* Connection from the Heavenly of Heavenlies until we are ready.

Unbeknown to most, defiance causes more harm to ourselves than good. Why? If there is disrespect running through our veins, rest assured, there is unrest surrounding us. So, allow me to align this accordingly: *"Let every soul be subject to the governing authorities. For there is no authority except from God, and the authorities that exist are appointed by God. Therefore, whoever resists the authority resists the ordinance of God, and those who resist will bring judgment on themselves. For rulers are not a terror to good works, but to evil. Do you want to be unafraid of the authority? Do what is good, and you will have praise from the same."* Romans 13:1-3.

Spirit to Spirit, here is something to think about before we go any further. Who knows our Divine Blueprint better than the Spirit of God? If we lack Spiritual Respect for our Creator, will we really respect the Divine Plan? Once we get what we

The Power of Oneness

want from God, will we respect those beneath us or look down on them? Why do we need to know this? It is because Spirit respects Spirit, period!

As It Pleases God, if our Spiritual Senses are not up to par, recognizing the Heavenly Anointed, then we have work to do. Until we get to this point in our Spiritual Relationship, respect everyone because we will never know who He is using to TEST our Spirit or our Anointing.

In pursuing a *Spirit to Spirit* Relationship with the Holy Trinity, our teachability becomes second to none. According to the Heavenly of Heavens, when we cast down worldliness, and embrace the Kingdom Mentality, we become the responsibility of the Holy of Holies to train us in the ways of the Spirit. Why do we need training? To ensure we do not intertwine worldliness into Kingdom Principles, and do not mislead others due to our lack of understanding.

If the truth is told, most of the wolves in sheep's clothing do not realize they are behaving like a wolf or turning their prayer into a session of witchcraft. As Believers, how is it possible NOT to know the impact of our prayers? It can easily happen when operating from conditioning, cultural biases, self-induced beliefs, and passed-on traditions without developing a *Spirit to Spirit* Connection.

When we do not have a full understanding of the Fruits of the Spirit, or we are not accustomed to exhibiting Christlike Character, we symbolically create what feels right to us, going through the motions. Once this happens, we cannot pinpoint the voids we feel, the trauma we cannot get over, the inner chatter that is running wild, the anger we are experiencing, the revenge we seek, and so on. As a result, this negativity spills over into our prayers without realizing what we are doing, causing us to pray amiss or have our prayers go unanswered.

The Power of Oneness

When we are obedient in our *Spirit to Spirit* Relationship, and when we stand steadfast on God's Word in the Spirit of Righteousness, He will defend us. With this knowledge, we can contend with the wiles of the enemy while putting on the Whole Armor of God in the Realm of the Spirit.

How do we get started on our *Spirit to Spirit* Journey with the Heavenly of Heavens on our side? The first step is to make a CHOICE to do so. Secondly, willfully invite the Holy Trinity (The Father, Son, and Holy Spirit) into our lives' equation, guiding us out of darkness to the Path of Light. Thirdly, REPENT of all known and unknown atrocities hindering our walk or blocking our path toward righteousness!

Why do we need to repent? Without repentance, we are symbolically telling God that we are perfect, we are not wrong about anything, all of our fruits are good, and the Spirit of Deception has clouded our sense of good judgment.

Listen, in our walk with God, we must constantly pay attention to '*What*' we are doing, '*Why*' we are doing it, '*Where*' we are doing it, '*When*' we are doing it, '*How*' we are doing it, and with '*Whom.*' By doing so, we are able to determine our motives of righteousness vs. unrighteousness when aligned with the Fruits of the Spirit.

Here is the Spiritual Decree set before us daily, but for some reason, the human psyche tries to forget it: *"See, I have set before you today life and good, death and evil, in that I command you today to love the LORD your God, to walk in His ways, and to keep His commandments, His statutes, and His judgments, that you may live and multiply; and the LORD your God will bless you in the land which you go to possess."* Deuteronomy 30:15-16. Some would say that was back then, and this is now. Well, the only difference from then to now, is the matter of TIME, but the Spirit of God or our Divine Blueprint has not changed!

The Power of Oneness

All in all, the *Ancient of Ancients* wants us to get back on track with our *Spirit to Spirit* Relationship, putting our worldliness on the back burner to possess what rightly belongs to us. Spiritually Speaking, according to *Divine Dominion: As It Pleases God*®, whatever we need is already, so do not become deceived by rationalizing and justifying the Word of God, primarily when it is already written on the heart of every person.

The Fight

Listen, my ears have been to the ground long enough to understand how the Kingdom operates, *As It Pleases God*. When someone does not fully understand Kingdom Principles and Laws, they will gravitate toward ANGRILY defending the Word of God. When in all actuality, we only need to STAND on the Word! Blasphemy, right? Wrong! The Word of God is ABSOLUTE.

When it comes down to the Holy of Holies, we must get out of our feelings, do what we have been called to do, and allow God to be God! *"And He said to me, 'Son of man, stand on your feet, and I will speak to you.' Then the Spirit entered me when He spoke to me, and set me on my feet; and I heard Him who spoke to me. And He said to me: Son of man, I am sending you to the children of Israel, to a rebellious nation that has rebelled against Me; they and their fathers have transgressed against Me to this very day. For they are impudent and stubborn children. I am sending you to them, and you shall say to them, 'Thus says the Lord GOD.'"* Ezekiel 2:1-4.

Here is a question: 'Do we see God physically fighting men?' No, we do not; everything with God is Spiritual in the Realm of the Unseen. However, He does ALLOW things to happen based upon the Systems, Cycles, and Laws already set in place, such as the Law of Gravity, Seedtime and Harvest, and so on. Now, to take this a step further, outside of what is already set

The Power of Oneness

in place, we will also see two things happening, especially if we DO NOT put the Holy Trinity at the forefront of our lives:

- ☐ We will see mankind fighting against each other.
- ☐ We will see mankind fighting against themselves.

If we are created in the Image of God, we must elevate ourselves to the Spiritual Realm. Frankly, this is where the battles are really taking place, causing us to feel as if it is real. When, in all actuality, we are really the culprit.

In our world, we are reacting to life; when in all actuality, life is reacting to us based on what we have set in motion with our thoughts, words, beliefs, actions, reactions, behaviors, and so on, giving life to our SEEDS, producing fruit after its own kind, positively or negatively.

When dealing in a *Spirit to Spirit* Relationship, we cannot sit around twiddling our thumbs, ignoring our Divine Blueprint, neglecting to build ourselves up from the inside out, or reacting to people, places, and things God has already delivered us from.

Is any of this Biblical? Of course, here is what Jesus said to Saul, who turned to Paul on the Road to Damascus, "*So I said, 'Who are You, Lord?' And He said, 'I am Jesus, whom you are persecuting.' But rise and stand on your feet; for I have appeared to you for this purpose, to make you a minister and a witness both of the things which you have seen and of the things which I will yet reveal to you. I will deliver you from the Jewish people, as well as from the Gentiles, to whom I now send you, to open their eyes, in order to turn them from darkness to light, and from the power of Satan to God, that they may receive forgiveness of sins and an inheritance among those who are sanctified by faith in Me.*" Acts 26:15-18.

Well, regardless of where we are in life, our ROAD may not lead us to Damascus, but it is going to definitely lead us

The Power of Oneness

somewhere. However, our somewhere will determine whether our ROAD leads us into Heaven or the Pit, based upon the choices we are making on a moment-by-moment basis. For this reason, it is always best to have the Holy Spirit guiding us as we cover ourselves with the Blood of Jesus to create a Spiritual Bumper for ourselves.

What is a Spiritual Bumper? It is our BOUNCE BACK ability through grace, mercy, and forgiveness hidden in our repentance and transparency. Unbeknown to most, by owning our truth and doing the right thing, even when the wrong things are happening, it really strengthens our 'Bounce Back' or 'Give Back.'

In Him

When we operate and reflect wholeheartedly *In Him*, we will defy human logic and science with our Gifts, Calling, Talents, Purpose, Creativity, and Understanding. However, this Level of Spirituality is only achieved by a few, but secretly and openly sought after by all, even if we are in denial. How is this possible when we all have a unique Blueprint? We were born with the desire to dominate or have dominion, according to the Book of Genesis. *"So, God created man in His own image; in the image of God, He created him; male and female He created them. Then God blessed them, and God said to them, 'Be fruitful and multiply; fill the earth and subdue it; have dominion over the fish of the sea, over the birds of the air, and over every living thing that moves on the earth.'"* Genesis 1:27-28.

Yet, amid the time in which we live, we have become accustomed to dominating the wrong, worldly, or negative things, leaving ourselves open to the lack of proper self-governing. To add insult to injury, we most often do not have a clue we are in dire need of righteous, Kingdomly, or positive governing from the inside out, bringing us in Purpose on purpose.

Furthermore, as a *Word to the Wise*, by functioning in the Spirit of Excellence, it squashes the Spirit of Curiosity by default. For those who do not know, ungoverned curiosity will cause us to experiment with everything or anyone without any form of Spiritual Discretion. For this Spiritual Journey, we must equip ourselves with the Spiritual Leverage needed to overcome evil with good.

In our own strength, our level of goodness is on a sliding scale of motives based upon the situation, circumstance, our understanding, or how we are feeling. If we do not use the Fruits of the Spirit and Christlike Character to govern the human psyche, we will find ourselves compromising without knowing we are doing so. Above all, it is still reflected in our heart and mind postures in the Eye of God.

According to the Heavenly of Heavens, *In Him* is eulogized in our Heaven on Earth Experience, but for some reason, we have forgotten the Spiritual Protocol of the Kingdom. We are into ourselves and not into God, our Heavenly Father, as we should. Unfortunately, it could result from our distractions, lack of understanding, unawareness on our behalf, conditioning, or from outright Spiritual Neglect. Who knows, besides the Spirit of God, right? Wrong, we know!

The Holy Spirit simply unveils that which is already. For this reason, we must stop playing pretend with ourselves, hoping or expecting someone to confirm or guide us on our journey through life, when the Blueprint is already written on the Tablet of the Heart.

What is the big deal about *In Him*? *In Him* was derived from our Forefather Abraham, when pleading for his Bloodline, *"And the LORD said, 'Shall I hide from Abraham what I am doing, since Abraham shall surely become a great and mighty nation, and all the nations of the earth shall be blessed in him?"* Genesis 18:17-18. The

The Power of Oneness

bottom line is that we are not of our own accord; we are the lineage of something, and it is our responsibility to get *In Him*, to receive Divine Instructions similar to Abraham having the Three Visitors in Genesis 18. Now, if we fast forward this up to today's day and age from the Ancient of Days, we have what we know as the Holy Trinity (The Father, Son, and Holy Spirit) in Three Persons of the ONE that is *In Him*.

Unbeknown to most, *In Him* resides within us all, and we do not need to go seeking what is already. We must AWAKEN ourselves from our slumber, making a conscious effort to become a work-in-progress. In order to stay AWOKE, we must operate *In Him* with the Fruits of the Spirit and Christlike Character. What does this mean? *In Him* is fed by good fruits, righteousness, and obedience.

In contrast, unrepentant or uncorrected rotten fruits, unrighteousness, and disobedience cause the Holy Spirit to lie dormant *In Him*. Meanwhile, deceptive Spirits take over, and we think we are operating *In Him* and we are NOT. How do we know the difference? Once again, we are known by our fruits!

How will operating *In Him* benefit us? When placing the Holy Trinity at the forefront of our lives, or better yet, by becoming Spiritually Awakened, covering ourselves with the Blood of Jesus, and making a conscious decision to operate *In Him*, here is the Spiritual Decree hidden in plain sight. *"Behold, I send an Angel before you to keep you in the way and to bring you into the place which I have prepared. Beware of Him and obey His voice; do not provoke Him, for He will not pardon your transgressions; for My name is in Him. But if you indeed obey His voice and do all that I speak, then I will be an enemy to your enemies and an adversary to your adversaries."* Exodus 23:20-22.

We can discount the relevance of operating *In Him* all we like, but we should never judge what we do not understand.

The Power of Oneness

"For You are my lamp, O LORD; The LORD shall enlighten my darkness. For by You I can run against a troop; by my God I can leap over a wall. As for God, His way is perfect; the word of the LORD is proven; He is a shield to all who trust in Him. For who is God, except the LORD? And who is a rock, except our God? God is my strength and power, and He makes my way perfect. He makes my feet like the feet of deer, and sets me on my high places." 2 Samuel 22:29-34.

What is the Spiritual Contingency Clause for remaining *In Him*? No idolatry, period. Now, if idolatry or the idolators have a chokehold on us Mentally, Physically, and Emotionally, we must willfully break it from the inside out. Why? Their sacred pillars become hidden in the human psyche; we must break them inwardly first, in order to see the manifestations outwardly. So, let us align this accordingly: *"You shall not bow down to their gods, nor serve them, nor do according to their works; but you shall utterly overthrow them and completely break down their sacred pillars. So, you shall serve the LORD your God, and He will bless your bread and your water. And I will take sickness away from the midst of you."* Exodus 23:24-25. Does this really work? Absolutely. Here is what the Bible says about Caleb, who operated in such a manner; *'But My servant Caleb, because he has a different spirit in him and has followed Me fully, I will bring into the land where he went, and his descendants shall inherit it."* Numbers 14:24.

We have all heard the abridged version of, 'In Him I live, and In Him I die,' right? But, according to Scripture, it says, *"For in Him we live and move and have our being, as also some of your own poets have said, 'For we are also His offspring.' Therefore, since we are the offspring of God, we ought not to think that the Divine Nature is like gold or silver or stone, something shaped by art and man's devising. Truly, these times of ignorance God overlooked, but now commands all men everywhere to repent, because He has appointed a day on which He will judge the world in righteousness by the Man whom He has ordained. He*

The Power of Oneness

has given assurance of this to all by raising Him from the dead." Acts 17:28-31. All in all, this means we have to die to our fleshly or worldly ways and walk in the Spirit of Righteousness, pray, repent, and delight *In Him* through Christ Jesus.

God is on our side, even if we make a mistake, when we are falsely accused of wrongdoings, or when people are looking down on us based on our condition. Here is a scripture bringing hope to all, *"He shall pray to God, and He will delight in him, He shall see His face with joy, For He restores to man His righteousness. Then he looks at men and says, 'I have sinned, and perverted what was right, and it did not profit me.' He will redeem his soul from going down to the Pit, and his life shall see the light. Behold, God works all these things, Twice, in fact, three times with a man, to bring back his soul from the Pit, that he may be enlightened with the light of life."* Job 33:26-30.

God is not expecting perfection; He expects obedience as we operate in the Spirit of Excellence. Is perfection and the Spirit of Excellence the same? No, they are not. In the Kingdom, perfection is being faultless and in need of no correction. On the other hand, the Spirit of Excellence is doing what it takes to get it right, build quality, develop durability, or create a win-win. Frankly, this is how we can operate *In Him*, amid our issues appearing real.

What appears as being real to us is really based upon our perceptions. For this reason, *In Him* allows our Spiritual Eye to become opened, ushering in Divine Illumination for us to see the win-win, especially when others are seeing defeat.

Our Spiritual Ears are opened to hear the Voice of God and tame the unknown voices of deception as we develop our Spiritual Language from the Heavenly of Heavens. Yet, to the natural man, this sounds like a fairytale of some sort, but to the Spirit Man, it will resonate, quickening the human psyche. How can we make this make sense? For example, I am indeed writing *In Him*, under a full Kingdomly Commissioned Anointing. So, if the reader needs what this book is offering,

The Power of Oneness

the inner man, *Spirit to Spirit*, will willfully STAND at attention. Meanwhile, those for whom it is not for, will lack the understanding because their Spiritual Eye is not open to receive as of yet.

When truly operating *In Him*, it will change the trajectory of our lives, giving us the ability to manifest on a level that causes our enemies to scratch their heads in disbelief or stand in awe. The key is, when operating *In Him*, we do not need to make a public spectacle out of it. Should we not represent God? Of course, we should. Keep in mind that worldly representation is not the same as Kingdom Representation.

The Kingdom is looking for the Fruits of the Spirit and Christlike Character, NOT what comes out of our mouths or what we put on public display. Why? We can say or do anything, masking our truth. In the interim, our fruits have their own language, speaking volumes without us having to say one word. When *In Him*, we must work on our fruits and character, like working a full-time job until we become well-versed in the Fruits of the Spirit and Christlike Character.

For the most part, we can look elsewhere for strength, but *In Him* resides what we need. Here is a scripture to keep close to the heart: *"The LORD is my strength and my shield; my heart trusted in Him, and I am helped; therefore, my heart greatly rejoices, and with my song I will praise Him. The LORD is their strength, and He is the saving refuge of His anointed."* Psalm 28:7-8.

What if the Vicissitudes of Life are pressing us to the max, and we do not know which way to turn? We must stand still for Divine Instructions while aligning ourselves with the Word of God, prayer, repentance, forgiveness, and positive affirmations. Once done, we can fervently say, *"Our soul waits for the LORD; He is our help and our shield. For our heart shall rejoice in Him, because we have trusted in His holy name."* Psalm 33:20-21.

Most often, when we are catching it from every angle, we feel compelled to do anything to make the pain or frustration

The Power of Oneness

go away. When, in all actuality, this is an indication that we need to get an understanding, period. Therefore, we do not need to engage in other things or with other people when we fail to understand the present situation, circumstance, events, or what is causing the uproar within our psyche.

Unbeknown to most, when we have an outward disturbance, it is really an inner disturbance manifesting itself outwardly to get our attention. Baloney, right? Wrong! Nothing makes it into the physical realm without having some form of Spiritual Manifestation first. And, if whatever it is was not connected to us from the inside out, we would not respond to it, nor would it provoke a reaction. Simply put, if we narrow down the inner SEED, we can deal with the outer manifestations provoking us to react, respond, or pay attention.

What if we are doing everything right, and things are still going wrong? If we are truthfully and faithfully operating *In Him*, while exhibiting the Fruits of the Spirit and Christlike Character with total humility and transparency, it often means that God is TESTING our patience, confidence, and staying power.

Why would God test us in this manner? Unfortunately, this is where most people give up, erecting a Golden Calf of idolatry, or they go to the dark side for the right now gratification. On the contrary, in the Kingdom, we must STAND on the Word of God without wavering, doing what we are called to do while being in Purpose on purpose, even if we are hurt, sick, traumatized, tattered, or torn.

If we stand for the Kingdom, *As It Pleases God*, without becoming divided, the Kingdom will have our backs, period. How will this benefit us amid oppression? We must view it as TRAINING for the next level of GREATNESS. Here are a few '*In Him*' pointers, but not limited to such:

The Power of Oneness

- ☐ *In Him*, we must not worry about those who plot wickedness. As long as we remain in a state of righteousness *In Him*, He has our backs, guaranteed! *"Do not fret because of evildoers, or be envious of the workers of iniquity. For they shall soon be cut down like the grass, and wither as the green herb."* Psalm 37:1-2.

- ☐ *In Him*, we must trust Him while doing everything in the Spirit of Excellence. *"Trust in the LORD, and do good; dwell in the land, and feed on His faithfulness."* Psalm 37:3.

- ☐ *In Him*, we must enjoy being in His presence, building a *Spirit to Spirit* bond to place a Spiritual Seal on the Divine Relationship and the go-ahead on our Divine Blueprint. *"Delight yourself also in the LORD, and He shall give you the desires of your heart."* Psalm 37:4.

- ☐ *In Him*, we must become committed to the Will of God, regardless of the distractions or mishaps we encounter along the way. *"Commit your way to the LORD, trust also in Him, and He shall bring it to pass."* Psalm 37:5.

- ☐ *In Him*, we must be ready, willing, and able to walk into our Divine Purpose when the timing is right or when we receive our Spiritual Cue. *"He shall bring forth your righteousness as the light, and your justice as the noonday."* Psalm 37:6.

- ☐ *In Him*, we must NOT worry about the Dream Killers. Just rest *In Him*, knowing all things will work together for our good. *"Rest in the LORD, and wait patiently for Him; do not fret because of him who prospers in his way, because of the man who brings wicked schemes to pass."* Psalm 37:7.

The Power of Oneness

- [ ] *In Him*, we must NOT be overcome with anger, forgive, let go, and move on, bearing no grudges. *"Cease from anger, and forsake wrath; Do not fret—it only causes harm."* Psalm 37:8.

- [ ] *In Him*, we must be patient. *"For evildoers shall be cut off; But those who wait on the LORD, they shall inherit the earth."* Psalm 37:9.

- [ ] *In Him* will cause our issues to vanish away like vapors when we least expect it. *"For yet a little while and the wicked shall be no more; Indeed, you will look carefully for his place, but it shall be no more."* Psalm 37:10.

- [ ] *In Him*, meekness will cause us to abound in a state of peacefulness, superseding human understanding. *"But the meek shall inherit the earth, and shall delight themselves in the abundance of peace."* Psalm 37:11.

- [ ] *In Him*, ushers in the day of reckoning for those who spitefully attempt to wreak havoc in our lives. *"The wicked plots against the just, and gnashes at him with his teeth. The Lord laughs at him, for He sees that his day is coming."* Psalm 37:12-13.

- [ ] *In Him*, when we are content with what we have, while operating in the Spirit of Righteousness, He will cause the weapons of warfare to ricochet, or He will outright deflect them from the intended target. *"The wicked have drawn the sword and have bent their bow, to cast down the poor and needy, to slay those who are of upright conduct. Their sword shall enter their own heart, and their bows shall be broken. A little that a righteous man has, is better than the riches of many wicked." Psalm 37:14-16.*

Regardless of where we are in life or what we have been through, we are safe *In Him*; we only need to trust *In Him* and the process it takes to extract the Greatness from Within. *"For You will light my lamp; the LORD my God will enlighten my darkness. For by You I can run against a troop, by my God I can leap over a wall. As for God, His way is perfect; the word of the LORD is proven; He is a shield to all who trust in Him. For who is God, except the LORD? And who is a rock, except our God? It is God who arms me with strength, and makes my way perfect." Psalm 18:28-32.*

Dr. Y. Bur

www.DrYBur.com

Chapter Twelve
The Clarion Call to Authority

Our Forefathers have gone to battle for us in ways we would never be able to comprehend because we are indeed living the Blessings from their sweat, blood, and tears. Yet, we have the nerve to become ungrateful for the good life in which we live. What is more, we pick on or bully those who appear to have less than us based on our biases, perceptions, or conditioning, especially when inner wealth is more valuable than anything known to man.

Unbeknown to most, in *The Clarion Call To Authority*, when there is something that money cannot buy, it creates exceptional VALUE for the Mind, Body, Soul, and Spirit. Our Forefathers knew about this, but what happened to us? We have become trapped by the ways of man, overlooking the Will of God, *As It Pleases Him*, only to please ourselves, forgetting all about Divine Dominion. For this reason, this chapter is designed to bring us into Spiritual Alignment with the *Grandfather Clause*, designed to help us recognize our Blessings in a whole new LIGHT.

The Clarion Call To Authority

Who knows the Mind of God, right? Wrong! It is written all over the Bible, hidden in plain sight. Yet, we miss it all the time. So, for the sake of the Ancient of Ancients, our Forefathers have a *Grandfather Clause* set in motion among the Realm of the Spirit on our behalf. How is this possible when we are in the NOW, and that was back then? Unfortunately, we are trapped in time, but the Mission of God must be fulfilled based upon a *Spirit to Spirit* Connection, not a man-to-man judicial system. According to *The Clarion Call To Authority*, we do not determine who makes it to Heaven, nor can we condemn someone to the abyss.

Regardless of how we point the finger, the number of curses we loom, or how many rocks we throw, we have all fallen short in the Eye of God and needed some form of forgiveness, mercy, or grace. Plus, we all have something to deal with; therefore, we should not judge the story of another man, or we will bring that same Spirit back to our house, especially without having all the facts. Blasphemy, right? Wrong. "*Judge not, that you be not judged. For with what judgment you judge, you will be judged; and with the measure you use, it will be measured back to you.*" Matthew 7:1-2.

In *The Clarion Call To Authority*, we are NOT speaking of our Judicial System governing the Laws of the Land; we are dealing with a Spiritual System governing mankind, *As It Pleases God*.

With all of this talk about the *Grandfather Clause*, what about the *Grandmother Clause*? In *Divine Dominion: As It Pleases God*®, we have had some fantastic grandmothers; however, the *Grandfather Clause* incorporates both because they are ONE with the Holy of Holies.

In the Kingdom, male and female are not divided; we are ONE. Listen, solid foundations are built and molded in Oneness with Divine Order set in place. Why? "*Every Kingdom*

The Clarion Call To Authority

divided against itself is brought to desolation, and every city or house divided against itself will not stand." Matthew 12:25.

Do we not have the free will to disagree? Of course, we do; however, it does not mean we must become divided in doing so. We must have respect for the opinions and differences of others without getting out of character while assuming responsibility to do the right thing regardless.

How can we strategically maximize the *Grandfather Clause* to help us with lifelong skills? Listed below are a few ways, but not limited to such:

- ☐ In *The Clarion Call To Authority*, we must have a desire to maximize our highest and greatest potential toward righteousness.

- ☐ In *The Clarion Call To Authority*, we must present ourselves appropriately in public and private arenas.

- ☐ In *The Clarion Call To Authority*, we must be faithful to our partners.

- ☐ In *The Clarion Call To Authority*, we must become pleasant to be around.

- ☐ In *The Clarion Call To Authority*, we must be willing to help, share, and teach others.

- ☐ In *The Clarion Call To Authority*, we must avoid becoming a drunkard, losing our sense of good judgment of soberness.

- ☐ In *The Clarion Call To Authority*, we must avoid becoming violent, abusive, or abrasive.

The Clarion Call To Authority

- ☐ In *The Clarion Call To Authority*, we must not become greedy, lustful, or reckless.

- ☐ In *The Clarion Call To Authority*, we must not become quarrelsome, chaotic, controversial, or instigators.

- ☐ In *The Clarion Call To Authority*, we must avoid becoming covetous, competitive, or manipulative.

- ☐ In *The Clarion Call To Authority*, we must avoid becoming unruly, ungoverned, or indecisive.

- ☐ In *The Clarion Call To Authority*, we must avoid becoming rebellious and prideful.

We can use this as a checklist, or we can use this scripture as a reference: *"This is a faithful saying: If a man desires the position of a bishop, he desires a good work. A bishop then must be blameless, the husband of one wife, temperate, soberminded, of good behavior, hospitable, able to teach, not given to wine, not violent, not greedy for money, but gentle, not quarrelsome, not covetous. One who rules his own house well, having his children in submission with all reverence (for if a man does not know how to rule his own house, how will he take care of the church of God?); not a novice, lest being puffed up with pride he fall into the same condemnation as the devil."* 1 Timothy 3:1-6.

As we move on, in an information-driven society, when we preface the mother or father with the word *Grand*, it is intended to take an ordinary mother and father to the next level of outstanding while propelling their Bloodline into *Greatness* on another level in the Spirit of Excellence. How is this possible? With a Spiritual Grandeur approach to our Bloodline, we determine the lifeline by building, pruning,

The Clarion Call To Authority

sowing, tilling, and growing it with the Spiritual Principles of Wisdom, *As It Pleases God*.

Furthermore, if we desire to LEAD our Bloodline with the *Grandfather Clause* in hand, we cannot go wrong in the Will of God, using the Fruits of the Spirit and exhibiting Christlike Character. In the Kingdom, the *Grandfather Clause* is predicated on our *Spirit to Spirit Relations* and people skills. If we perfect those, becoming a work-in-progress, our Divine Blueprint will be fulfilled, paving the way to the Kingdom from generation to generation to prepare our NEXT.

With *The Clarion Call To Authority*, we are here to complete our Divine Missions, not judging or degrading another based on our conditioning, biases, and perceptions.

God loves us all, and He is the Creator of it all, and we cannot determine what He is doing in the life of another without the utterance of the Holy Spirit. Therefore, we should not judge, circumvent the Will of God, or place ourselves above Him. For this reason, He requires outright love, humility, and respect.

Now, on the other hand, we are required to examine our fruits or charactorial traits and those of another to judge ourselves, perfect the Fruits of the Spirit, exhibit Christlike Character, or get an understanding of what or who we are dealing with. We must know the difference to avoid bringing condemnation back to our house.

How do we know the difference? The moment we begin to negatively point the finger, criticize, degrade, blame, or turn up our noses without the correction of the Holy Spirit, this is an indication of Spiritual Contempt. Here is a scripture, *"Therefore whoever eats this bread or drinks this cup of the Lord in an unworthy manner will be guilty of the body and blood of the Lord. But let a man examine himself, and so let him eat of the bread and drink of the cup. For he who eats and drinks in an unworthy manner eats and drinks judgment to himself, not discerning the Lord's body. For this reason, many* are weak and sick among you, and many sleep. For if we would judge ourselves, we would not be judged. But when we are judged, we are chastened by the Lord, that we may not be condemned with the world." 1 Corinthians 11:27-32.

All in all, Jesus is the Spiritual Atonement for our sins, ensuring we do not have to make any more bloody sacrifices. If, for some reason, we are making them, it is not for the God Almighty of the Heavenly of Heavens!

The Holy Spirit is our Spiritual Guide and Teacher, leading us to the Light or placing us into a Spiritual Classroom. Yet, amid all, we are used in Earthen Vessel in cultivating or facilitating such tasks, but we are not the enforcers of the Divine Covenant. The Spiritual Covenant is written within each person, and they are accountable for their own due diligence.

How can we make this make sense, especially when we cannot see our hearts to read what the Divine Covenant is? We need a *Spirit to Spirit* Connection, *As It Pleases God* to unveil the veiled. Please allow me to Spiritually Align: *"For this is the covenant that I will make with the house of Israel after those days, says the LORD: I will put My laws in their mind and write them on their hearts; and I will be their God, and they shall be My people. None of them shall teach his neighbor, and none his brother, saying, 'Know the LORD,' for all shall know Me, from the least of them to the greatest of them. For I will be merciful to their unrighteousness, and their sins and their lawless deeds I will remember no more. In that He says, 'A new covenant,' He has made the first obsolete. Now what is becoming obsolete and growing old is ready to vanish away."* Hebrews 8:10-13.

How can we capitalize on the *Grandfather Clause?* Strategically and *As It Pleases God!* If the goal is to please ourselves, in due time, we will 'get got' by the wiles of the enemy. We cannot violate Spiritual Laws or Covenants. What if we do not know them? Then it behooves us to stick

The Clarion Call To Authority

to using the Fruits of the Spirit and exhibiting Christlike Character; they provide a Spiritual Safety Net for us.

If we pride ourselves on living fancy-free, creating all types of atrocities in the Eye of God due to ignorance or the lack of understanding, we will become easy BAIT without knowing it. Now, what the BAIT is or is not becomes based on our weakest, denied, or traumatized link, so it will not be the same for everyone.

What is the purpose of becoming BAIT for the enemy? The enemy is trying to get us to void the *Grandfather Clause* over our lives because the enemy lacks the authority to cancel what is DIVINE. Nonetheless, if we do it to ourselves or know nothing about it, then who gets the last laugh?

The Divine Mindset

As it relates to *Divine Dominion: As It Pleases God*®, if we dare to get out of the system of worldliness and into God's Head, He will restructure our Mindset into a Heavenly Stratosphere, putting our enemies to boot. With a *Divine Mindset* as such, our Creative Genius can come forth, strategizing in ways that our enemies can never articulate, period.

However, they can emulate, but CANNOT outdo the Creator of it all. He is always a step ahead, step above, and step beyond whatever is designed to distort our Divine Blueprint; thus, we need to know this beyond a shadow of a doubt. If not, we open ourselves up for deception, distortion, dismantling, or disenfranchising. Listed below are a few ways to maximize a *Divine Mindset*, but not limited to such:

- ☐ With a *Divine Mindset*, we must trust God for '*Safety.*' "Preserve me, O God, for in You I put my trust." Psalm 16:1.

The Clarion Call To Authority

- [ ] With a *Divine Mindset*, we must train the human psyche to *'Understand'* that everything *'Good'* comes from Above. "*O my soul, you have said to the LORD, 'You are my Lord, my goodness is nothing apart from You.'*" Psalm 16:2.

- [ ] With a *Divine Mindset*, we must be *'In the Spiritual Know'* about being Spiritually Chosen by God for a specific PURPOSE while doing everything in the Spirit of Excellence. "*As for the saints who are on the earth, They are the excellent ones, in whom is all my delight.*" Psalm 16:3.

- [ ] With a *Divine Mindset*, we must *'Cast Down'* idolatry while avoiding putting anything or anyone above the Holy Trinity or the Kingdom of God. "*Their sorrows shall be multiplied who hasten after another god; their drink offerings of blood I will not offer, nor take up their names on my lips.*" Psalm 16:4.

- [ ] With a *Divine Mindset*, we must *'Involve'* God in our Divine Blueprint, *As It Pleases Him*, because only He has all the unadulterated and unbiased instructions. "*O LORD, You are the portion of my inheritance and my cup; You maintain my lot.*" Psalm 16:5.

- [ ] With a *Divine Mindset*, we must *'Heed'* to the Divine Instructions given in our *Spirit to Spirit* Relationship, as well as when He drops the information right in our laps, guiding us in the right direction to take possession of our Birthrights. "*The lines have fallen to me in pleasant places; yes, I have a good inheritance.*" Psalm 16:6.

- [ ] With a *Divine Mindset*, we must *'Exalt'* God and the Heavenly of Heavens. Why? It is a formal *'Give-Back'*

The Clarion Call To Authority

for Divine Counsel from the Holy Spirit and the Covering of the Blood of Jesus. With this sort of reverence, it will guide us to the Light in our moments of darkness, especially when the Vicissitudes of Life put us in a Spiritual Classroom or when it puts us to the test to see what we are made of. *"I will bless the LORD who has given me counsel; my heart also instructs me in the night seasons."* Psalm 16:7.

- ☐ With a *Divine Mindset*, we must 'Place' God first before all things; it helps clear our Spiritual Eyes, Ears, and Mouth, allowing us to see people, places, and things from His point of view. *"I have set the LORD always before me; because He is at my right hand I shall not be moved."* Psalm 16:8.

- ☐ With a *Divine Mindset*, we must 'Exhibit' authentic happiness and joy in all things, regardless of how it may appear to the naked eye. Why? God hides a win-win in everything! We simply must *know* it exists, *find* it, *understand* its purpose, and *share* our findings as a Spiritual Seed, sowing back into the Kingdom without becoming restless and hopeless in doing so. *"Therefore, my heart is glad, and my glory rejoices; my flesh also will rest in hope."* Psalm 16:9.

- ☐ With a *Divine Mindset*, we must 'Know' God will deliver us, especially if we use the Fruits of the Spirit and Christlike Character as our Weapon of Warfare. *"For You will not leave my soul in Sheol, nor will You allow Your Holy One to see corruption."* Psalm 16:10.

The Clarion Call To Authority

- ☐ With a *Divine Mindset*, we must '*Ask*' and '*Trust*' God for Divine Direction, Information, or Revelation, leading the way of our Spiritual Path for our Heaven on Earth Experience. *"You will show me the path of life."* Psalm 16:11a.

- ☐ With a *Divine Mindset*, we must '*Focus*' on the *Fullness* of the Kingdom, without falling prey to the emptiness or negativity of the worldly system in which we live. If we stay on the positive side of the spectrum, we give ourselves a fighting chance from the inside out. *"In Your presence is fullness of joy; at Your right hand are pleasures forevermore."* Psalm 16:11b.

When truly walking in the Gifts of the Spirit, Matthew 10:8 says, *"Freely you have received, freely give."* Not doing so freely, leads to one of the biggest Spiritual Woes of them all: DISOBEDIENCE. *"Woe to the rebellious children, says the LORD, who take counsel, but not of Me, and who devise plans, but not of My Spirit, that they may add sin to sin; who walk to go down to Egypt, and have not asked My advice, to strengthen themselves in the strength of Pharaoh, and to trust in the shadow of Egypt!"* Isaiah 30:1-2. From a Spiritual Perspective, this is how most of us zap our own Spiritual Gifts without realizing it, only to covet that of another.

Listen, most of our Spiritual Battles surround our Spiritual Gifts, the pouncing on those who proclaim to possess them, and the misuse of them for selfish reasons. Amid whatever or with whomever, we put on the Whole Armor of God, only to unawaringly fight against ourselves due to our lack of understanding of all things Spiritual.

If we are at war from within, we must resolve our inner battles first before contending with the wiles of the enemy to avoid cursing our hands. Why must we resolve inner conflict

The Clarion Call To Authority

first? It prevents us from becoming yoked by self-induced tactics, prematurely revealing our rotten fruits or acts of coveting. Here is what the scripture says, *"Woe to those who devise iniquity, and work out evil on their beds! At morning light they practice it, because it is in the power of their hand. They covet fields and take them by violence, also houses, and seize them. So, they oppress a man and his house, a man and his inheritance."* Micah 2:1-2.

In *Divine Dominion: As It Pleases God®*, the Heavenly of Heavens frown upon those who withhold to oppress, especially when it is within our power to give, help, or share with no strings attached. The more we use our Giftings, Callings, or Talents to give or to become a Blessing to others, the more we receive.

According to *Divine Dominion: As It Pleases God®*, if we want God's Divine Hand, Provisions, and Protection over our Divine Purpose, Birthrights, or Blueprint, we must confront the hidden quirks of our psyche. With a *Divine Mindset*, we cannot leave them AS-IS. The hidden quirks in our psyche can manifest as limited beliefs, unresolved traumas, negative thoughts, or ingrained patterns of behavior that hinder us Mentally, Physically, Emotionally, or Spiritually. These aspects of our subconscious can cloud our sense of good judgment, create barriers, zap our authenticity, and prevent us from fully accessing the Spiritual Gifts and Blueprint that are rightfully ours.

We can point the finger all we like, but once again, we all have quirks! This is what makes us different, and it also contributes to our Purpose or Passion, linking us to our Divine Blueprint. In order for the enemy not to use our hidden quirks against us, we must know them, work on them, regraft them to a positive, perfect them, and then share them as our '*Give Back*.'

Of course, confronting our veiled idiosyncrasies requires courage and honesty. Our weaknesses, often perceived as

The Clarion Call To Authority

burdens, hold the potential to become our GREATEST TEACHERS if we allow them to do so. They are like seeds lying dormant, waiting for us to nurture them in the right conditions. How do I know? I am living proof. All of my strengths were weaknesses hidden in plain sight.

Once again, I will say that our Divine Blueprint is already—the only person who determines its readiness is the one who possesses it. What about God? He placed the Tree of Life within us, and He will not violate the free will of mankind. We as individuals must step *'Into the Spiritual Know'* about that which is already.

Just imagine if we think we have it going on right now without God. We will be astonished by what we can achieve with Him, being in Purpose on purpose, getting Divine Clarity, and solidifying our Spiritual Knowing *In Him*.

In conclusion, in this book, *Divine Dominion: As It Pleases God*®, I have provided you with everything you need to gain your rightful DOMINION. I encourage you to embrace these Spiritual Principles wisely, and I PROMISE you that they will REVOLUTIONIZE your life for the Greater Good. From me to you, *Spirit to Spirit*, you got this! Grow Great...May the Peace of God be with you and BLESS your every step.

Dr. Y. Bur

www.ingramcontent.com/pod-product-compliance
Lightning Source LLC
Chambersburg PA
CBHW071703160426
43195CB00012B/1564